An Introduction to the Osteology of the Mammalia

AN INTRODUCTION

TO THE

OSTEOLOGY OF THE MAMMALIA.

AN INTRODUCTION

TO THE

OSTEOLOGY OF THE MAMMALIA:

BEING THE SUBSTANCE OF THE COURSE OF LECTURES
DELIVERED AT
THE ROYAL COLLEGE OF SURGEONS OF ENGLAND IN 1870.

BY

WILLIAM HENRY FLOWER, F.R.S., F.R.C.S.,

HUNTERIAN PROFESSOR OF COMPARATIVE ANATOMY AND PHYSIOLOGY, AND CONSERVATOR
OF THE MUSEUM OF THE COLLEGE.

WITH NUMEROUS ILLUSTRATIONS.

London:

MACMILLAN & CO.

1870.

PREFACE.

THE desire to acquire a knowledge of the structure of some portion at least of the Animal Kingdom, now becoming so general, is often checked by the difficulty of determining where to make a beginning amid the vast extent and variety of the materials at hand.

I have selected for my first course of lectures on Comparative Anatomy at the Royal College of Surgeons, the structure and modifications of the Skeleton, because, as the framework around which the rest of the body is built up, it gives, more than any other system, an outline of the general organization of the whole animal, and also because it is the most convenient for study, on account of the facility with which it can be preserved and examined.

Moreover, Osteology has special importance in comparison with the study of any other system, inasmuch as large numbers of animals, all in fact of those not at present existing on the earth, can be known to us by little else but the form of their bones.

In endeavouring to gain anatomical knowledge, it signifies little with which group of animals a commencement is made.

The structure of Man has undoubtedly a, more universal interest than that of any other organized being, and has, therefore, been more thoroughly worked out; and as the majority of terms used in describing the parts composing the bodies of Vertebrate animals were originally bestowed on account of their form, relation, or real or fancied resemblance to some object, as they were met with in Man, there are advantages in commencing with members of the highest class, and mastering their essential characters before proceeding to acquire knowledge of the other groups.

But as human anatomy may be taken as a point of departure from which to set out in the study of that of other Vertebrates, so, on the other hand, those whose special duty it is to become familiar with its details, will find themselves greatly assisted by some knowledge of the structure of lower forms. Thus the essential characters of the human skull will be much better understood if the student will also make himself acquainted with those of some simpler condition of Mammalian cranium, as that of the dog or sheep.

Although the present work contains the substance of a course of lectures, the form has been changed, so as the better to adapt it as a handbook for students. Theoretical views have been almost entirely excluded; and while it is impossible in a scientific treatise to avoid the employment of technical terms, it has been my endeavour to use no more than are absolutely necessary, and to exercise due care in selecting only those that seem most appropriate, or which have received the sanction of general adoption.

With very few exceptions, all the illustrations have been drawn expressly for this work, with great care and fidelity, by Mr. R. W. Sherwin, from specimens in the Museum of the Royal College of Surgeons.

September 24th, 1870.

CONTENTS.

AN INTRODUCTION

TO THE

OSTEOLOGY OF THE MAMMALIA.

CHAPTER I.

CLASSIFICATION OF THE MAMMALIA.

It is not the object of the present work to enter in detail into the subject of the Classification of the Mammalia ; but, as it will be necessary to refer frequently to the principal subdivisions in which the various animals treated of are arranged, a brief outline of the system adopted will be necessary.

A perfect arrangement of any group of animals can only be attained simultaneously with a perfect knowledge of their structure and life's history. We are still so far from this that any classification now advanced must be regarded as provisional, and merely representing our present state of knowledge. Moreover, as naturalists will estimate differently the importance to be attached to different structural modifications as indicative of affinity, it must be long before there will be any general agreement upon this subject.

B

The classification and the names of the subdivisions used throughout this work correspond, in the main, with those given by Professor Huxley in his " Introduction to the Classification of Animals," 1869.

The whole of the animals composing the class are arranged primarily in three natural divisions, which, presenting very marked differentiating characters, and having no existing intermediate or transitional forms, may be considered as *sub-classes* of equivalent value, taxonomically speaking, though very different in the numbers and importance of the animals composing them.

These three groups, to adopt the names originally proposed for them by De Blainville, are :—1. MONODELPHIA ; 2. DIDELPHIA ; and 3. ORNITHODELPHIA.

I. **Monodelphia,** sometimes called *Placentalia,* comprises the great bulk of the class. The main characteristic of the animals composing it is, that their young are nourished for a considerable period within the uterus of the mother by means of an organ called the *placenta,* a villous and vascular development from the outer surface of the fœtal envelopes, which, being in contact with corresponding vascular developments from the inner wall of the uterus, permits an interchange of materials between the circulating fluids of mother and young, thus brought into the closest proximity. This organ varies much in shape and structure in the different minor divisions of the sub-class.

It is very difficult to subdivide the Monodelphia into any groups larger than orders, or to arrange these orders in anything like a linear series, as most of them have affinities in many directions.

One group may be placed apart as having no distinct

relationship with any of the others, and chiefly distinguished by negative characters. This is the order EDENTATA, comprising the Sloths, the Armadillos, the Ant-eaters of America, and the Pangolins and Orycteropus, or Cape Ant-eater of the Old World. These are animals of generally low organization for the division to which they belong.

The remaining Monodelphian Mammals are:— 1. PRIMATES, the highest order, culminating in the genus *Homo* of Linnæus, and comprising also all the animals commonly known as Monkeys. With these are generally united a group of very inferior structure (*Lemurina*), containing the various species of Lemurs and allied animals, which, without question, connect the Primates on the one hand with the Insectivora, Carnivora, and Chiroptera on the other; though it is doubtful, at present, whether they should be associated with the Monkeys, or should constitute a distinct order by themselves. 2. CHIROPTERA, or Bats. 3. INSECTIVORA, or Hedgehogs, Shrews, Moles, &c. 4. CARNIVORA, divided into the Terrestrial Carnivora, or *Fissipedia*, Cats, Dogs, and Bears, and the various modifications of these types; and the Aquatic Carnivora, or *Pinnipedia*, Seals, Walrus, and Eared Seals, or Sea Lions. 5. CETACEA, containing two sub-orders, the *Mystacoceti*, or Whalebone Whales, and the *Odontoceti*, Cachalots, Narwhals, Dolphins, and Porpoises. 6. SIRENIA, a small order of aquatic vegetable-feeding animals, of which the Manati (*Manatus*) and Dugong (*Halicore*) are the sole living representatives. 7. UNGULATA, the very large order of hoofed quadrupeds, divided into the *Perissodactyla*, or "odd-toed" Ungulates, containing the Horse, Tapir, and Rhinoceros; and the *Artiodactyla*, or "even-toed," again subdivided into four sections. *a*. The non-ruminating, or *Suina*, consisting of the Pigs, Peccaris, and Hippopotamus.

b. The cushion-footed, or *Tylopoda*, the Camels and Llamas. *c.* The *Tragulina*,. or Chevrotains, a group of little deer-like animals formerly associated with the Musk-deer. *d.* The *Pecora*, or true Ruminants, comprising the Deer, Giraffes, Antelopes, Sheep, Goats, and Oxen. The last three divisions constitute the order *Ruminantia* of Cuvier. 8. HYRA-COIDEA, an order consisting of a single genus, *Hyrax*, a small animal having many affinities with the Perissodactyle Ungulata, with which it is often associated. 9. PROBOSCIDIA, represented at present only by the two species of Elephant; and 10. RODENTIA, a well-marked group, but with varied affinities, both to the Insectivora and Primates on the one hand, and to the Ungulata and Proboscidia on the other, and also to the Didelphia. This order contains the Hares, Rats, Guinea-pigs, Porcupines, Beavers, Squirrels, &c.

II. The sub-class **Didelphia** comprises only one order, MARSUPIALIA, consisting of animals presenting great diversity of superficial appearance and habits of life, although all united by many essential anatomical and physiological characters. The young are born in an exceedingly rudimentary condition before the formation of a placenta, and are transferred to the nipple of the mother, to which they remain firmly attached for a considerable time, nourished by the milk injected into the mouth by compression of the muscle covering the mammary gland. The nipples are nearly always concealed in a fold of the abdominal integument, or "pouch" (*marsupium*), which serves to support and protect the young in their early helpless condition. The existing species are entirely confined to Australia, its neighbouring islands, and the American continent; though, in former times, they had a more extensive geographical range. The Wombats, Kangaroos, Phalangers, Koalas,

Bandicoots, Dasyures, Thylacines, and Opossums, are the best known representatives of this group.

III. The **Ornithodelphia**, equivalent to the order MONOTREMATA, consist of only two existing genera; and hitherto, no extinct animals which can be referred to other genera of this remarkable and well-characterised group have been discovered. These two isolated forms, in many respects widely dissimilar, yet having numerous common characters which unite them together and distinguish them from the rest of the Mammalia, are the *Ornithorhynchus* and the *Echidna*, both restricted in their geographical range to the Australian continent and the island of Tasmania. Many of the characters in which they differ from the two other sub-classes tend to connect them with the inferior group of Vertebrates, the SAUROPSIDA, especially the Lacertians; for though the name *Ornithodelphia* owes its origin to the resemblance of the structure of the female reproductive organs to those of birds, there is nothing specially bird-like about them; all the Sauropsida (Birds and Reptiles) agreeing in these respects.

The accompanying diagram (page 6) is intended to exhibit the relationships which appear to exist between the different groups of the Mammalia. If all known extinct forms were inserted, many of the intervals between the boundary lines of the groups would be filled up; otherwise no great modification would be required in their relative position. But our knowledge of the systematic position and relations of the past forms of Mammalian life is in general so imperfect and fragmentary, that it seemed better to confine the diagram to a representation of the present condition of Mammalian life upon the earth.

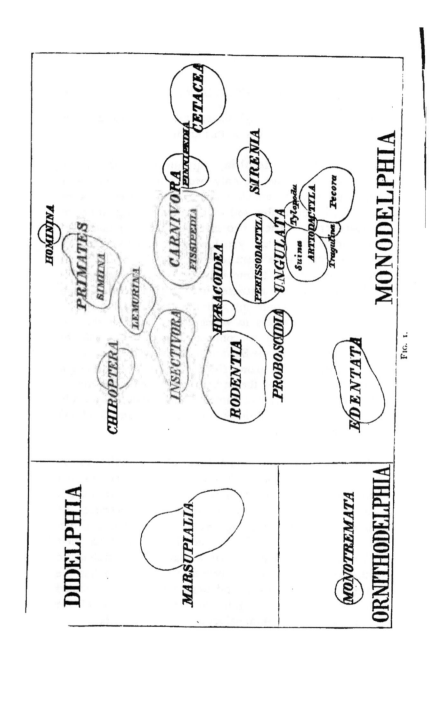

FIG. 1.

CHAPTER II.

THE SKELETON.

THE term *Skeleton*, in its widest sense, is used to denote a system of hard parts forming a framework which supports or protects the softer organs and tissues of the body, and which may be either entirely external or superficial as regards those organs and tissues, or may be more or less embedded in enveloping softer structures. In the former case it is called an *Exoskeleton*, in the latter an *Endoskeleton.*

It is of the Endoskeleton alone that this work proposes to treat, as in the class Mammalia the external skeleton, when it exists, performs a relatively subordinate part in the economy.[1]

The branch of anatomy called *Osteology* is commonly restricted to a study of such parts of the endoskeleton as are composed of bony or osseous tissue, a tissue characterized by a peculiar histological structure and chemical composition, being formed mainly of a gelatinous basis, strongly impregnated with phosphate and carbonate of lime, and disposed in a definite manner, containing numerous minute nucleated spaces or cavities called *lacunæ*, connected together by delicate channels called *canaliculi*,

---

[1] The Armadillos and their extinct allies are the only known mammals which have an ossified exoskeleton.

which radiate in all directions from the sides of the lacunæ. This structure is readily recognized when a thin section of bone is examined under a moderately high magnifying power.

Parts composed of bone are, of all the tissues of the body (with the exception of the teeth), the most imperishable, often retaining their exact form and intimate structure ages after every trace of all other portions of the organization has completely disappeared ; and thus in the case of extinct animals affording the only means of attaining a knowledge of their characters and affinities.

It must, however, be remembered that, at one period of life, the parts composing the skeleton exist in a fibrous or a cartilaginous form, that their transformation into bone is a subsequent and gradual process, and that even in the Mammalia, though in a less degree than in some of the other Vertebrata, the whole of the internal skeletal system is never entirely osseous, but that portions may remain permanently in a cartilaginous or fibrous condition.

The different bones composing the skeleton are connected together either by *sutures*, or by moveable *joints* or *articulations*.

In the first, the edges of the bones are in close contact, often interlocking by means of projections of one bone fitting into corresponding depressions of the other, and are held together by the *periosteum*, or fibrous membrane investing the bones, passing directly from one to the other, permitting no motion, beyond, perhaps, a slight yielding to external pressure. The bones of the cranium are connected together in this manner. In old animals there is a great tendency for such bones to become joined together by the extension of ossification from one to the other and consequent obliteration of the suture. This process is called *ankylosis*.

The various forms of joints may be arranged under two principal heads. In one, the contiguous surfaces of the bones are connected by interposed fibrous tissue, passing directly from one to the other, filling up the space between them, and allowing of only a limited amount of motion, as is the case with the bodies of the vertebræ.

The other and more frequent and more perfect form of joint is that in which the contiguous extremities of the bones are covered by a thin layer of very smooth cartilage, surrounded by a capsular ligament, attached only round the edges of the articular surfaces, and which is lined by a *synovial membrane,* so called from its secreting a viscid lubricating fluid termed *synovia.* The amount of motion permitted in these " synovial joints " varies according to the form of the opposed articular surfaces and the arrangement of the ligaments which hold them together. When the two surfaces are nearly flat, and the bones firmly bound by strong short ligaments, as in those which compose the carpus and tarsus, the motion is reduced to an extremely slight gliding of one on the other. Joints in the form of a hinge, as at the elbow, allow of a free motion in one plane only. Ball and socket joints, as at the shoulder and hip, allow of the greatest variety of movements.

The Endoskeleton is divided into an *axial* portion, belonging to the head and trunk, and an *appendicular* portion, belonging to the limbs. There are also certain bones called *splanchnic,* being developed within the substance of some of the viscera. Such are the *os cordis* and *os penis* found in some Mammals. These, however, are more appropriately treated of with the anatomy of the organ of which they form a part.

The Axial Skeleton consists of the vertebral column, the skull, the sternum, and the ribs.

CHAPTER III.

General Characters.—The *Vertebral Column* consists of a series of distinct bones called *Vertebræ*, arranged in close connection with each other along the dorsal side of the neck and trunk, and in the median line. It is generally prolonged posteriorly beyond the trunk to form the axial support of the appendage called the tail. Anteriorly it is articulated with the occipital region of the skull.

The number of distinct bones of which the vertebral column is composed varies greatly among the Mammalia, the main variation being due to the elongation or otherwise of the tail. Apart from this, in most Mammals, the number is not far from thirty; though it may fall as low as twenty-six (as in some Bats) or rise as high as forty (*Hyrax* and *Cholæpus*).[1]

The different vertebræ, with some exceptions, remain through life quite distinct from each other, though closely connected by means of fibrous structures which allow of a certain, but limited, amount of motion between them.

The exceptions are,—near the posterior part of the trunk, in nearly all Mammals which possess completely developed

[1] These numbers are not exact, owing to the uncertainty in the mode of reckoning the sacral vertebræ.

hinder limbs, two or more vertebræ become ankylosed together to form the "*sacrum*," the portion of the vertebral
column to which the pelvic girdle is attached. As a rule,
none of the other vertebræ are normally united by bone,
but in some species there are constant ossific unions of
certain vertebræ, more particularly in the region of the
neck. These will be specially noticed presently.

Although the vertebræ of different regions of the column
of the same animal, or of different animals, present great
diversities of form, there is a certain general resemblance
among them, or a common plan on which they are constructed, which is more or less modified by alteration of
form or proportions, or by the superaddition or suppression
of parts to fit them to fulfil their special purpose in the
economy.

An ordinary vertebra (see Fig. 2) consists in the first place
of a solid piece of bone, the body or *centrum* (*c*), of the form

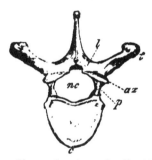

FIG. 2.—Anterior surface of human thoracic vertebra (fourth), ⅓ ; *c* body or centrum ;
nc neural canal ; *p* pedicle and *l* lamina of the arch ; *t* transverse pro cess ; *az*
anterior zygapophysis.

of a disk or short cylinder. The bodies of contiguous
vertebræ are connected together by a very dense, tough, and
elastic fibrous material, called the *intervertebral substance*, of
peculiar and complex arrangement. This substance forms

the main, and in some cases the only, union between the vertebræ. Its elasticity provides for the vertebræ always returning to their normal relation to each other and to the column generally, when they have been disturbed therefrom by muscular action.

A process (*p*) rises on each side from the dorsal surface of the body. These meeting in the middle line above form together an arch, surrounding a space or short canal (*nc*). As in this space lies the posterior prolongation of the great cerebro-spinal nervous axis, or spinal cord, it is called the *neural canal*, and the arch is called the *neural arch*, in contradistinction to another arch on the ventral surface of the body of the vertebræ, called *the hæmal arch*.[1] The last is, however, never formed in mammals by any part of the vertebra itself, but only by certain bones, placed more or less in apposition with it, and which will not here be considered as parts of the vertebral column, strictly speaking.

The lower portions of each side of the arch (*p*), usually thick and more or less vertical in direction, constitute its *pedicles*. The upper more compressed and more horizontal portions (*l*) are the *laminæ*. The pedicles are usually notched in front and behind, but most deeply behind, to form the sides of the *intervertebral foramina* for the transmission of the nerves issuing from the spinal cord. Occasionally the foramina for these nerves perforate the pedicles, instead of being truly intervertebral.

The laminæ meet in the median line above, at a more or less open angle. At the point of their junction there is usually a single median process projecting dorsally, called the *spinous process* or *neural spine*.

In most cases upon the anterior and posterior edges of the

[1] So called because it encloses the heart and the great central blood-vessels.

laminæ of the arch are flattened, slightly projecting, more or less oval, smooth surfaces or facets, which in the natural state are covered with a thin layer of cartilage, and come into contact and articulate (by synovial joints) with the corresponding surfaces of the immediately antecedent and succeeding vertebræ. These have been called by Professor Owen *zygapophyses ;* that placed on the front edge of the arch being the *anterior zygapophysis,* that on the hinder edge the *posterior zygapophysis.* As a general rule the latter have their faces directed downwards, overlying the upward directed anterior zygapophyses of the vertebra next behind. This is a useful rule to remember in ascertaining which is the front and which the posterior surface of a vertebra. Sometimes the posterior zygapophyses have their faces directed outwards, in which case the corresponding anterior zygapophyses look inwards (Fig. 3, *as*).

These articular surfaces on the arch constitute a second mode by which the vertebræ are united, and their size and conformation aids to regulate the amount of motion allowed between the component parts of the column. They are often entirely wanting when flexibility is more needed than strength, as in the greater part of the caudal region of long-tailed animals.

In addition to the body and the arch, there are certain projecting parts called *processes,* more or less developed in different vertebræ. Many difficulties exist about the signification, homologies, and terminology of these processes. Probably, when more is known of the development of the vertebræ in a large series of animals, some further light will be thrown on the subject ; but at present it does not appear that there is that uniformity in the plan of construction of all vertebræ which has often been supposed, and definitions of the different parts applicable in every case have not yet been arrived at, and it may even be doubted whether this will ever be possible.

The principal processes commonly met with are as follow :—

1. From the middle of the upper part of the arch a process generally single, but sometimes bifid at the end, grows out vertically. This is the *spinous process*, or *neural spine* already mentioned ; about its homology in different vertebræ there never can be any question. It may however be completely absent, when the arch is round or smooth above, as in the cervical region in some animals ; on the other hand, it may grow out into a very long conspicuous rod of bone, as in the anterior dorsal region of others.

2. Occasionally a process grows in the median line from the under-surface of the body. This may be single and long and slender, as in the anterior lumbar vertebræ of the Hare (Fig. 3, *h*), or a sharp median ridge, as in the cervical vertebræ

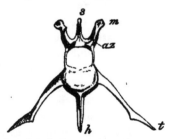

Fig. 3.—Anterior surface of the lumbar vertebra of Hare (*Lepus timidus*). *s* spinous process ; *m* metapophysis ; *az* anterior zygapophysis ; *t* transverse process : *h* hypapophysis.

of many Ungulata, and the cervical and caudal vertebræ of the Ornithorhynchus, or double, as in the atlas vertebræ of the last-named animal, and the caudal vertebræ of many others. This is termed a *hypapophysis*. Most commonly there is not even a trace of any such process.

3. From the sides of the lower part of the arch, or from the body, lateral processes project more or less directly outwards. These are called *transverse processes*. There may be but one, or there may be two, superior and inferior, on each side of a vertebra. In the latter case the superior is sometimes called a *diapophysis*, and the inferior a *parapophysis;* though it is questionable whether the processes to which these terms have been applied can always be regarded as strictly homologous.

4. Besides these principal laterally projecting processes, there are often others arising from the side of the arch, more especially developed in the lumbar region, though by no means constant even there. Of these there may be one or two on each side. They have been often called *accessory processes;* but in a more precise system of nomenclature, the one which is situated highest on the arch (see Fig. 4, *m*), pro-

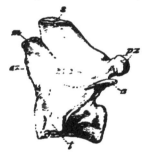

FIG. 4.—Side view of first lumbar vertebra of Dog (*Canis familiaris*), ⅓ *s* spinous process ; *az* anterior zygapophysis ; *pz* posterior zygapophysis ; *m* metapophysis ; *a* anapophysis ; *t* transverse process.

jects more or less forwards as well as outwards, is usually thick and rounded, and is nearly always in relation with the anterior zygapophysis, is termed *metapophysis;*[1] the one

[1] It is also called "mammillary process" in some works on Human Anatomy.

placed rather lower (Fig. 4, *a*), and which projects more or less backwards, and is generally rather slender or styliform, is called *anapophysis.*

These, with the *zygapophyses* before mentioned, sometimes called *oblique processes,* but which are rather articular surfaces than true processes, are all the processes commonly met with on any Mammalian vertebra.

Development of the Vertebræ.—The first indication of the formation of a vertebral column in the embryo, is the appearance of a longitudinal *primitive dorsal groove* in the germinal membrane, the edges of which (*laminæ dorsales*) rise up and meet above, so as to convert the groove into a canal. From the tissue lining this canal (uppermost layer of the germinal membrane) the brain and spinal cord are developed, and in its walls are formed anteriorly the cranium, and posteriorly the vertebral column ; the canal itself becoming the cerebral cavity and the neural canal of the spine.

In the floor of this canal, formed by a horizontal lamina which separates it from another and larger, ventral or hæmal canal (formed by the approximation in the middle line below of the *laminæ ventrales*), a slender rod of peculiar structure is developed. This is the *notochord* or *chorda dorsalis,* around which the bodies of the future vertebræ are developed. In the Mammalia it almost completely disappears at a very early period, traces only remaining in the axis of the intervertebral substance, though in many of the inferior Vertebrata it is persistent as a continuous rod for a longer period, and sometimes permanently.

The formation of the arches of the vertebræ in the *laminæ dorsales* is preceded by the appearance of dark-looking cellular masses called *proto-vertebræ* or *somatomes,* corresponding in number, though not exactly in situation, to the future vertebræ, and which undergo a series of changes (for a description of which the student is referred to special treatises on embryology) out of which ultimately results a vertebra, of the precise shape it presents in adult life, but formed of a continuous piece of hyaline cartilage.

The mode of ossification of this cartilaginous vertebra in the different groups of Mammals still offers an interesting field for investigation, but the following is a summary of the most important facts ascertained regarding it.

Leaving out for the present the greatly modified two anterior vertebræ, the atlas and the axis, which must be specially considered afterwards, and also the comparatively rudimentary vertebræ of the caudal region, each vertebra consists at one period of three pieces of bone, as distinct from each other, and remaining so for as long a period, as many of the separate elements of the skull.

One constitutes the greater part, but usually not the whole, of the body or centrum. Each of the others forms one side of the arch, and usually more or less of the upper lateral part of the body. These last ultimately unite to each other in the middle line above, and to the central piece on each side below. The line of union between them and the central piece is readily distinguishable in all vertebræ up to the time the animal is about half-grown, and is named by Professor Huxley the *neuro-central suture.* (See Fig. 8, p. 27, *ncs.*)

As a general rule all the processes (except the hypapo-physes) arise from the part of the vertebra situated above the neuro-central suture, but there are notable exceptions.

The body of the vertebra is nearly always completed by the addition of a thin disk-like epiphysis at each end, which for a considerable period after it is fully ossified remains adhering by a rough surface to the central or main part of the body, and is easily separated from it by maceration.

Its coalescence with the remainder of the body, especially in the thoracic region, is one of the last acts in the completion of the bony skeleton, and does not take place until after all the epiphyses of the limb bones are firmly united. Hence it may be taken as a safe indication that the animal is thoroughly adult.

It must be noted that the epiphysis covers the whole surface of the end of the body, whether ossified from the centrum or the arch, and is therefore quite independent of the position of the neuro-central suture.

These terminal epiphyses to the bodies of the vertebræ are peculiar to the Mammalia, but not found universally throughout the class, as they appear to be wanting in the Ornithodelphia and the Sirenia. In Man, the highest Apes, and also in some of the Didelphia, they have less solidity and importance than in other Mammals, being mere thin osseous rings, representing the circumferential portion only of the ordinary epiphysis.

The various processes of the vertebræ have been divided into those that are *autogenous*, or formed from separate ossific centres, and *exogenous*, or outgrowths from either of the just-mentioned primary vertebral constituents.

There can be no doubt but that an endogenous process of one vertebra of an animal may be serially represented by an autogenous process in another vertebra of the same animal ;[1] and likewise that the corresponding processes of the same vertebra may be developed endogenously in one animal and autogenously in another.

In nearly all the more prominent processes, moreover, whether formed by exogenous or autogenous ossification, the

---

[1] Even the arches of some of the caudal vertebræ appear to be ossified directly from the body, and not independently, as is the rule with the thoracic and lumbar vertebræ.

extreme tip remains cartilaginous for a considerable time ; and
at a comparatively late period in developmental life (near the
approach of maturity) a small ossific centre forms in it. This
spreads through the cartilage, and then constitutes an epiphysis, which ultimately unites to, and becomes indistinguishably incorporated with, the remainder of the process.[1]

The spinous process is either formed by the coalescence
of outgrowths from the two pieces forming the neural arch,
or the greater part of it may be (as in the long spines of the
anterior thoracic vertebræ of Ungulates) formed by a very
early autogenous ossification, which soon becomes united
to the upper part of the arch. In either case it is usually
completed by an epiphysis of comparatively late ossification.

There is one part connected with certain vertebræ which
requires some particular consideration, on account of the
great modifications it presents, being in some regions a largely
developed independent bone, articulated with the vertebra
by synovial joints, and in other regions a small rudiment,
early and firmly united to, and incorporated with the vertebra
itself.

The ribs in the thoracic region, though primarily formed
from a rod of cartilage continuous with that of the vertebra,
always become distinct, independent, and moveably articulated bones; after their original segmentation they can
never be properly said to constitute part of the vertebra.
But it frequently happens that in certain of the vertebræ
anterior to the thoracic region, and in certain of those
posterior to it, there are bony elements formed at an early
period, which, though very different from ribs in the ordinary

---

[1] These epiphyses are sources of considerable difficulty in tracing
homologous parts, as it is questionable whether they should be treated
as separate elements of the skeleton, and, if not, where to draw the line
between an epiphysis and an element.

sense of the word, yet occupy a somewhat similar position
in relation to the vertebræ to that which the ribs do in the
thoracic region.   These have hence been considered as
modified conditions of the same part, and have been called
pleurapophyses by Professor Owen.

Perhaps the clearest case of the presence of rib elements
in the vertebræ in any Mammal is afforded by the cervical
vertebræ of the Ornithodelphia, where the greater part of each
transverse process ossifies separately from the rest of the
vertebra, and remains a long time only suturally connected

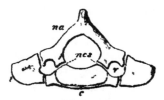

FIG. 5.—Third cervical vertebra of a nearly full-grown Echidna (*E. hystrix*), the
different pieces of which it is composed being slightly separated from one
another. *na* neural arch; *c* centrum; *t* transverse process; *v* vertebrarterial
canal; *ncs* neuro-central suture.

with it (Fig. 5).   They thus closely correspond to the cervical ribs of reptiles, which are unquestionably homologous
serially with the thoracic ribs.

The anterior, or more properly inferior, bar of the transverse process of the seventh, and occasionally of some of the
other cervical vertebræ in Man, is autogenously developed,
and has some characters by which it may be placed in the
category of rudimentary ribs.

The transverse processes of the anterior lumbar vertebræ
of certain Mammals, as the Pig, are originally autogenous
elements, though coalescing very early with the rest of the
vertebræ.

In the sacral region, the separate lateral ossifications which

connect the ilium with the vertebral column present many
characters allying them to ribs.   (See Fig. 6.)

FIG. 6.—Anterior surface of first sacral vertebra (human) showing mode of development. *na* neural arch; *c* centrum; *p* distinct (pleurapophysial) ossification for
attachment of ilium.

Finally, the transverse processes of the caudal vertebræ of
some animals (as the Manati and Beaver) are separately
developed, though it is doubtful whether this circumstance
alone is sufficient to entitle them to be considered as costal
elements.

Division of Vertebral Column into Regions.—For con-
venience of description the whole vertebral column has
been divided into five regions, the *cervical, thoracic,*[1] *lumbar,
sacral,* and *caudal.*

This division is useful, especially as it is not entirely
arbitrary, and in most cases is capable of ready definition,
at least in the Mammalia; but at the contiguous extremities of the regions, the characters of the vertebræ of one
are apt to blend into those of another region, either normally, or as peculiarities of individual skeletons.

1. The *Cervical* region constitutes the most anterior portion
of the column, or that which joins the cranium.

The vertebræ which belong to it are either entirely

---

[1] Generally called *dorsal,* but it would be better to reserve this term
in morphology as relating to the upper surface of the body and opposed
to *ventral.*

destitute of moveable ribs, or, if they have any, these are small, and do not join the sternum.

As a general rule they have a considerable perforation through the base of the transverse process (the *vertebrarterial canal*, Owen), or, as it is sometimes described, they have two transverse processes, superior and inferior, which, meeting at their extremities, enclose a canal. (See Fig. 7 ; Fig. 8, p. 27 ; and Figs. 17 and 18, p. 39.)   This,

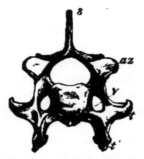

FIG. 7.—Anterior surface of sixth cervical vertebra of Dog, ¾. *s* spinous process ; *az* anterior zygapophysis ; *v* vertebrarterial canal ; *t* transverse process ; *t'* its inferior lamella.

however, rarely applies to the last vertebra of the region, in which only the upper transverse process is usually developed.

The transverse process moreover very often sends down near its extremity a more or less compressed plate (*inferior lamella*, Fig. 7, *t'*), which being considered to be serially homologous with the ribs of the thoracic vertebræ (though not developed autogenously) is often called " costal" or " pleurapophysial" plate.   This is usually largest on the sixth, and altogether wanting on the seventh vertebra.

The first and second cervical vertebræ, called respectively *atlas* and *axis*, are specially modified for the function of supporting, and permitting the free movements of the head.

They are not united together by an "intervertebral substance," but connected only by ordinary ligaments and
synovial joints.

The cervical region in Mammals presents the remarkable
peculiarity that, whatever the length or flexibility of the
neck, the number of vertebræ is the same, viz. seven, with
very few exceptions, which will be particularized further on.

2. The *Thoracic* or *Dorsal* region consists of the vertebræ
which succeed those of the neck, having ribs moveably
articulated to them.   These ribs arch round the thorax, the
anterior one, and most usually some of the others, being
attached below to the sternum.

The characters of the ribs and their mode of articulation
with the vertebræ will be considered further on, but it may
now be stated that in the anterior part of the thorax the
vertebral extremity of each rib is divided into "head" and
"tubercle;" that the former is attached to the side of the
body of the vertebra, the latter to its transverse process;
and that the former (capitular) attachment corresponds to
the interspace between the vertebræ, the head of the rib
commonly articulating partly with the hinder edge of the
body of the vertebra antecedent to that which bears its
tubercle.   Hence the body of the last cervical vertebra
supports part of the head of the first rib.   In the posterior
part of the series the capitular and tubercular attachments
commonly coalesce, and the rib is attached solely to its corresponding vertebra.

3. The *Lumbar* region consists of those vertebræ of the
trunk in front of the sacrum (to be afterwards defined) which
bear no moveable ribs.   It may happen that as the ribs
decrease in size posteriorly, and the last are sometimes
more or less rudimentary, the step from the thoracic to the
lumbar regions may be gradual and rather undetermined in

a given species. But most commonly this is not the case, and the distinction is as well defined here as in any other region.

As a general rule there is a certain relation between the number of the thoracic and the lumbar vertebræ, the whole number being tolerably constant in any given group of animals, any increase of the one being at the expense of the other. Thus in all known Artiodactyle Ungulata there are 19 thoracico-lumbar vertebræ; but these may consist of 12 thoracic and 7 lumbar, or 13 thoracic and 6 lumbar, or 14 thoracic and 5 lumbar.

The smallest number of thoracico-lumbar vertebræ in Mammals occurs in some Armadillos, which have but 14. The number found in Man, the higher Apes, and most Bats, viz. 17, is exceptionally low; 19 prevails in the Artiodactyles, nearly all Marsupials, and very many Rodents; 20 or 21 in Carnivora and most Insectivora, 23 in Perissodactyla. The highest and quite exceptional numbers are in the two-toed sloth (*Cholœpus*), 27, and Hyrax, 30.

The prevailing number of rib-bearing vertebræ is 12 or 13, any variation being generally in excess of these numbers.

4. The *Sacral* region offers more difficulties of definition, especially at its posterior portion.

Taking the human "*os sacrum*" as a guide for comparison, it is generally defined as consisting of those vertebræ, between the lumbar and caudal regions, which are ankylosed together in the adult state to form a single bone. It happens, however, that the number of such vertebræ varies in different individuals of the same or nearly allied species, especially as age advances, when a certain number of the tail vertebræ generally become incorporated with the true sacrum.

A more certain criterion is derived from the fact that some

of the anterior vertebræ of the sacral region have distinct additional (pleurapophysial) centres of ossification, between the body and the ilium (see Fig. 6, p. 21). To these perhaps the term *sacral* ought properly to be restricted, the remaining ankylosed vertebræ being called *pseudo-sacral*, as suggested by Gegenbaur. Our knowledge of the development of the sacrum in different animals is not sufficient at present to apply this test universally, but it appears probable that two is the most usual number of true sacral vertebræ, as thus defined in the Mammalia.

5. The *Caudal Vertebræ* are those placed behind the sacrum, and terminating the vertebral column. They vary in number greatly, being reduced to 5, 4, or even 3, in a most rudimentary condition, in Man, some Apes and Bats, and being numerous and powerfully developed, with strong and complex processes in many Mammals, especially among the Edentata, Cetacea, and Marsupialia. The highest known number, 46, is possessed by the African Long-tailed Manis.

CHAPTER IV.

SPECIAL CHARACTERS OF THE CERVICAL VERTEBRÆ IN THE MAMMALIA.

Order PRIMATES.—The human cervical vertebræ (excluding for the present the first and second) have short, wide, depressed bodies, hollowed in front from side to side, and behind from above downwards,[1] with wide neural canals, and short, broad, and usually bifid spines (considerably longer in the seventh vertebra than in the others), well marked, broad, flat, anterior and posterior zygapophyses, and short, sub-bifid, widely perforated transverse processes.

These vertebræ are, as usual, developed mainly from three centres, one for each side of the arch, and one for the centrum (see Fig. 8), but it will be observed that the whole of the body is not formed from the latter, but that its lateral parts, with the transverse processes, are ossified from the arches.

Besides these main centres of ossification there are thin and imperfect disk-like epiphyses on the ends of the body, very late in making their appearance, and not joined until long after the rest of the vertebra is completed. A small

---

[1] The body is supposed to be placed horizontally, so that the same terms of relative position may be used as when speaking of the vertebral column of the ordinary less modified animals of the class.

epiphysis is also formed on the end of the spinous process.

Lastly, the inferior or ventral bar of the transverse process of the seventh vertebra is developed from a separate centre of ossification, and occasionally the same part of the sixth or fifth has its own separate nucleus. This bar of bone is connected internally with a projection from the side of the body, ossified from the arch ; externally with the end of the

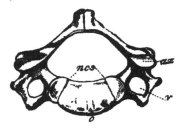

FIG. 8.—Sixth cervical vertebra of a child, ı. *c* centrum ; *ncs* neuro-central suture ; *v* vertebrarterial canal ; *as* anterior zygapophysis.

upper or true transverse process, which is an exogenous growth from the arch, so that it is attached to the vertebra entirely above the neuro-central suture. Occasionally it acquires an abnormal development, and grows into a considerable rib-like bone, in which case it is usually united at its distal extremity with the first thoracic rib.

The first vertebra or *atlas* (Fig. 9) is little more than an oval ring, thickened on each side into the so-called "lateral mass," which bears an articular surface before and behind. The anterior surfaces are very large, elongated from above downwards, and hollowed for the reception of the condyles of the occiput. The posterior articular surfaces are subcircular, flattened, or slightly concave. The transverse processes are

short, stout, and perforated; the arch presents scarcely a
rudiment of a spinous process.   On its anterior edge
immediately above the articular surface is a deep notch or
groove (*g*) of some importance, as it corresponds with the
slight notch in front of the pedicle in other vertebræ, which
contributes with the deeper notch in the hinder border of
the pedicle of the preceding vertebra to form the "inter-

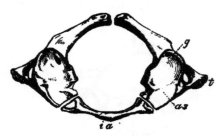

FIG. 9.—Human atlas, young, showing development, ⅔. *ia* inferior arch; *as* articular
surface for occiput; *t* transverse process; *g* groove for first spinal nerve and
vertebral artery.

vertebral" foramen for the exit of a spinal nerve, and because
occasionally in man, and constantly in many animals, it is
converted by a bridge of bone into a canal, through which
the first cervical (or *suboccipital*) nerve passes out.   The
inferior arch of the atlas (*ia*) differs entirely from the bodies
of the other vertebræ, being a simple, depressed, slightly
curved bar of bone, with a smooth facet on its *neural* or
upper surface, for articulation with the odontoid process of
the axis.

The second cervical vertebra, *axis, epistropheus,* or *vertebra
dentata* (Fig. 10), consists of a body terminating anteriorly
in a large subconical median projection, the *odontoid process* (*o*), which is received into, and articulates with, the concavity of the inferior arch of the atlas.   It is retained in its

place by means of a strong transverse ligament passing between the lateral masses of that bone, and separating its canal into an upper or neural portion for the passage of the spinal cord, and an inferior portion for the reception of the odontoid process.

The axis has posterior zygapophyses placed on the arch, serially continuous with those of the rest of the vertebræ, but its anterior articular facets, like those of the atlas, do not belong to the arch proper, but partly to the body and partly to the arch, and are therefore not exactly serially homologous with the zygapophyses of the other vertebræ. The transverse processes are short, single, and perforated. The arch is high, with a stout bifid spine.

The development of the atlas and axis offer some important points for consideration.

The arch of each is ossified from two centres, one on each side, as in other vertebræ; but if the axis is examined a year

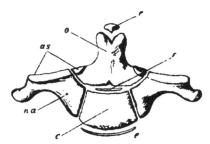

FIG. 10.—Diagram showing mode of ossification of human axis (hæmal or ventral surface). *o* odontoid process, or centrum of atlas ; *c* proper centrum of axis ; *na* neural arch ; *as* anterior articular surface ; *eee* epiphyses, completing the ends of the centra.

or two after birth (Fig. 10), its body appears to be composed of two parts, one placed in front of the other, the first including the odontoid process and the anterior part of the body, the second all the remainder of the body. The arch is united

to both.   On the other hand, the atlas at the time of birth
has nothing corresponding to the centrum of other vertebræ,
its inferior arch being still cartilaginous.

It is therefore a generally received opinion among anatomists that the anterior ossification of the axis is essentially the body of the atlas, which unites with both arch
and centrum of the vertebra behind it. It must be observed,
however, that in its mode of ossification, at least in man, it
differs from the centra of all the other vertebræ, as at one
period it consists of two distinct lateral pieces, which after
a while coalesce in the middle line.   The usual disk-like
epiphyses of the vertebral bodies are represented by one at
the posterior extremity of the body, by a small osseous
nodule, which completes the odontoid process in front, and
by some irregular ossifications found between the two main
portions of which the body is composed.

The inferior arch of the atlas ossifies soon after birth from
one or more centres, and the resulting piece of bone (Fig.
9, *ia*) ultimately unites with the two pieces forming the
neural arch about the same time as that at which they join
together in the middle line above. This piece may probably
be regarded as a detached " hypapophysial " segment of the
first vertebral centrum, the remainder of which forms the
odontoid portion of the body of the axis.

The cervical vertebræ of the other PRIMATES resemble
those of Man generally, the most noticeable deviations being
the following :—

In the atlas the groove for the first cervical nerve is usually
converted into a foramen ; and a median hypapophysial
tubercle or spine often projects backwards from its inferior
arch under the axis (especially in *Mycetes* and *Lagothrix*).

The spinous processes, especially of the third, fourth,
fifth, and sixth cervical vertebræ, are immensely elongated in

the Gorilla, and considerably so in the Chimpanzee and Orang. These processes as a rule are not bifid, as in Man, but occasionally (as in *Mycetes*) they are trifid, having a pair of lateral backward projecting processes developed near their extremity.[1]

The inferior lamellæ of the transverse processes are generally larger proportionally than in man, especially in the *Lemurina*. In the seventh vertebra, the transverse processes vary much as to their perforate or imperforate condition.

In the CARNIVORA, the atlas (Fig. 11) has very deep anterior articular surfaces for the condyles of the skull. The

FIG. 11.—Inferior surface of atlas of dog, *l.* ar foramen or first spinal nerve *v* vertebrarterial canal.

first spinal nerve passes through a complete foramen. The transverse processes are large, wing-like, flattened from above downwards, and perforated by the vertebrarterial canal.

The axis (Fig. 12) has a long conical odontoid process, and a large compressed neural spine, greatly extended from before backwards, and especially produced forwards.

The remaining cervical vertebræ have small, narrow, compressed, usually simple spines, gradually lengthening to the seventh, large transverse processes, with greatly developed inferior lamellæ (see Fig 7, p. 22) especially large in the fifth and sixth. In the latter the lower edge of this lamella is

---

[1] These are named *hyperapophyses* by Mr. Mivart, who has called particular attention to them : "On the Axial Skeleton in the Primates ;" Proc. Zool. Soc. 1865, p. 545.

frequently hollowed in the middle, and produced at each extremity, so that the transverse process has a trifid appearance. This is especially marked in the *Felidæ.* The transverse process of the seventh vertebra has no inferior lamella, and its base is imperforate.

FIG. 12.—Side view of axis of dog, ⅓. *s* spinous process ; *o* odontoid process ; *pz* posterior zygapophysis ; *t* transverse process ; *v* vertebrarterial canal.

Metapophyses are generally more or less developed on the cervical vertebræ of the Carnivora, and there are also in some genera small backward projecting tubercles (*hyperapophyses*, Mivart) situated on the laminæ of the arch, rather internal to the posterior zygapophyses, not usually found in other vertebræ.

In the INSECTIVORA, the cervical vertebræ vary considerably in their characters. The atlas has usually short transverse processes. Generally the spinous process of the axis is large and prominent, and that of the other vertebræ very small, but in *Centetes* and *Potamogale* they are all more or less elongated. The neural arches in some (as *Myogale* and *Sorex*) are reduced to mere filaments. In the mole (*Talpa*) the transverse processes of the fourth, fifth, and sixth vertebræ are much expanded antero-posteriorly, and overlap each other. Large single hypapophyses are developed from the inferior surface of most of the cervical vertebræ in the Shrews (*Sorex*) and some of their allies, and in *Galeopithecus* each vertebra bears at its hinder end a pair of hypapophysial tubercles.

In the CHIROPTERA all the cervical vertebræ are broad, very short from before backwards, with slender neural arches, from which (except in the axis) no distinct spinous processes are developed. In certain forms (as *Scotophilus*) some of the vertebræ have distinct double hypapophysial spines project. ing backwards.

In the RODENTIA the atlas has usually broad, moderately long, wing-like transverse processes. The odontoid process is long and slender ; the spinous process of the axis is much developed, while as a rule that of the other cervical vertebræ is exceedingly small. The transverse processes of the fifth and sixth have large inferior lamellæ ; the seventh is some-times perforated at the base (as in *Lepus*), and sometimes imperforate (as in *Hydrochærus*).

In the Capybara (*Hydrochærus*) and some others, the side of the arch of the atlas is perforated near its anterior border for the exit of the first spinal (sub-occipital) nerve, and also near its hinder border for the second cervical nerve.

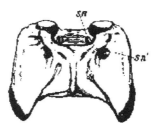

FIG. 13.—Inferior surface of atlas of Red Deer (*Cervus elaphus*). *sn* foramen for superior branch of first spinal nerve ; *sn'* foramen for inferior branch of the same nerve.

In the Jerboas (*Dipus*) a very exceptional condition of the cervical vertebræ occurs. The atlas is free, but all the others are ankylosed together by both bodies and arches, and the bodies are very wide and depressed, as in the Armadillos.

Among the UNGULATA, the atlas (Fig. 13) in the *Pecora* is very long, with deep articular cavities for the occipital condyles. The transverse processes are not wide, but much extended from before backwards, and flattened from above downwards. Each is perforated by a foramen (*sn'*) which gives exit to the inferior division of the first cervical nerve, but not by the vertebral artery, which usually enters the neural canal between the arches of the second and third vertebræ. The odontoid process of the axis (Fig. 14) is of peculiar shape, being like a spout, or hollow half-cylinder, with a prominent

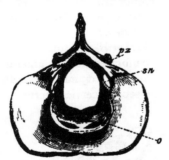

FIG. 14.—Anterior surface of axis of Red Deer, ⅜. *o* odontoid process *sn* foramen for second spinal nerve ; *pz* posterior zygapophysis.

sharp semicircular rim. The canal for the second cervical spinal nerve pierces the lamina of the axis near its anterior border. The other vertebræ have more or less elongated bodies, which are *opisthocœlous*, i.e. concave behind and convex in front. They are keeled below, the keel being often developed into a hypapophysial spine posteriorly ; the neural spines are moderately long, and inclined forwards. The transverse processes of the fifth, and especially of the sixth have large inferior lamellæ. That of the seventh is usually imperforate.

In the Giraffe the bodies of the cervical vertebræ are very long ; the transverse processes are short, but so extended from before backwards as to become divided into two, one at the anterior and one at the posterior end of the vertebra. That of the seventh is perforated.

In the *Tylopoda* (Camels and Llamas) the vertebrarterial canal passes obliquely through the anterior part of the pedicle of the arch, being in its posterior half confluent with the neural canal. A similar condition occurs in *Macrauchenia*, an extinct South American Perissodactyle Ungulate.

The Pig and Hippopotamus differ from the ruminating Ungulates in the form of the odontoid process, which is conical ; while on the other hand the Horse and Tapir among the Perissodactyles have this process wide, flat, and hollowed above, approaching the form it presents in the Ruminants. In the Pig, the broad pedicles of all the cervical vertebræ are perforated by canals for the passage of the upper division of the spinal nerves.

The bodies of the cervical vertebræ in the Rhinoceros, Tapir, and Horse are markedly opisthocœlous, but in the Pig and Hippopotamus very slightly so.

In the Horse the bodies of the cervical vertebræ are elongated, with a strong keel and hypapophysial spines. The neural laminæ are very broad, the spines almost obsolete, except in the seventh, and the transverse processes not largely developed. The seventh is perforated by the vertebrarterial canal.

In the Rhinoceros, on the other hand, the bodies are comparatively short, and not keeled, the laminæ narrow, the spines well marked, and the transverse processes greatly developed, especially those of the atlas.

In the Elephant (order PROBOSCIDIA), the atlas much resembles the human atlas. The axis has a short conical odontoid process, a very massive spine, broad above and bifid posteriorly. The bodies of the other vertebræ are very short, flattened, sub-circular disks, very slightly opisthocœlous. Excepting the seventh they all have short spinous processes, and short, broad, and largely perforated transverse processes. The seventh has a high spine, an imperforate transverse process, and on the hinder edge of its body a very distinct articular cavity for the head of the first rib. In the young animal this is divided into two equal parts by the neurocentral suture.

In the order SIRENIA, the Dugong (*Halicore*) has seven cervical vertebræ, as in the Mammalia generally. The atlas has short imperforate conical transverse processes. The axis has a high arch and massive neural spine, a short rounded odontoid process, and very rudimentary transverse processes. The others have short and wide bodies, small spines, and irregularly developed transverse processes, often not completely enclosing a vertebrarterial canal.

The *Rhytina*, a large animal of this order, which became extinct towards the close of the last century, had also seven cervical vertebræ.

The Manatis (genus *Manatus*), of which there are two well-marked species, one inhabiting the west coast of Africa, and the other the east coast of Central and South America, never have more than *six* vertebræ in the cervical region. These resemble generally those of the Dugong, having short and wide bodies, and very irregular transverse processes. In a specimen of *M. senegalensis*, in the Museum of the College of Surgeons, the second and third are ankylosed by their bodies, and the neural arches of most of the others are widely open above. In the skeletons of *M. americanus*, in the same museum, the vertebræ are all free, and the arches, though slender, are complete, and with very slightly developed spinous processes.

In the *Cetacea* the seven cervical vertebræ usually found in the Mammalia are always present, though often so short and blended together, that it is not easy at first sight to recognize their existence. In some genera of both sub-orders all the vertebræ are free, though never allowing of much motion between them; but more commonly certain of them are firmly united together by bone. Even where the atlas and axis are separate the odontoid rarely forms a distinct process (most distinct in *Platanista*), but still it is developed from an ossific centre of its own, as in other Mammals.

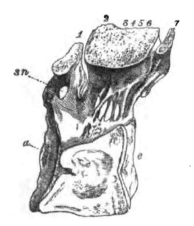

Fig. 15.—Section through middle line of united cervical vertebræ of Greenland Right Whale (*Balæna mystutus*), ½. *a* articular surface for occipital condyle ; *e* epiphysis on posterior end of body of seventh cervical vertebra ; *sn* foramen in arch of atlas for first spinal nerve ; 1 arch of atlas ; 2 3 4 5 6 coujoined arches of the axis and four following vertebræ ; 7 arch of seventh vertebra.

Among the *Mystacoceti*, in the Right Whales (genus *Balæna*) the whole of the seven cervical vertebræ are usually united into one mass by their bodies, though sometimes the seventh is free.   The arches are also more or less united above, though generally not in a continuous mass.   Small slit-like openings between the narrow pedicles of the arches permit the exit of the cervical spinal nerves, and in the adult condition afford the only indication by which the number of the united vertebræ can be ascertained.   Already before birth most of the bodies have coalesced, and it is even doubtful whether they ever exist in a separate condition.

The Fin Whales or Rorquals (genus *Balænoptera*) present a totally different condition of cervical vertebræ, as these are, as a rule, all distinct and free, though occasionally, as an individual peculiarity, an irregular ankylosis may take place between two or more of them.

In the common large Fin Whale of our coasts (*B. musculus*) the atlas (Fig. 16) has short, stout, conical, imper-

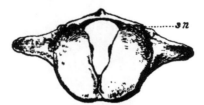

FIG. 16.—Anterior surface of atlas of common Fin Whale (*Balænoptera musculus*), ⅟₇. *sn* foramen for first spinal nerve.

forate transverse processes.   The axis (Fig. 17) has a broad oval body, high massive arch, very short odontoid process, and very wide, oblong wing-like transverse processes directed somewhat backwards, and with an oval perforation near the base.   The other cervical vertebræ (Fig. 18) have similar broad, very short bodies, small arches, without spines, and very long transverse processes, composed of a slender upper and lower bar, widely separated at their bases, but united at their extremities so as to enclose a very large space between them. In the seventh only the upper process exists, and the lower one is occasionally imperfect in the sixth. In very young animals these processes are only formed in cartilage ; and as ossification takes place gradually from within out-

FIG. 17.—Anterior surface of axis of common Fin Whale (*Balænoptera musculus*), ⅟₂. *o* odontoid process.

wards, and does not reach the outer extremity until the animal approaches maturity, specimens are frequently met with in museums, which, instead of completely annular

FIG. 18.—Anterior surface of ourth cervical vertebra of the same animal, ⅟₂. *az* anterior of zygapophysis ; *t* upper transverse process ; *t'* lower transverse process.

transverse processes, show only truncated upper and lower bars. In some species, however (as in *Megaptera longimana*), most of the cervical vertebræ remain permanently in this condition.

Among the *Odontoceti*, all the cervical vertebræ are free in the Gangetic Dolphin (*Platanista*), and in the allied South American genera *Inia* and *Pontoporia*, also in the Arctic Narwhal (*Monodon*) and the *Beluga*, or the White Whale. In most of these genera the atlas has a large hypapophysial process, projecting under and articulating with the body of the axis, which develops no distinct odontoid. In the Narwhal irregular ankyloses between the bodies of the cervical vertebræ are very frequent. In all the other *Delphinidæ* (including *Delphinus, Orca, Pseudorca, Globiocephalus, Pho-cæna,* &c.), at least the first and second cervical vertebræ are united by both body and spine, and most commonly some of the succeeding vertebræ are joined to them. If any are free, it is always those situated most posteriorly, and they have extremely thin, sub-circular disk-like bodies, and irregular and comparatively rudimentary transverse processes.

In *Hyperoodon,* and most of the other Ziphioids, the whole of the cervical vertebræ are ankylosed together ; but the allied Cachalot, or Sperm Whale (*Physeter*), presents a condition not met with in any other known Cetacean : the atlas is free, and all the other neck vertebræ are completely united.

Among the various members of the order EDENTATA, the cervical vertebræ present very different conditions.

In the Armadillos (*Dasypodidæ*) the bodies are extremely short, broad, and depressed, and several are commonly anky-losed together ; the corresponding neural arches being also united, the neural and vertebrarterial canals form continuous tubes. The orifices for the spinal nerves perforate the united pedicles. The atlas is always free. The vertebræ that are united are the second and third, or the second, third, and fourth, and in some species the fifth also. The spinous process of the axis is very large, but the neural arches of the hinder free vertebræ are extremely narrow, and the spinous processes rudimentary. The transverse process of the seventh has an inferior lamella, nearly as large as that of the sixth, but it is usually not perforated.

In *Orycteropus*, the Pangolins (*Manis*), and the Anteaters (*Myrmecophaga*), the neck vertebræ are more normal in form, and are not ankylosed. In the last-named genus, the vertebrarterial canal of several of the vertebræ perforates the pedicle obliquely, and enters the neural canal posteriorly, much as in the Camels.

Among the leaf-eating Edentates, or Sloths, the neck vertebræ present some remarkable peculiarities, especially as to number.

All the known species of three-toed Sloths (genus *Bradypus*) have nine cervical vertebræ, *i.e.* nine vertebræ in front of the one which bears the first thoracic rib (or first rib connected with the sternum, and corresponding in its general relations with the first rib of other Mammals), but the ninth, and sometimes the eighth, bears a pair of short moveable ribs. The eighth is perforated by the vertebrarterial canal, but not the ninth.

The common species of two-toed Sloth (*Cholœpus didactylus*) has seven cervical vertebræ, but a closely allied species (*C. hoffmannii*) has but six.

In the very heterogeneous order MARSUPIALIA (sub-class *Didelphia*) the cervical vertebræ vary much in their characters, though the number is always seven, as in the great majority of the Mammalia.

One of the most important variations is in the mode of ossification of the atlas. In the Wombat (*Phascolomys*), Koala(*Phascolarctos*), *Phalangista*, and Kangaroo (*Macropus*), there is no distinct ossific nucleus in the inferior arch of the bone, which remains either permanently open in the middle line below, or (as in some of the smaller Kangaroos) is completed by the union of prolongations of the arches inwards. This, however, is not the case with the carnivorous Marsupials. In the Thylacine (see Fig. 19) there is a distinct

heart-shaped piece of bone in the centre of the inferior arch
of the atlas, which appears never to become united to the
remainder, as it is still attached by ligament in skeletons
otherwise perfectly mature, and is commonly lost in mace-

FIG. 19.—Inferior surface of atlas of Thylacine (*Thylacinus cynocephalus*), ⅔. *h* distinct ossification in centre of inferior arch, with pointed hypapophysial projection.

ration. In *Perameles* and *Didelphys* the atlas is completely
ossified below by a wide intermediate piece, quite as in
ordinary Mammals.

As to the other vertebræ, in the Kangaroos the transverse
processes are long and slender, and (including the seventh)
have a very small perforation close to the base. The inferior
lamella arises near the base of the process, and is very large
in the sixth, but quite absent in the seventh vertebra.

In the Wombat, the bodies are wide and depressed. The
transverse processes are perforated in all, the inferior lamella
of the sixth much developed antero-posteriorly; the spines
of all are rather short.

In *Perameles lagotis* the greater part of the transverse process of the axis is ossified separately from the rest of the
vertebra, and remains some time distinct, as in the Monotremata. In this genus, as in the other carnivorous Marsupials, the inferior lamellæ of the transverse processes of the
fourth, fifth, and sixth vertebræ, but especially of the latter,
are particularly large.

Some species of American Opossums (as *Didelphys
virginiana* and its nearest allies) have the spinous processes

of the second, third, fourth, and fifth cervical vertebræ, very high, square, and massive, and being closely applied to each other by flattened surfaces form a solid wall of bone along the top of the neck.

In both genera of MONOTREMATA (sub-class *Ornitho-delphia*) the cervical vertebræ are seven in number, and in both the inferior arch of the atlas is completely ossified, apparently from a separate centre ; but in *Ornithorhynchus* a large bifurcated hypapophysis is developed, which is quite wanting in *Echidna*.

In *Ornithorhynchus* also all the other cervical vertebræ have a single median hypapophysial spine, equally wanting in *Echidna*.

In both, the axis has a high compressed spine, and the odontoid portion remains long distinct from the true centrum of the bone. In both, the transverse processes are of auto-genous formation, and remain suturally connected with the remainder of the vertebra until the animal is nearly full-grown (see Fig. 5, p. 20) ; that of the axis is still distinct in an adult *Ornithorhynchus*. Though in this respect they present an approximation to the *Sauropsida* (Reptiles and Birds), they differ from that group, inasmuch as there is not a gradual transition from these autogenous transverse pro-cesses of the neck (or cervical ribs, as they may be con-sidered) into the thoracic ribs, for in the seventh vertebra the costal element is much smaller than in the others, indicative of a very marked separation of neck from thorax, not seen in the *Sauropsida*.

CHAPTER V.

SPECIAL CHARACTERS OF THE THORACIC AND LUMBAR VERTEBRÆ.

IT will be most convenient to consider the vertebræ of these two regions together.

In Man, there are seventeen trunk vertebræ, twelve thoracic or rib-bearing, and five lumbar.

The bodies increase in size from before backwards,[1] and also change their form. The first is like a cervical vertebra, broad and depressed. They soon become more compressed, especially at the lower part, so as to be subtriangular when seen from one end (Fig. 2, p. 11); after the middle of the thoracic region they become more circular in outline, and in the lumbar region they are wide transversely. The ends of the bodies are flat or slightly concave.

The neural canal does not alter greatly in size throughout this region, though it does somewhat in form. In the first vertebra it is wider in proportion to its height than in any of the others.

The arches have comparatively narrow pedicles, arising from the anterior half of the body, deeply notched behind, for the canal for the exit of the spinal nerves. The laminæ are broad. The spines are moderately long, subequal

[1] As before, the vertebral column is supposed to be in the horizontal position.

throughout the series, rather slender, and sloping backwards in the thoracic region ; broader (in the antero-posterior direction) and more upright in the lumbar region, and presenting but scarcely any indication of that convergence towards a point in the posterior thoracic region so frequently seen in other Mammals.   They are generally simple and slightly dilated at their ends ; but in the lumbar region, the posterior edge is often more or less bifid.

The zygapophyses are well developed throughout.   In the thoracic region they are oval, flat facets, looking pretty nearly directly upwards (the anterior) and downwards (the posterior) : the anterior, developed on the top of the pedicle and projecting forwards, being supported by the " oblique process ; " the posterior is placed on the under-surface of the hinder part of the lamina.   In the lumbar region, their form and position change, the anterior having their outer edges turned upwards, and supported by a short rounded metapophysis (*mammillary process*).   The posterior ones have undergone a corresponding change, so that their faces, instead of looking downwards, are directed obliquely outwards ; they are also much curved.

The transverse processes project throughout the series from the arch, near the junction of the pedicle with the lamina.   In the greater part of the thoracic region they are tolerably long, project somewhat upwards, and slightly forwards, and are dilated and tuberous at the extremities, on the under-surface of which (except in the two last) they show a smooth concave facet for the attachment of the tubercle of the rib.   In the posterior part of the thoracic region they are shorter, and begin to resolve themselves into three distinct processes, generally conspicuous in the first lumbar. One of these projects outwards, and, elongating in the second and third lumbar, it forms its principal transverse process.

One projects upwards and forwards, by the side of the anterior zygapophysis ; this is the *metapophysis*, or mammillary process. The other projects backwards, and represents in a rudimentary condition the process so largely developed in many animals called *anapophysis*. It gradually becomes smaller in the second and third lumbar vertebræ, and generally disappears in the fourth.

The lumbar transverse processes are thus not serially homologous with the thoracic ribs, but with the part of the transverse process of the thoracic vertebræ to which the tubercle of the rib is attached, and are complementary to the ribs, becoming greatly augmented in size directly these cease. Neither are they normally developed autogenously.[1]

The sides of the bodies of the thoracic vertebræ bear facets for the articulations of the heads of the ribs. Except the last three or four, each vertebra supports a portion of the heads of two ribs, having a large facet near its anterior edge (placed partly on the body and partly on the side of the pedicle) for the head of its own rib (*i.e.* the rib which articulates also with the transverse process), and on the hinder border of the upper angle of the body a small facet to receive the anterior edge of the succeeding rib. In the hinder part of the thoracic region the rib is connected only with its corresponding vertebra, and not with the one in front.

Among the remaining Primates, 19 is the prevailing number of trunk vertebræ, of which usually 12 to 14 bear ribs. The Gorilla and Chimpanzee (genus *Troglodytes*), and Orang (*Simia*), agree with Man in having but 17. The Gibbons (*Hylobates*) and Spider Monkeys (*Ateles*) have

[1] There are several specimens in the College Museum which show the co-existence, on the first lumbar vertebra, of a rudimentary (supplemental) rib, with a transverse process serially homologous with the transverse processes of the other lumbar vertebræ.

mostly 18. Among the *Lemurina*, *Loris* and *Nycticebus* have as many as 23 or 24.

Of thoracic vertebræ, the Gorilla has 13, the Chimpanzee usually 13, the Orang 12, the Gibbons 12 or 13 ; other Old World Monkeys from 11 to 13 ; the American Monkeys from 12 to 15 ; the Lemurs from 12 to 16.

As a general rule the vertebral column, taken as a whole, is straighter than it is in Man, showing a much less marked sigmoid curve.

Except in the most anthropoid Apes, and a few others, the spinous processes of the anterior thoracic vertebræ lean backwards, and those of the lumbar and some of the posterior dorsal vertebræ forwards, so that they converge to a point near the hinder part of the thoracic region, sometimes called " *the centre of motion* " of the vertebral column.[1] This may be between two vertebræ, but more often there is one, which has an upright spine, towards which the others are directed ; this is the " *anticlinal vertebra.*" It is at this point that the thoracic vertebræ begin to change their characters, and assume those of the lumbar vertebræ ; and the simple elongated transverse processes break up as it were into the metapophyses, anapophyses, and lumbar transverse processes, all of which are conspicuous in these animals.

The transverse processes of the lumbar vertebræ are usually placed lower on the sides of the vertebræ than in Man.

In *Galago* the hinder edges of the neural spines of the lumbar vertebræ bear a pair of backward-projecting processes, which clasp the anterior edge of the succeeding spine. Similar processes are developed, but to a less extent, in the Howling Monkeys (*Mycetes*) and in *Lagothrix*.

---

[1] This disposition of the spines of the trunk vertebræ is still more marked in many of the inferior mammals, especially the terrestrial Carnivora.

The foramina for the exit of the spinal nerves, instead of being "intervertebral," perforate the pedicles of the arches in the Potto (*Perodicticus*). In the same genus, two or three of the anterior thoracic vertebræ have very long slender spinous processes, which in the living animal project beyond the general level of the skin, forming distinct conical prominences, covered only by an exceedingly thin and naked integument.

In the CARNIVORA, the trunk vertebræ are nearly always 20 or 21 in number. The genera *Felis*, *Canis*, and *Viverra* have 13 thoracic and 7 lumbar, *Hyæna* 15 and 5, *Mustela*, *Nasua*, *Procyon*, and *Ursus* 14 and 6, *Meles* 15 and 5; *Mephitis* has the exceptionally high number of 16 and 6, and *Mellivora* but 14 and 4. Among the Seals, *Cystophora* and *Otaria* have 15 and 5, *Trichecus* 14 and 6, and *Phoca* 14 and 5.

The spines of the anterior thoracic vertebræ are long and slender, and slope back to about the eleventh (the *anticlinal*), after which they are shorter, thicker (from before backwards), and lean forwards. From this point also metapophyses and anapophyses become distinctly developed; the latter are especially large in the *Felidæ*. The lumbar vertebræ have long transverse processes directed forwards and rather downwards, and short, stout, compressed spinous proconcesses.

In the Seals, the trunk vertebræ present much the same characters, but the anapophyses are very slightly developed, or altogether absent, and the spinous processes show no convergence to a "centre of motion."

Among the INSECTIVORA, the number of the trunk vertebræ varies much in the different genera, from 18 (13 thoracic and 5 lumbar) in *Tupaia*, 19 (13 and 6) in *Talpa* and most *Sorecidæ*, 19 (14 and 5) in *Galeopithecus*, 21 (15 and 6) in

Erinaceus, 22 (19 and 3) in *Chrysochloris*, to 24 (19 and 5) in *Centetes*.

There are also great differences in the development of the processes of the vertebræ, which appear to accord with the diversities in the habits and movements of the animal. The transverse processes of the lumbar vertebræ are very short in the comparatively slow moving, running, or burrowing Hedgehogs (*Erinaceus*), Shrews (*Sorex*) and Moles (*Talpa*), but they are very long, broad, and inclined downwards in the jumping *Macroscelides* and *Rhynchocyon*, where the lumbar muscles are greatly developed and the hinder extremities disproportionately large.

In the Mole, there are distinct, small, oval, flat ossicles on the under-surfaces of the interspaces between the lumbar vertebræ. Similar ossicles, but in a more rudimentary condition, are occasionally found in the same situation in some other Insectivora, as the Hedgehog, but not in any other Mammals.

The usual number of thoracic and lumbar vertebræ in the CHIROPTERA is 17, being either 12 and 5, or less commonly 11 and 6. The transverse processes of the lumbar vertebræ are almost obsolete, as are also the spinous processes throughout the series.

Among the RODENTIA, the most prevalent number is 19; but it falls as low as 16 (13 thoracic and 3 lumbar) in *Fiber zibeticus*, and rises as high as 23 (17 and 6) in *Capromys*, and even as 25 (17 and 8) in *Loncheres*.

The characters of the vertebræ vary much in the different genera, as among the Insectivora. In the Hares (genus *Lepus*) the anterior thoracic vertebræ have long slender spinous processes; the lumbar vertebræ (see Fig. 3, p. 14) have very long and slender transverse processes directed downwards and forwards and widening at their extremities;

E

long metapophyses projecting upwards and forwards, small anapophyses, and remarkably long, single, compressed median hypapophyses. These latter are not found in the Rodentia generally.

In the UNGULATA, the bodies of the trunk vertebræ are generally slightly opisthocœlous. The spinous processes in the anterior thoracic region are exceedingly high and compressed. The transverse processes of the lumbar vertebræ are long, flattened, and project horizontally outwards or slightly forwards from the arch. The metapophyses are moderately developed, and there are no anapophyses. The canals for the exit of the spinal nerves frequently pierce the pedicle of the neural arch.

In the Artiodactyle sub-order the number of thoracic and lumbar vertebræ together is always 19, though the former may vary from 12 to 15. Among the Perissodactyles, the number 23 is equally constant, the Horse and Tapir having 18, and the Rhinoceros 19 thoracic vertebræ.

Some species of Hyrax have as many as 22 thoracic and 8 lumbar vertebræ, making altogether 30, the highest number in any terrestrial Mammal.

The Elephants have 23 in all, 19 or 20 of which bear ribs.

In the order SIRENIA, the thoracic vertebræ are numerous and the lumbar very few; thus the Dugong (*Halicore*) has 19 thoracic and 4 lumbar, and the Manati (*Manatus*) 17 and 2. The bodies are rather triangular, being compressed and keeled below, and in the young state have no distinctly ossified terminal epiphyses. The bodies of all the thoracic vertebræ bear articular facets for the heads of the ribs. The spinous processes are not very high, but the zygapophyses are well developed throughout the series. The metapophyses are rudimentary, and there are no distinct anapophyses.

As there is no sacrum in the CETACEA the lumbar region passes directly into the caudal, and they can only be distinguished by the presence of " chevron bones " in the latter.

The thoracic vertebræ vary in number from 9 in Hyperoodon, to 15 and occasionally 16 in some Fin-Whales (*Balænoptera*), and the lumbar vertebræ from 3 in *Inia* (the Amazonian fresh-water Dolphin) to 24 or even more in some of the true Dolphins (*Delphinus*).

The bodies are short in the anterior part of the thoracic region, but afterwards are more or less elongated and cylindrical. Their terminal epiphyses are strongly ossified disks, very distinct in young animals, but coalescing completely with the rest of the body in adult age. The spinous processes are high and compressed. The zygapophyses are very little developed, and only found in the anterior thoracic region. The metapophyses are distinct (see Fig. 20, *m*), placed at first near the ends of the transverse processes, but gradually rising on the arch, are ultimately transferred to the sides of the anterior edge of the neural spine, from which they project forwards, clasping between them the hinder edge of the spine of the vertebra in front.

In most Cetacea the transverse processes of the anterior thoracic region arise rather high on the side of the neural arch of the vertebra, but in the hinder part of the same region become gradually placed lower, until finally they are transferred to near the middle of the side of the body, which position they occupy in the lumbar region (see Fig. 20). The transverse processes of the lumbar vertebræ are thus evidently serially homologous with the transverse processes of the anterior dorsal vertebræ, which, in their turn, continue backwards the upper series of cervical transverse processes.

In the *Physeteridæ* (comprising *Physeter, Hyperoodon,*

Ziphius, and the allied forms) a very different and peculiar
arrangement occurs (Fig. 21). The transverse processes in the
anterior thoracic region (*t*) are placed quite similarly to those
of the ordinary Dolphins; but passing backwards, instead
of changing their position on the vertebræ, they gradually
become smaller, and finally disappear; while simultaneously
with their diminution in size, other processes (*t'*) rise from the
body of the vertebra, in the situation of the capitular attach-

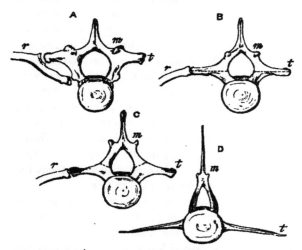

FIG. 20.—Anterior surface of vertebræ of Dolphin (*Globiocephalus melas*), ⅓. A fifth
thoracic; B seventh thoracic; C eighth thoracic; D first lumbar; *r* rib; *m* metapophysis; *t* transverse process. The dotted lines indicate the position of the
neuro-central suture.

ment of the rib, which, rapidly increasing in length, become
continuous serially with the lumbar transverse processes. In
two or three vertebræ the two co-exist (Fig. 21, B and C),
resembling the upper and lower transverse processes of the
neck, and sometimes even meeting at their extremities so as
to enclose a canal. The lumbar transverse processes in this

case therefore are not serially homologous with the transverse processes of the anterior thoracic region, and of the upper transverse processes of the neck, as in the former case, but rather with the lower transverse processes of that region ; and yet tried by every other test, the special homology of the transverse processes of the lumbar vertebræ of a Dolphin (Fig. 20, D *t*) and a Sperm Whale (Fig. 21, D *t*) is perfectly evident.

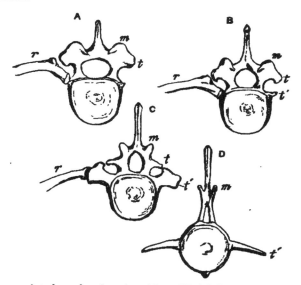

FIG. 21.—Anterior surface of vertebræ of Sperm Whale (*Physeter macrocephalus*), ¼. A eighth thoracic ; B ninth thoracic ; C tenth thoracic ; D fifth lumbar ; *r* rib ; *m* metapophysis ; *t* upper transverse process ; *t'* lower transverse process.

The mode of ossification of the thoracic and lumbar vertebræ of the Cetacea, appears, so far as it has been ascertained, to differ from that of all other Mammals, inasmuch as the neuro-central suture (see Fig. 20) is always placed a little above the junction of the arch and the body, the whole of the latter, with any process which may arise from it, being ossified from the central nucleus. Consequently, in the thoracic vertebræ of the Dolphins, the transverse process is anteriorly an outgrowth from the arch, then partly from the arch and partly from the body, and finally from the body alone—a condition quite unknown in other Mammals.

It would appear, from the conflicting statements on the subject, that the transverse processes of the lumbar region are sometimes ossified autogenously, and sometimes exogenously from the centrum.

The members of the order EDENTATA present some great peculiarities in the condition of the trunk vertebræ, especially those of the lumbar region.

As to numbers, the Three-toed Sloths (*Bradypus*) have 20 altogether (either 17 and 3, or 15 and 5) ; and the Two-toed Sloths (*Cholœpus*) have sometimes as many as 24 thoracic and 3 lumbar, making altogether 27 trunk vertebræ. The Great Anteater (*Myrmecophaga*) has 18 (15 and 3) ; the little Two-toed Anteater (*Cyclothurus*), 17 (15 and 2). The Armadillos have 15 to 19, the Pangolins (*Manis*) commonly 18 (13 and 5), and the Cape Anteater (*Orycteropus*) 21 (13 and 8).

The vertebral column of the Sloths is remarkable for the extremely broad, flat laminæ and short neural spines, lying backwards on the next succeeding vertebræ, throughout the whole column down to the sacrum. All the processes are very short, and the spines are bifid in the lumbar region.

In these animals a small (anapophysial) process projects backwards from the hinder edge of the transverse process of each lumbar vertebra, having on its inner surface a facet, which articulates with a corresponding facet on the anterior edge of the arch of the succeeding vertebra, below the ordinary zygapophysis.

In *Megatherium, Myrmecophaga, Cyclothurus,* and *Dasypus* (in fact, all the remaining American Edentates), a disposition thus slightly indicated in the Sloths is carried out to a great extent, and results in a very complex and altogether peculiar method of articulation between the vertebræ.

It will be most convenient to describe it from one species, the Great Anteater (*Myrmecophaga jubata*), but it is the same in principle in all the above-named genera.

The anterior thoracic vertebræ articulate in a perfectly normal manner by large anterior and posterior zygapophyses.

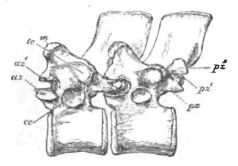

Fig. 22.—Side view of twelfth and thirteenth thoracic vertebræ of Great Anteater (*Myrmecophaga jubata*), ⅓. *m* metapophysis ; *tc* facet for articulation of tubercle of rib ; *cc* ditto for capitulum of rib ; *az* anterior zygapophysis ; *az¹* additional anterior articular facet ; *pz* posterior zygapophysis ; *pz¹* and *pz²* additional posterior articular facets.

These retain the horizontal position of their facets throughout. On the eleventh dorsal vertebra, the upper surface of the backward projecting process which bears the posterior zygapophysis (*pz*) below, develops an articular surface (*pz¹*) which looks upwards, and articulates with a corresponding downward directed process (*az¹*) developed on the upper part of the arch of the following vertebra, rather below the metapophysis (*m*). Thus the vertebra has a process projecting backwards, with flattened articular facets on its upper and under surface, fitting into a deep recess on the anterior edge of the arch of the vertebra behind, and the articulation is now by two zygapophysial surfaces on each side of the arch instead of one.

In the thirteenth thoracic vertebra a third articular facet (pz^2) is developed on the hinder margin of the lamina of the arch, still higher than the last additional one (pz^1), and separated from it by a deep notch. This looks mainly outwards, and articulates with a corresponding facet (az^2, Fig. 24) on the anterior edge of the arch of the fourteenth

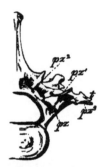
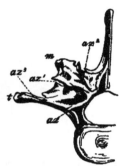

Fig. 23.—Posterior surface of second lumbar vertebra of Great Ant-eater, ⅓. *t* transverse process ; *pz* posterior zygapophysis ; pz^1, pz^2, and pz^3, additional posterior articular facets.

Fig. 24.—Anterior surface of third lumbar vertebra of Great Ant-eater, ⅓. *t* transverse process ; *m* metapophysis ; *az* anterior zygapophysis ; az^1, az^2, and az^3, additional anterior articular facets.

vertebra, placed to the inner side of the metapophysis, which is now situated on a process projecting forwards into the notch between the two upper articular facets of the antecedent vertebra. So that there are now three distinct articulations connecting the arches of the vertebræ on each side, the processes of the vertebræ which bear them interlocking in a " tenon and mortice " fashion.

This condition continues as far as the second lumbar, in

which, in addition to these three facets, a fourth (p^3) is developed on the under-surface of the hinder edge of the transverse process near its outer extremity, which articulates with a similar facet (az^3) on the upper surface of the transverse process of the third lumbar, so that there are now four pairs of articular facets, or zygapophyses, on each arch. The same occurs also between the third lumbar and the first sacral vertebra.

In the Armadillos the lumbar metapophyses are very long, and project upwards, outwards, and forwards, supporting the bony carapace, while the broad transverse processes are exceedingly reduced.

An allied extinct genus, Glyptodon, had the greater number of the trunk vertebræ completely ankylosed, a condition altogether unique in the Mammalia.

In neither of the Old World Edentates, *Manis* and *Orycteropus*, is there any development of the articular facets other than the ordinary zygapophyses. In the former genus, the metapophyses (contrary to the usual rule) project rather backwards than forwards. The anterior zygapophyses of the lumbar and posterior thoracic region are largely developed, and very concave, completely embracing the semicylindrical surfaces of the posterior zygapophyses. There are no distinct anapophyses. In *Orycteropus* the lumbar vertebræ are numerous (8), with carinated bodies, long and slender spines leaning forwards, long, broad, and flat transverse processes pointing forwards and downwards, well developed metapophyses and rudimentary anapophyses.

In the MARSUPIALIA, the number of thoracico-lumbar vertebræ is invariably 19, although there are some apparent exceptions, in which the last lumbar assumes the form of a sacral vertebra. The rib-bearing vertebræ are always 13, except in the Koala (*Phascolarctos*), which has but 11, and one species of Wombat (*Phascolomys vombatus*), which has 15. The Hairy-nosed Wombat (*P. latifrons*) has the ordinary number.

In the Kangaroos, the lumbar vertebræ have largely developed metapophyses and anapophyses, and moderate-sized transverse processes much curved forwards.

In the running and jumping Bandicoots (*Perameles*) the lumbar vertebræ have very slender, long, forward-directed spines, and long transverse processes. In the climbing Opossums (*Didelphys*), on the other hand, the spines are very short and broad from before backwards.

The MONOTREMATA agree with the Marsupials in the total number of trunk vertebræ, but those that bear ribs are more numerous, viz. 16 in *Echidna*, and 17 in *Ornithorhynchus*.

The spinous and transverse processes are very short, and the ribs have no articulation with the latter, but are attached to the bodies only, the greater part of the articular surface being below the neuro-central suture, the reverse of what occurs in the higher Mammals. In the thoracic vertebræ the canals for the exit of the spinal nerves perforate the neural arch.

CHAPTER VI.

SPECIAL CHARACTERS OF THE SACRAL AND CAUDAL VERTEBRÆ.

Sacral Vertebræ.—The difficulties in defining the sacral vertebræ have been noticed at p. 24. Their essential character is best illustrated by tracing it up from the simple condition it presents in the tailed Amphibians (as *Menopoma*). In these animals a series of similar small straight ribs are moveably articulated to the ends of the transverse processes of all the trunk vertebræ, which are not distinctly divisible into separate regions. To the distal extremity of one of these the ilium is attached. This vertebra with its rib thus constitutes the "sacrum," and the ilium is clearly seen not to be a "pleurapophysis," as it is sometimes called, or any part of a vertebra, but a something distinct and superadded. In the Crocodiles there are two vertebræ with strongly developed rib-like bones connecting them to the ilium, and remaining long only suturally united to their vertebræ.

The inferior ossification of the transverse processes of the true sacral vertebræ in Mammals (see Fig. 6, p. 21) is clearly of the same nature, though more rudimentary in character, and coalescing at an earlier period with the remainder of the vertebra. It is not yet known that it exists in all Mammals, but this may be considered probable, as it is certainly found, at least in the first sacral vertebra, in such different forms as

Man, the Chimpanzee, Orang, Cat, Sheep, Elephant, Sloth, and Wombat.

The ankylosis of additional vertebræ in the Mammalia is probably related to the greater fixity and more complete attachment of the pelvis to the vertebral column in this class ; [1] for the innominate bone is not only articulated by its iliac portion to the true sacral vertebræ, but it has also a posterior connection with the vertebral column by its ischial portion, by means either of very strong ligaments, or in some cases by bony union.

In Man there are usually five ankylosed vertebræ, constituting the "*os sacrum*" of anthropotomy, but only two, or perhaps sometimes three, have distinct costal elements. The remainder may be called *pseudo-sacral,* and belong more properly to the caudal series. The sacrum as a whole is broad, strongly curved in the longitudinal direction, with the concavity downwards, and its anterior extremity forms with the body of the last lumbar vertebra a more prominent "sacro-vertebral angle" than in other Mammals.

In the Gorilla, Chimpanzee, and Orang, there are generally five ankylosed vertebræ, to which the last lumbar not unfrequently becomes united in old animals. The whole sacrum thus formed is long and narrow, gradually tapering posteriorly, and much less curved than in Man. In the other Monkeys, there are usually two or three, rarely four, ankylosed vertebræ; the first two, or true sacrals, are broad, and behind these the sacrum suddenly contracts.

In the *Lemurina* the number of united vertebræ varies from 2 to 5.

In the CARNIVORA, as a general rule, there appears to be but one true sacral vertebra, though one or more are ankylosed

---

[1] This is carried to a still greater extent in birds.

to it behind, especially in the Bears and Seals, where as many as 4 or 5 may be united by bone in old animals. In the Dog there are usually 3 ankylosed vertebræ.

In most UNGULATA and RODENTIA the sacrum consists of one broad vertebra joining the ilia, and a series of narrow ones varying in number with age, gradually diminishing in width, ankylosed to it behind.

In the Beaver among Rodents, the Cape Anteater (*Orycteropus*) among Edentates, and the Wombat among Marsupials, the sacrum consists of numerous ankylosed vertebræ, with widely-expanded transverse processes, which are longer in the hindermost vertebræ, and nearly meet the ischia.

In most other EDENTATA, as the Sloths, Anteaters, and Armadillos, this modification is carried further, and the transverse processes of the hinder pseudo-sacral vertebræ form a complete bony union with the ischia, converting into a foramen what is usually the sacro-sciatic notch. In some of the Armadillos as many as 10 vertebræ are thus most firmly fused together, and with the innominate bones.

In MARSUPIALIA usually but one vertebra supports the iliac bones, though another is commonly ankylosed with it.

In the MONOTREMATA, the Echidna has 3, and the Ornithorhynchus 2 ankylosed vertebræ.

The CETACEA having no iliac bones, have no part of the vertebral column specially modified into a sacrum ; but in the SIRENIA, the rudimentary ilia are attached by ligament to the end of the transverse processes of one vertebra, which may hence be regarded as sacral.

Caudal Vertebræ.—The vertebræ of the tail vary greatly in number and in characters in different animals. When it is well developed, as, for example, in the long-tailed Carnivora, from one of which the accompanying figures are taken, the anterior vertebræ (Figs. 25 and 26) are comparatively short and broad, with complete neural arches, though without distinct spines, prominent metapophyses, and anterior and posterior zygapophyses (the latter especially being raised on pedicles), and well-developed

FIG. 25.—Anterior surface of third caudal vertebra of Leopard (*Felis leopardus*), ⅔. *az* anterior zygapophysis; *pz* posterior zygapophysis; *m* metapophysis; *t* transverse process.

single transverse processes. But a gradual change takes place in these characters (see Figs. 27 and 28), the body lengthens out and becomes more and more cylindrical; the neural arch diminishes and finally disappears, leaving for a

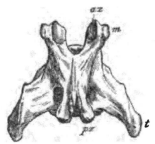

FIG. 26.—Upper surface of the third caudal vertebra of Leopard, ⅔. *az* anterior zygapophysis; *pz* posterior zygapophysis; *m* metapophysis; *t* transverse process.

while a pair of processes at each extremity of the vertebra, the remains of the parts of the arch which bore the zygapophyses; the transverse process is much reduced, and confined to the posterior extremity of the body, a second one

appearing at the anterior extremity.   Even these rudiments
of processes gradually cease to be perceptible, and nothing
is left but a cylindrical rod of bone, representing the centrum
alone of the vertebra.   These diminish in size towards the
apex of the tail, the last being usually a mere rounded nodule.

Connected with the under-surface of the caudal vertebræ
of many animals which have the tail well developed, are

FIG. 27.—Anterior surface of twelfth
caudal vertebra of Leopard, ⅓. *m*
metapophysis; *p* processes serially
continuous with those which support
the posterior zygapophyses in the anterior vertebra; *h* hypapophyses. The
process on the side of the body between *m* and *h* is the anterior transverse process.

FIG. 28.—Upper surface of twelfth caudal
vertebra of Leopard, ⅓.   *m* metapophyses; *p* processes serially continuous
with those which support the posterior
zygapophyses in the anterior vertebra.
t transverse process ; *t'* anterior transverse process.

certain bones, formed more or less in the form of an inverted arch (Fig. 29), called *chevron bones* (French, *Os en V;*
German, *Unterbogen; hæmapophyses,* Owen).   These are
always situated nearly opposite to an intervertebral space, and
are generally articulated both to the vertebra in front and the
vertebra behind ; but sometimes chiefly or entirely either
to one or the other.   They are usually articulated moveably
to prominences (*hypapophyses*) on the lower surface of the
body of the vertebra, but occasionally become ankylosed to
it.   They ossify from two centres, one on each side, which

usually coalesce in the median line below, though not unfrequently, especially at the beginning and end of the series,
where they are less developed, the two lateral portions remain
permanently separate. They serve to give a larger surface of
attachment for the inferior muscles of the tail, and also to
protect the caudal vessels, which run within the canal formed
by the series of these bony arches. They are always best

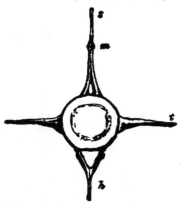

FIG. 29.—Anterior surface of fourth caudal vertebra of Porpoise (*Phocæna com-
munis*), ¼. *s* spinous process; *m* metapophysis; *t* transverse process; *h* chevron
bone.

developed near the anterior extremity of the tail, and are
never found under the posterior rudimentary vertebræ.

In Man the caudal vertebræ are quite rudimentary;
usually 4 in number all ankylosed together, and constituting
the *coccyx*, or *os coccygis*, of anthropotomy. The first is sometimes ankylosed to the sacrum.

Among the *Simiina* there are but 4 to 5 caudal vertebræ
in the Anthropoid Apes, and only 3 in the Barbary Ape
(*Inuus*), no more than 5 in some Baboons, as many as 31
in *Semnopithecus*, and 33 in some of the Spider Monkeys
(*Ateles*).

In the latter the tail is prehensile, and the vertebræ are altogether more strongly developed than in the weak, pendant, though almost equally long tails of the Old World monkeys.

Chevron bones are found in all except those species that have the tails quite rudimentary. They are most fully developed in *Ateles*, where the extremities are often bifurcated. They are attached to a pair of projections on the anterior end of the lower surface of the vertebra.

In the *Lemurina*, the number of the caudal vertebræ varies from 5 to 29.

Among the CARNIVORA, the Bears have very short tails, with from 8 to 10 vertebræ, the Seals from 9 to 14; some of the Lynxes have but 13, but most of the animals of the order have tails of moderate or great length; the greatest number of vertebræ being found in *Paradoxurus*, which may have as many as 36.

Chevron bones are usually not much developed; they are articulated (sometimes ankylosed) to the front end of the vertebra, as in the Primates.

In the INSECTIVORA, the tail is very variable. It is short and simple in *Erinaceus* and *Centetes*, long in *Solenodon, Gymnura, Potamogale, Tupaia* and *Rhynchocyon;* in the last-named genus the chevron bones are well developed and bifid.

In the CHIROPTERA, the tail is sometimes exceedingly rudimentary, as in *Desmodus;* sometimes elongated, but composed of long, simple, slender, cylindrical vertebral bodies; and generally enclosed in the interfemoral cutaneous expansion.

Among the different members of the order RODENTIA, there are great differences in the condition of the caudal vertebræ.

In the Hares, Guinea Pigs, Capybara, &c., the tail is almost rudimentary. In the Cape Jumping Hare (*Pedetes*) it is nearly as long and powerful as that of a Kangaroo, with well-developed chevron bones.

In the true Porcupines the tail is generally short; but in some allied genera (Tree Porcupines) it is much elongated and prehensile.

In the Beaver (*Castor*) there are 25 caudal vertebræ, all short, broad, and depressed, and with wide transverse processes, becoming double (anterior and posterior) about the middle of the tail, not by development of a new process, but by gradual division of the one existing in the anterior region.

In the UNGULATA, the tail is variable in length, but of simple character and function; it is never prehensile, nor has it ever chevron bones, although occasionally, as in the Ox, there is a pair of well-developed hypapophyses which may be produced so as to meet in the median line, enclosing a small canal. The vertebræ are most numerous in the Oxen, and least so in some Deer, especially *Moschus*, in which animal the tail is quite rudimentary.

The Elephant has a long tail, composed of 31 vertebræ of simple character, without chevron bones.

In the Hyrax the tail is almost rudimentary.

As the tail is the principal organ of locomotion in the CETACEA, it is always very well developed, and consists of numerous (from 18 to 30) vertebræ.

Chevron bones are always present, and of simple character, though with long compressed median spines (see Fig. 29, p. 64). They are mainly attached to the posterior extremity of the vertebra immediately in front of them.

The characters of the caudal vertebræ in the various animals of the order are tolerably uniform, the tail having the same function in all. In the anterior part of the region the bodies are very massive and cylindrical ; the arches have high spines, with metapophyses on their anterior edges, and the transverse processes are tolerably long, and directed straight outwards. In passing backwards the arches and all the processes gradually disappear, and the bodies become much compressed, and elevated vertically. Suddenly a change takes place (at the spot where the end of the vertebral column becomes enclosed in the horizontal, laterally extended cutaneous expansions, constituting the "flukes" of the tail), and the vertebræ altogether alter their characters, becoming much smaller, wide transversely and depressed. There is always one vertebra which is transitional in its character between these two forms. Most of the caudal vertebræ are perforated by a vertical canal on each side, at first passing through the base of the transverse process, but posteriorly through the body of the vertebra itself. This transmits an ascending branch of the caudal artery.

The SIRENIA have numerous, much depressed caudal vertebræ, with wide transverse processes, gradually diminishing in length from the commencement towards the apex. They are thus very different from those of the Cetacea.

Among the EDENTATA, the Sloths have a quite rudimentary tail, consisting of from 6 to 10 depressed vertebræ without chevron bones.

In the allied *Megatherium* the tail was greatly developed, with long processes and large chevron bones, as is the case with nearly all the Entomophagous Edentates, but mostly so in the Pangolins (*Manis*), one species of which (*M. longicauda*) has 46 tail vertebræ, the highest number known in any Mammal. *Cyclothurus* has a prehensile tail of 40 vertebræ. The little *Chlamydophorus* has a rather short tail of 15 vertebræ, remarkable for being expanded, depressed and spatulate towards the end, the transverse processes actually increasing in size instead of gradually diminishing, as is almost universally the case.

The chevron bones are usually much developed. They are Y-shaped, having long, simple, compressed spines in *Orycteropus;* simple V-shaped in Manis and most Armadillos; but in *Priodontes,* they have wide, diverging, lateral processes, instead of a median spine. They are attached rather to the vertebra in front than to that behind them.

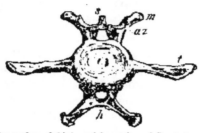

Fig. 30.—Anterior surface of third caudal vertebra of Great Armadillo (*Priodontes gigas*), ⅓. *s* spinous process; *m* metapophysis; *az* anterior zygapophysis; *t* transverse process; *h* chevron bone with diverging processes.

In the MARSUPIALIA, as might be supposed in so heterogeneous a group, there is great diversity in the condition of the caudal vertebræ.

In the Wombat (*Phascolomys*) and Koala (*Phascolarctos*) the tail is comparatively rudimentary.

In the Kangaroo, on the other hand, it is very large, and serves as an organ of support when standing upright. It is composed of from 21 to 25 vertebræ, the first few with short bodies and large processes; afterwards the bodies lengthen out, becoming cylinders contracted in the middle. The zygapophyses soon cease, but the metapophyses continue longer. The neural arch is not continued longer than about the middle of the tail ; the transverse processes are gradually placed further and further back on the vertebra, and then a new one arises near the anterior end, so that they become double.

The chevron bones are placed quite between the vertebræ so that it is difficult to say to which they most properly belong In the proximal part of the tail their free edge is compressed and develops a process forwards and backwards, giving a hatchet shape when seen sideways. Further back they also send out broad processes laterally, so as to be cruciform, with a flat inferior surface.

In some Marsupials the tail is prehensile, as in the Opossums (*Didelphys*), with from 19 to 35 vertebræ, and the Phalangers (*Phalangista*), with from 21 to 31.

Chevron bones are generally present in the tails of all the Marsupials, except the Wombat and Koala. In the Thylacine they are few and comparatively rudimentary.

The tails of the two animals composing the order MONOTREMATA differ considerably.

The Echidna has 12 caudal vertebræ. These have no hypapophyses, but there are two single median chevron bones near the middle of the tail, more like the lumbar subvertebral ossicles of the Mole than ordinary chevron bones. The Ornithorhynchus has 20 or 21 caudal vertebræ, with wide transverse processes, a single median hypapophysis, and no chevron bones.

CHAPTER VII.

THE STERNUM.

THE *Sternum* of Mammals is a bone, or generally a series of bones, placed longitudinally in the mesial line, on the inferior or ventral aspect of the thorax, and connected on each side with the vertebral column by a series of more or less ossified bars called ribs.[1]

It is present in all Mammals, but varies much in character in the different groups.

When in its usual and most complete form (see Fig. 31), it may be divided into three parts, called respectively,—

1. *Presternum*, or "Manubrium sterni" of human anatomy.

2. *Mesosternum*, body of the sternum or gladiolus.

3. *Xiphisternum*, xiphoid or ensiform process of the sternum.

The mesosternum is usually composed of several distinct segments, which may become ankylosed together, but more often permanently retain their individuality, being connected either by fibrous tissue or by synovial joints.

The ribs are attached to the sides of the sternum : the first pair to the presternum; the second to the presternum and the mesosternum at their point of junction; the

---

[1] For much valuable information upon the structure and development of the sternum see W. K. Parker's "Monograph on the Shoulder-girdle and Sternum of theVertebrata," published by the Ray Society, 1868.

remainder to the mesosternum, opposite the interspaces between each segment, though two or more pairs are often clustered round the last segment. The xiphisternum bears no ribs.

Development.—The osseous sternum is preceded by a continuous or non-segmented piece of cartilage ; and as the

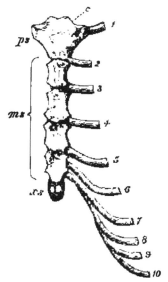

Fig. 31.—Human sternum and sternal ribs, ½. *ps* presternum; *ms* mesosternum; *xs* xiphisternum; *c* point of attachment of clavicle; 1 to 10 the cartilaginous sternal ribs.

portion of the body in which this is developed is formed by the union in the middle line of the two " ventral laminæ" of the embryo, traces of this original median division are generally seen in very young sterna, and are often persistent through life in the form of fissures or fenestræ in the middle line of the sternum. Each segment ossifies from a single nucleus, or from two nuclei placed

one on each side of the middle line, and which usually
become blended together in the course of growth. Sometimes epiphyses are added to the ends of the segments. The
terminal portion of the xiphisternum generally remains cartilaginous through life.

Special Characters of the Sternum in the various Orders.
Order PRIMATES.—In Man (see Fig. 31, p. 71) the *presternum*
is broad and flat, hollowed in the middle line in front, and
expanded laterally to give large surfaces for the attachment

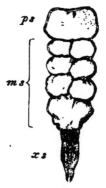

of the clavicles and the first pair of
ribs. The *mesosternum* is elongated,
but is also comparatively broad and
flattened. It consists of four distinct
segments. The *xiphisternum* is a
more or less elongated posterior appendage, varying somewhat in form
and size in different individuals.

The ossification of the human
sternum is *endosteal*, or commencing
within the substance of the primative
hyaline cartilage. The presternum
ossifies from one, or sometimes two,
centres, which may be placed side by
side, or one in front of the other.

FIG. 32.—Sternum of young
Orang (*Simia satyrus*): *ps*
presternum; *ms* mesosternum;
xs xiphisternum.

Each of the segments of the mesosternum has a distinct
centre, though these may be double in their earliest condition, and sometimes remain so for a long period.

The segments of the mesosternum usually unite together
so as to form one continuous bony piece, to which the presternum often remains throughout life connected only by
fibrous tissue, although it is not unfrequently ankylosed in
old age.

The xiphisternum ossifies irregularly and imperfectly.

The Gorilla, Chimpanzee, Orang, and Gibbons, resemble Man, and differ from the other monkeys in the breadth and flatness of the sternum. It is broadest in proportion to its length in the Siamang (*Hylobates syndactyla*). In the Orang (Fig. 32), each segment of the mesosternum is developed from a pair of lateral ossifications, which commonly remain separate until the animal is about half-grown.[1]

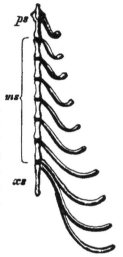

In the lower Monkeys the presternum is somewhat broad, but the bones constituting the mesosternum are elongated and compressed, and are not ankylosed together as in Man and the highest Apes. Their number varies from three to five. In the Howling Monkey (*Mycetes*) the presternum has in front of it two large diverging horns (*pro-ostea*, Parker), which ossify separately and support the clavicles and either the whole or part of the first pair of ribs.

In the CARNIVORA, the sternum (Fig. 33) is generally composed of eight or nine pieces altogether, including the presternum and the xiphisternum.

FIG. 33.—Sternum and sternal ribs of Dog (*Canis familiaris*), ⅓: *ps* presternum; *ms* mesosternum; *xs* xiphisternum.

The presternum, or manubrium, is long and narrow, somewhat expanded near the front for the attachment of the first pair of sternal ribs, and terminating anteriorly in a conical rounded projection.

[1] The sternum of a young Gorilla in the Museum of the College of Surgeons presents the same condition.

The segments of the mesosternum are elongated, and more or less four-sided, contracted at the middle, and widening at each extremity. They ossify, according to Parker, *ectosteally*, or from without inwards, the bony deposit commencing in the inner layer of the perichondrium, as in the shafts of long bones; and they remain permanently distinct from each other.

The xiphisternum is long, narrow, and flat, and generally ends in an expanded, flattened cartilage.[1]

In the *Pinnipedia*, the presternum is produced considerably in front of the attachment of the first pair of ribs.

In the INSECTIVORA, the sternum is variable in form, but always more or less elongated and segmented. The presternum is always more or less expanded laterally in this claviculated group of animals. It is bilobate in front in the Hedgehog (*Erinaceus*), trilobate in the Shrews (*Sorex*). In *Rhynchocyon* it is broad in front, narrow posteriorly, strongly keeled below, and with two horn-like processes projecting outwards and forwards between the attachment of the clavicles and the first pair of ribs.

The mesosternum is usually narrow, as in the Carnivora, but in the Hedgehog, where it consists of three segments, it is broad and flat posteriorly. In this genus the xiphisternum is rudimentary, whereas in the Shrews it is long and ends in a flat expanded cartilage.

The Mole (*Talpa*) and its nearest allies have a remarkably developed presternum, which is longer than the whole of the mesosternum (Fig. 34). It is strongly keeled below, except at the front part, which is much thickened. On its superior or inner surface it is grooved in the middle line. Laterally it gives off a pair of wing-like processes, behind which the first pair of ribs are attached. It is distinctly separated from the

[1] This is not preserved in the specimen figured.

mesosternum, which consists of five segments of nearly equal width. The xiphisternum has a broad oval cartilaginous expansion posteriorly, not shown in the figure, which is taken from a dried specimen.

As the clavicle is supported at the anterior extremity of the elongated presternum, it is widely separated from the first rib, and the anterior extremities are brought into such close juxtaposition with the head, that the animal appears to have no neck.

In the CHIROPTERA, the sternum presents a considerable general resemblance to that of Man. The presternum is large, trilobate in front, and strongly keeled. In many of the Insectivorous Bats the segments of the mesosternum are (at least in adults) firmly ankylosed together, but in the frugivorous Bats (*Pteropus*, &c.) they continue separated.

FIG. 34.—Sternum of Common Mole (*Talpa europæa*): *ps* presternum; *ms* mesosternum; *xs* xiphisternum; *c* point of attachment of clavicle.

In the RODENTIA, the sternum is long and narrow, consisting of a presternum (which is generally broad in the forms which have the clavicle well developed, as the Rats, Beavers, &c.), a mesosternum of three, or more usually four, segments, and a long xiphisternum, with a broad cartilaginous terminal expansion. The segments of the mesosternum often have epiphyses at each end.

The presternum is compressed and produced forwards in those species in which the clavicle is absent or rudimentary, as the Aguti, the Hares, and the Capybara. In the latter it much resembles that of the Horse or Tapir.

Order UNGULATA.—In the *Ruminantia* there are usually seven segments altogether in the sternum (Fig. 35). The presternum is narrow, rounded in front, and bearing the

first pair of sternal ribs close to its apex. The succeeding
pieces gradually widen, the posterior segments of the mesosternum being square, flat, and rather massive (especially in
the Giraffe); they are hollowed at the middle of their
lateral borders. The xiphisternum is thin and flat.

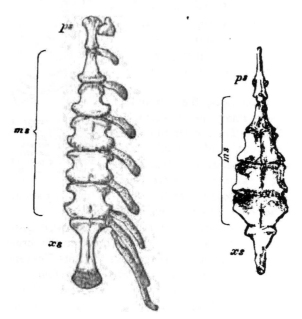

FIG. 35.—Sternum and sternal ribs of
the Red Deer (*Cervus elaphus*), ⅓. *ps*
presternum; *ms* mesosternum; *xs*
xiphisternum.

FIG. 36. — Sternum of the Pig (*Sus
scrofa*), ¼: *ps* presternum; *ms* mesosternum; *xs* xiphisternum.

In the Pig (Fig. 36) and Hippopotamus the presternum
is compressed and keeled; the articular facets for the first
pair of ribs are close together on its upper surface; but
the mesosternum is broad and flat, the first segment being

transitional, compressed in front, and broad posteriorly. The xiphisternum is narrow and pointed. The sternum of the Pig very often retains indications of the primordial median fissure through life.

The Horse and the Tapir have a very peculiar sternum. The presternum is extremely compressed and projects forward like the prow of a boat. In the Tapir, its anterior portion is originally, and commonly remains, a distinct ossification (*pro-osteon*, Parker). The segments which follow gradually widen, and the hinder part of the sternum is broad and flat. The last mesosternal segment in the Tapir is generally divided in the middle line, and is not followed by a xiphisternal element.

The sternum of the Rhinoceros, on the other hand, is very narrow throughout, with a long, rather spatulate xiphisternum.

Order CETACEA.—Each of the two primary divisions of this order has a distinct form of sternum.

Among the *Odontoceti*, the typical Dolphins have a very broad presternum of peculiar form, emarginate in the middle line in front, and with a pair of lateral proceesses behind the attachment of the first pair of ribs. This is followed by two or three mesosternal segments, but no xiphisternum. An indication of the primordial median fissure can generally be traced, except in very old animals, either as a hole in the presternum, or as a division of the posterior mesosternal segment.

In the Porpoise (*Phocæna*) the sternum is shorter and broader than in most Dolphins, and its various elements early coalesce into a single bone.

In the Cachalot (*Physeter macrocephalus*) the sternum ossifies from three distinct pairs of nuclei, and a large median fontinelle remains between the first and second

pair.[1] In the specimen in the Museum of the Royal College
of Surgeons, which is very nearly adult, each half of the

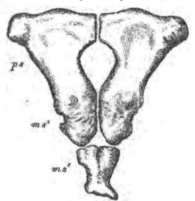

FIG. 37.—Sternum of Cachalot or Sperm Whale (*Physeter macrocephalus*), ⅒.

presternum (ps) has coalesced with the corresponding
half of the first segment of the mesosternum (ms^1), but the

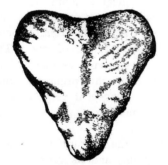

FIG. 38.—Sternum of Greenland Right Whale (*Balæna mysticetus*), ⅒.

resulting pieces are not united by bone across the middle
line, while the second or last pair of mesosternal segments

---

[1] I have observed this in animals evidently of great age.

(ms^2) are ankylosed together mesially, but not with the portion of the sternum in front of them.

In the Whalebone Whales (*Mystacocéti*) the sternum is comparatively rudimentary, consisting only of a broad, flattened presternum, produced posteriorly into a xiphoid process in some species.   There are never any mesosternal segments, and consequently no ribs, other than the first pair, are attached to it.

The presternum is ossified from one, or perhaps a pair of symmetrical nuclei.   In the Right Whales (*Balæna*, Fig. 38) it is heart-shaped, or longitudinally oval.   In the Fin Whales

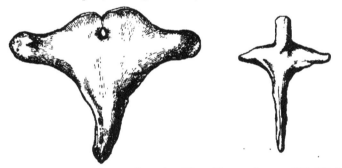

FIG. 39.—Sternum of Common Rorqual or Fin Whale (*Balænoptera musculus*), ⅒.   FIG. 40.—Sternum of Pike Whale (*Balænoptera rostrata*), ⅒.

(*Balænoptera*) it is transversely oval or trilobate, with a backward projecting xiphoid process.[1]   In young animals ossification of the cartilaginous sternum advances forwards on each side of the middle line, so that the ossified portion at one period appears deeply notched in front ; as the bone meets across the middle line anteriorly, this notch usually

[1] In the cartilaginous sternum of a young *Balænoptera sibbaldii*, Professor Turner found the xiphisternum to be quite distinct from the presternum, and connected with it by fibrous tissue. (*Journal of Anatomy*, May 1870.)   In most Whales the sternum shows no such evidence of segmentation.

becomes converted into a hole (see Fig. 39), which finally
closes with complete maturity.

In the Pike Whale (*B. rostrata*) the sternum is cross-
shaped (Fig. 40), the first ribs being attached behind the
lateral arms of the cross.

In the SIRENIA the sternum is a simple, flattened, somewhat elongated bone, which in the adult shows no trace of
segmentation.

In a young Dugong (*Halicore*), Fig. 41, there are two
distinct ossifications,—a presternum, to which the first pair of

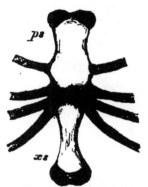

FIG. 41.—Sternum of a young Dugong (*Halicore indicus*), ½. From a specimen in
the Leyden Museum.

ribs are attached, and a xiphisternum. The second, third,
and fourth pairs of sternal ribs are attached to the intermediate unossified portion, representing a rudimentary
mesosternum.

In the Manati (*Manatus*) the sternum is of somewhat
similar form, and has three pairs of ribs attached to its
lateral margins near the middle.

Among the EDENTATA there is considerable variation in
the characters of the sternum.

In the Cape Anteater (*Orycteropus*) the sternum is of quite a normal form. The presternum is trefoil-shaped, expanding laterally near the front to meet the largely developed clavicles, then contracting to the width of the mesosternal segments, which are four in number, simple, flattened, oblong, with lateral margins nearly parallel, rather broader above than below, united together by fibrous tissue, and succeeded posteriorly by a moderately developed xiphisternum.

In *Manis dalmannii* the sternum is flat, consisting of seven segments, several of which are sometimes divided in the middle line by synovial cavities. The xiphisternum is very long, partially cleft in the middle line, and ending in a large, flattened, cartilaginous expansion. In the Long-tailed Pangolin (*Manis longicauda*) the xiphisternum is of a remarkable form, being prolonged into a pair of cartilaginous processes, each about nine inches long, and connected posteriorly with some rudimentary abdominal ribs.[1]

In the Anteaters (*Myrmecophaga*), the presternum is broad, flat, and oval. The segments of the mesosternum (Fig. 42) are eight in number, short, deep, broad above, and sending a club-shaped process downwards ; each is ossified from a principal endosteal centre and eight epiphyses, is connected by synovial articulations with the segment before and behind, and has at either end an upper and lower hollowed surface, which, with the corresponding surfaces on the contiguous segment, form articulating facets for the double-headed sternal ribs. This mode of articulation curiously resembles that at the vertebral end of the rib. The xiphisternum is rather long and simple.

In the small Tree Anteater (*Cyclothurus didactylus*) the presternum is very broad and trilobate, sending out lateral

[1] Parker, *op. cit.*

G

expansions behind the attachment of the clavicles to meet
the first pair of ribs. The hinder, narrow part of the manu-

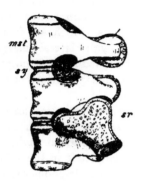

FIG. 42.—Side view of three mesosternal segments from a young Anteater
(*Myrmecophaga tamandua*), showing the mode of articulation of the sternal rib
(*sr*), copied from Parker's figure: *mst* the upper or inner surface of the mesosternal
segment; *sy* the synovial articulation between the segments.

brium is segmented off from the larger anterior part, and
resembles a mesosternal segment ; but it is in front of the
attachment of the second pair of ribs. The true mesosternal
segments are six in number, of nearly equal width, high,
rounded above, and compressed below, with a synovial
cavity between each. The sternal ribs are articulated by a
single oval condyle. The xiphisternum is long, stout, and
styliform.

In the Armadillos (*Dasypodidæ*) the presternum is broad,
and in *Priodontes gigas* (Fig. 44, p. 92) strongly keeled. The
mesosternal segments, four to six in number, are broad above,
but very narrow below ; and, according to Mr. Parker, each
ossifies from eleven centres. They are connected by synovial joints to each other, and to the strongly ossified sternal
ribs, which have broad, sub-bifid heads. The xiphisternum
expands posteriorly into a wide cartilaginous flap.

In the Sloths the sternum is long and narrow.   The three-
toed species (*Bradypus*) have a rather broad presternum, but
with no prolongation in front of the attachment of the first
rib.   This is followed by eight small mesosternal segments,
and a very small rounded xiphisternum.   In the two-toed
Sloths (*Cholæpus*), the presternum is narrow, slightly keeled,
and forms a considerable projection in front of the attach-

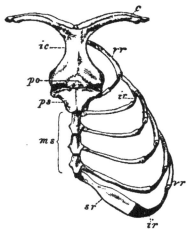

FIG. 43.—Sternum and adjacent parts of the skeleton of a young Ornithorhynchus
(*O. paradoxus*): *c* clavicle ; *ic* interclavicle ; *po* pro-osteon (a part of the true
sternum) ; *ps* presternum ; *ms* mesosternum ; *sr* sternal ribs ; *ir* intermediate ribs;
vr vertebral ribs.

ment of the first rib.   The mesosternum has twelve segments, and the xiphisternum is rudimentary or absent.

In the MARSUPIALIA the sternum presents no especial
aberrant characteristics.   The presternum is rather broad at
the point of attachment of the first pair of ribs.   Its anterior
extremity often does not ossify.   There are usually four
quite distinct, elongated segments to the mesosternum,
connected by fibrous tissue, and sometimes completed at

each end by epiphyses. The xiphisternum has an elongated, narrow, ossified portion, and terminates in a laterally expanded cartilage, which may contain one or two endosteal bony patches.

In the MONOTREMATA the Ornithorhynchus (Fig. 43) has a broad presternum (*ps*), with a small partially ossified *pro-osteon* (*po*) in front of it; three keeled mesosternal segments (*ms*), which commence to ossify in pairs, and no xiphisternum. The Echidna agrees in all important respects, but it has an ossified xiphisternum.

The T-shaped bone, *Interclavicle* or *episternum* (*ic*) in front of the presternum, which connects it with the clavicle, and which appears to have no homologue among the other Mammalia, belongs more properly to the shoulder-girdle than to the sternal apparatus.

CHAPTER VIII.

THE RIBS.

THE ribs form a series of long, narrow, and more or less flattened bones, extending laterally from the sides of the vertebral column, curving downwards towards the median line of the body below, and mostly joining the sides of the sternum.

Free ribs are normally only attached to the thoracic vertebræ, although, as before shown, certain parts, which may be serially homologous with ribs, are found in other regions of the vertebral column; but in such cases they become ankylosed with their corresponding vertebræ. In the thoracic region the ribs are never normally ankylosed with the vertebræ, but are articulated to them by synovial joints, which permit a certain, though limited, amount of motion.

As a general rule, the first thoracic rib joins the presternum or manubrium; sometimes, as in the Whalebone Whales, this is the only rib united below to the sternum, but usually a larger number are so connected, while the more posterior are either attached by their extremities to the sides of the ribs in front of them, and thus indirectly join the sternum, or else they are quite free below, meeting no part of the skeleton. These differences have given rise to the division into *true* ribs and *false* ribs (by no means good expressions), or those that join the sternum directly and those that do not ; and of the latter, those that are free below are called *floating* ribs.

Each primary piece of cartilage, out of which one of the half hoops or ribs is developed, is, moreover, divided transversely into two portions, which assume different characters, as they usually undergo a different mode of ossification, and remain more or less distinguishable from each other during life. The portion nearest the vertebral column is called the *vertebral* rib. This is the larger segment, and becomes firmly ossified at an early period by *ectostosis;* it is the bone commonly spoken of as a "rib."

The portion towards the sternal extremity or *sternal* rib is usually imperfectly ossified, and always at first (except in Monotremes) by *endostosis.* Sometimes it remains permanently in a cartilaginous state ; but, on the other hand, in some cases it becomes as firmly ossified as the vertebral ribs.

The vertebral ribs are variously connected with the sternal ; by continuous cartilage ; by intercalation of fibrous tracts ; or by synovial joints.

Occasionally, in the Mammalia, an "intermediate" portion of the rib is segmented off, as in Reptiles ; this is best developed in the Monotremata (Fig. 43, *ir*), where, however, it is only partially ossified by *endostosis.* In all other instances in which it occurs it is quite rudimentary.

The vertebral ribs, when in their most typical condition, have two points of attachment to the vertebra ; the tubercle (*tuberculum*) and the head (*capitulum*). The former is superior and posterior, and attached to the transverse process of the vertebra ; the latter, inferior and anterior, and attached to the body of the vertebra, or the inferior part of the arch near the body, and always very near the neurocentral suture. Commonly, in fact, the articular surface is

cut by this suture. Sometimes, as in Man, the greater part
of the articulation is above the suture ; or, on the other hand,
it may be, as in the *Monotremes*, below the suture. The distinction between the two points of attachment is most
marked in the anterior ribs ; in passing backwards they
approach nearer to each other, sometimes becoming blended,
or sometimes either one or the other (generally the
tubercular) attachment is lost in the hindermost ribs.

The tubercle articulates, by a nearly flat or slightly convex
surface, to a facet on the under-surface of the extremity of
the transverse process of the corresponding vertebra, but the
more rounded capitulum (at least in the anterior ribs) is
placed opposite to the intervertebral space in front of this
vertebra, and portions of two vertebræ commonly contribute
to form the articular cavity for its reception. Thus the first
rib is articulated by its tubercle to the transverse process of
the first thoracic vertebra, and by its head to the hinder part
of the seventh cervical, and front part of the first thoracic
vertebra, and so on. The posterior ribs, as a rule, are connected solely with their own corresponding vertebræ.

The amount of motion permitted by these articulations
is sufficient to allow the thorax to expand and contract in
respiration. In inspiration the ribs are drawn forwards, and
approach nearer to a right angle with the vertebral column ;
while in expiration they fall back, and occupy a more
oblique position to the axis of the column.

The sternal ribs are connected with the sternum either by
interposed fibrous tissue, or by distinct synovial joints. The
first is attached to the side of the presternum, the second
opposite to the junction of the presternum and the first
mesosternal segment, and the succeeding ones opposite to
the interspaces between the other mesosternal segments ;
though two or more may be attached to the hinder end of

the last of these segments. The inferior ends of the so-
called "false ribs" are attached by fibrous tissue, or by
synovial joints, to the hinder borders of the sternal ribs
in front ; though, as before said, the most posterior are free
or "floating."

The ribs of Mammals never have "uncinate processes,"
like those found in Birds and Reptiles.

The most prevalent number is thirteen pairs ; the lowest
is nine (in *Hyperoodon*), the highest twenty-four (in the two-
toed Sloth, *Cholæpus*).

*Special Characters of the Ribs in the various Groups of
Mammalia.* Order PRIMATES.—In Man there are normally
twelve pairs of ribs, of which the first seven are reckoned as
true ribs, and the last two as floating ribs. The last pair
may be rudimentary or absent ; or, on the other hand, the
seventh cervical or the first lumbar vertebra may have an
additional moveable rib articulated with it.

The first vertebral rib is much shorter, broader, flatter,
and more curved than the others. These gradually increase
in length until the seventh, after which they again diminish
to the twelfth. In breadth they gradually decrease from the
first to the last.

The portion of the rib between the head and the tubercle
is called the *neck ;* it is wanting in the last two ribs, in
which the two attachments are blended. The greatest point
of curvature on the external surface of the rib is called the
angle.

Each vertebral rib has a main centre of ossification and
two epiphyses, one for the head, and (except in the last two)
one for the tubercle.

The sternal ribs generally remain cartilaginous throughout
life, being only partially ossified by endostosis in old age
or under abnormal conditions. They are not distinctly

separated from the vertebral ribs except by their difference of structure; but synovial joints are (except in the first) interposed between their inferior extremities and the sternum.

Among the higher *Simiina* the ribs do not differ very notably from those of Man, except in number; but in the lower forms, and especially in the *Lemurina*, they more resemble those of the Carnivora. Among the Old World Monkeys, the number varies from 11 to 13 pairs. The Gorilla and Chimpanzee (*Troglodytes*) have 13, and the Orang (*Simia*) 12. In the American Monkeys there are from 12 to 15 pairs; in the Lemurs from 12 to 16 pairs.

In the most typical forms of CARNIVORA, the vertebral ribs are comparatively slender, subcylindrical, and little curved. The most anterior especially are short and straight, the thorax being thus more compressed in front than it is in Man and the higher Primates. The sternal ribs (see Fig. 33, p. 73) are long, slender, have a feeble granular ossification, and are not otherwise segmented off from the vertebral ribs. In all the *Felidæ* and *Canidæ* there are 13 pairs, in the *Viverridæ* 13 or 14, in the *Hyænidæ* 14 or 15, in the *Mustelidæ* 14 to 16, in the *Procyonidæ* 14, in the *Ursidæ* 14 or 15, in the *Pinnipedia* 14 or 15.

In the UNGULATA, the ribs are generally more or less flattened and broad, notably so in the Ox and Camel, and least so in the *Perissodactyla*. The anterior ribs have scarcely any curve, the thorax being very narrow in this region. The sternal ribs (see Fig. 35, p. 76), especially those near the front of the series, are short, stout, rather flattened or prismatic, tolerably well ossified, and articulated with the vertebral ribs by a cup and ball synovial joint. The Artiodactyles have from 12 to 15 pairs of ribs, the Horse and Tapir 18, the Rhinoceros 19, the Elephant 19 or 20, and the Hyrax 20 to 22.

In the SIRENIA, the total number of ribs is very great, though but few are attached to the sternum. In the Manati they acquire an extraordinary thickness and solidity of texture. This animal has seventeen pairs, of which but three are attached by flexible cartilages to the sternum.

Order CETACEA.—In the Whalebone Whales the ribs differ greatly from those of the rest of the Mammalia in their extremely loose connection, both with the vertebral column above and with the sternum below, probably to allow of greater alteration in the capacity of the thorax in respiration, necessitated by the prolonged immersion beneath the surface of the water which these animals undergo.

At their vertebral extremities they are attached only by their tubercle to near the end of the transverse process, but apparently not by synovial articulation. The heads of only a few of the anterior ribs are developed, and are rarely sufficiently long to reach the bodies of the vertebræ, their place being supplied by a ligamentous band. The first rib is the only one connected with the sternum, either directly or indirectly, the whole of the remainder being free or floating ribs. The sternal ribs are mere cartilaginous rudiments, connected by an intermediate layer of fibrous tissue to the inferior extremity of the vertebral rib ; at least such is their condition in the fœtus of *Balæna mysticetus*, as described by Eschricht and Reinhardt.

Balænoptera rostrata, the smallest of the Whalebone Whales, has but 11 pairs of ribs, *Megaptera longimana* 14 pairs, the Greenland Right Whale (*Balæna mysticetus*) usually 13, and the larger Fin Whales (*Balænoptera musculus* and *sibbaldii*) 15, and occasionally 16, the highest number known in any cetacean. In these last, it not unfrequently happens that the hindermost rib, having only the middle or lower portion developed, is separated by a wide interval from the vertebral column, a very rare condition, as in most other cases where the hinder ribs are rudimentary, the part in immediate connection with the vertebra remains.

The first rib presents a very anomalous condition in some Whalebone Whales, being apparently double, probably owing to the coalescence of a supplemental cervical rib with the ordinary first thoracic rib. In some species (as *Balænoptera laticeps*) this appears to be of constant occurrence ; in others, it is occasional.

In the *Odontoceti* or Toothed-whales, as the common Dolphin and Porpoise, the ribs (usually 12 or 13 pairs) are long and slender. The first 4 or 5 have tubercles, by which they articulate with the transverse process of the thoracic vertebræ, and long necks and heads, reaching to the side of the antecedent vertebra, near the junction of the body and the arch (see Fig. 20, p. 52). The posterior ribs, however, lose the neck, and are solely articulated by the tubercle to the transverse process. There are usually 7 pairs of rather short, straight, but strongly ossified sternal ribs, and often small intermediate ribs, sometimes distinctly ossified.

In the aberrant *Physeteridæ*, including the Sperm Whale, Hyperoodon and various forms of Ziphioids, the ribs are connected to the vertebræ throughout the greater part of the series by both head and tubercle ; but a few of the most posterior have only a single point of attachment in consequence of the changes which take place in the condition of the transverse processes of the vertebræ, described at p. 53. In this family the sternal ribs are either permanently cartilaginous, or very imperfectly ossified. The Hyperoodon has but 9 pairs of vertebral ribs, the smallest number known in any mammal, the Sperm Whale (*Physeter*) 11, of which the last is quite rudimentary; *Ziphius* 10, and *Kogia* 14.

Among the EDENTATA, the Sloths have very numerous ribs (from 15 to 24 pairs). In the anterior part of the thorax the sternal ribs are firmly ossified, and indistinguishable from the vertebral ribs (at least in adult age), but posteriorly they are separated from the latter by a less perfectly ossified intermediate rib.

In the Armadillos the ribs are comparatively few (10 to 12 pairs), and are broad and flat, the first extremely so. The first sternal rib is very short and incorporated with the

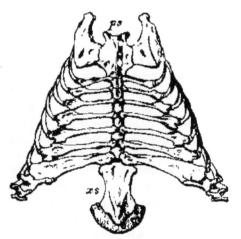

FIG. 44.—Sternum and ribs of the Great Armadillo (*Priodontes gigas*), ⅓ : *ps* presternum ; *xs* xiphisternum.

vertebral rib, but the others are very strongly ossified, and articulated by synovial joints with the sternum, with each other, and with the vertebral ribs.

The peculiar double articulation of the sternal ribs with the sternum in the Anteater (*Myrmecophaga*) has been already described (see p. 82). The ribs of the small climbing Two-toed Anteater (*Cyclothurus didactylus*) are remarkable for a thin lamelliform expansion of their hinder border, overlapping the succeeding rib. This animal has 15 pairs, the great Anteater 16, the Cape Anteater (*Orycteropus*) 13.

The MARSUPIALIA have nearly always 13 pairs of ribs ; the Koala (*Phascolarctos*) with but 11, and the common Wombat (*Phascolomys vombatus*) with 15, being the only known exceptions. The sternal ribs are articulated by synovial joints with the sternum, but are not distinctly segmented from the vertebral ribs, and are but feebly ossified by endostosis. There are no intermediate ribs.

In the MONOTREMATA the intermediate ribs are well marked (see Fig. 43, p. 83), and only partly ossified by endostosis, while the sternal ribs (except the first) are, according to Parker, strongly ossified *ectosteally*, as in Birds. The hinder sternal ribs are very broad and flat. The echidna has 16, and the Ornithorhynchus 17 pairs of vertebral ribs ; they do not divide above into head and tubercle, but are attached only to the sides of the bodies of the vertebræ.

CHAPTER IX.

THE skull is the term commonly applied to the portion of the axial skeleton situated within the head.

It consists mainly of the *cranium*, a strong bony case or frame, enclosing the brain, and affording support and protection to the organs of smell, sight, hearing, and taste, and formed by the close union, either by sutures or by ankylosis, of numerous bones.

To the inferior surface of the cranium are suspended (1) the *Mandible*, or lower jaw, moveably articulated by a synovial joint; and (2) a group of skeletal structures called the *hyoidean apparatus*.

The table on pp. 104 and 105 is intended to show, at a single view, the names applied to the various bones of which the skull is composed, and to give some idea of their relative position.

It will be well to commence the study of the skull by describing that of a Dog, as a good average specimen of the class, and one which is easily procurable at various ages; and I would strongly advise the student to follow the description with a skull in his hand, or two would be better, in one of which a longitudinal median section has been made. In the other, the various bones should be separated from each other.   For this purpose a young animal, still retaining the milk teeth, will be best.[1]

The skull has a longitudinal central axis (*the cranio-facial*

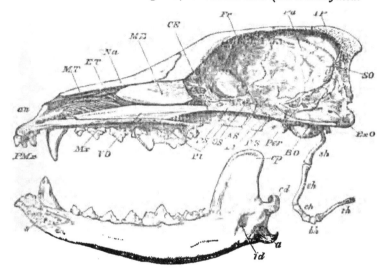

FIG. 45.—Longitudinal and vertical section of the skull of a Dog (*Canis familiaris*), with mandible and hyoid arch, ½. *an* anterior narial aperture ; *MT* maxillo-turbinal bone ; *ET* ethmo-turbinal ; *Na* nasal ; *ME* ossified portion of the mesethmoid ; *CE* cribriform plate of the ethmo-turbinal ; *Fr* frontal ; *Pa* parietal ; *IP* interparietal ; *SO* supraoccipital ; *ExO* exoccipital ; *BO* basioccipital ; *Per* periotic ; *BS* basisphenoid ; *Pt* pterygoid ; *AS* alisphenoid ; *OS* orbitosphenoid ; *PS* presphenoid ; *Pl* palatine ; *Vo* vomer ; *Mx* maxilla ; *PMx* premaxilla ; *sh* stylohyal ; *eh* epihyal ; *ch* ceratohyal ; *bh* basihyal ; *th* thyrohyal ; *s* symphysis of mandible ; *cp* coronoid process ; *cd* condyle ; *a* angle ; *id* inferior dental canal ; the mandible is displaced downwards to show its entire form ; the * indicates the part of the cranium to which the condyle is articulated.

axis, Huxley), around which all its parts are arranged, and its structure will be best understood by commencing with the description of the bones forming this axis.

[1] When the zoologist wishes to throw into the strongest relief the distinctive characters of different species, he selects for comparison fully adult examples ; when the anatomist wishes to trace their community of structure and their resemblances, younger specimens are better adapted for his purpose.

When the skull remains in connection with the vertebral column, it will be seen that its axis is a continuation forwards of the axis of that column, consisting of the bodies of the vertebræ; and that its hinder termination is placed in the same line with the odontoid process of the second cervical vertebra, the anterior termination of the axis of the spinal column.

The large cavity above the axis of the skull (cerebral cavity) is in direct continuity with the spinal canal above the axis of the vertebral column.

Beginning at the posterior end of the axis, the section will be seen to have passed through a flat, elongated bone (Fig. 45, *BO*), terminating freely behind at the inferior margin of the great opening (*foramen magnum*) at the hinder end of the cerebral cavity, by which this cavity is continued into the vertebral canal, and through which the backward prolongation of the brain (the medulla spinalis) passes. This bone is the *basioccipital*.

Immediately in front of this is a bone (the *basisphenoid*, *BS*) not quite so elongated from before backwards, but of greater vertical depth; the interior being more or less cellular in structure. The under-surface is flat, but the upper surface is hollowed in the middle, and raised at each extremity. This hollow corresponds to the part called " *sella turcica* " in the human skull, and lodges the pituitary body of the brain.

Further forwards, and likewise separated by a ·vertical fissure, is a bone (*PS*) of about the same length as the last, but still more elevated, and very cellular within. Its inferior contour is perfectly straight, but above it is somewhat irregular. This is the *presphenoid*.

So far the cranio-facial axis consists of bones placed in a continuous line, more or less depressed, and broad from side to side, and forming the floor of the cranial cavity; but the continuation of the axis forward is of a different character. The anterior end of the presphenoid narrows considerably, and the segment in front of it, in very young skulls, is a much compressed vertical plate of cartilage, of very considerable size, both from before backwards and from above downwards. Ossification of this cartilage commences in the posterior end and upper part, and spreads forwards and downwards, but it never or very rarely reaches its anterior extremity; and in the animal now described a narrow inferior margin remains permanently cartilaginous. The ossified portion of this cartilage (*ME*) constitutes the "*lamina perpendicularis*" of the ethmoid bone, the anterior unossified portion, the septal cartilage of the nose, which is the anterior termination of the cranio-facial axis. The term *mesethmoid* may be applied to the whole of this element of the skull, whether ossified or not.

Above all the posterior, or *basicranial*, part of this axis, constituted by the three first-mentioned bones, is the cerebral cavity, the walls of which constitute the "brain-case."

These walls are formed by several more or less expanded and curved bones, which rise up from the sides of the axis or floor of the cavity below, and, meeting in the middle line, roof in the cavity above. These bones are arranged in three sets from behind forwards, each corresponding with one of the axial bones, and with the latter constituting one of the three segments or bony rings into which the brain-case may be divided.

The hindermost (or occipital) segment consists of the basioccipital below; next on each side the *exoccipitals* (*EO*), and a large, median, flat bone above, with its upper extremity prolonged forwards in the middle line between the bones of the next segment, called the *supraoccipital* (*SO*).

H

These four bones surround the *foramen magnum* behind, and
all take share in its circumference, though the exoccipitals,
which bound it laterally, contribute most. On each side of
the foramen, and rather below than above, are the *occipital
condyles*, by which the skull articulates with the first cervical
vertebra; and externally to these, separated by a deep
depression, is a prominent process for muscular attachment,
called the *paroccipital* (or *paramastoid*) process. The condyles in the Dog are formed by the exoccipitals alone. The
part (*IP*) which appears to be an anterior prolongation of the
upper extremity of the supraoccipital, wedged in between
the parietals, is ossified from a separate centre, and in some
animals remains permanently as a distinct bone. It is then
called *interparietal*.

The middle (or parietal) segment is formed by the basisphenoid below. From the sides of this a pair of wing-
like bones (*AS*) extend outwards and upwards, called *alisphenoids;* and above these are large square-shaped bones
(*Pa*), meeting in the middle line above, the *parietals*.

The occipital and the parietal segments are in contact
below and above, but there would be a considerable open
space between them laterally were it not for the interposition
of a group of bones, which do not form part of the segmented
wall of the brain-case proper, but are more or less connected
with the organ of hearing, and will therefore be described
hereafter. These are the bones which, being all united into
one in Man, constitute the so-called *temporal bone* of human
anatomy.

The anterior (or frontal) segment is formed by the presphenoid below; then by the wing-like bones (*OS*) projecting
from its sides, smaller than those of the second segment,
called *orbito-sphenoids;* and finally by two greatly expanded
bones (*Fr*), curving inwards above and in front, to close in

the cerebral cavity in these directions, by meeting in the middle line.   These are the *frontal bones.*

Between the middle bones of the parietal and frontal segments (alisphenoid and orbitosphenoid) is an irregular vacuity, called the *foramen lacerum anterius,* or sphenoidal fissure, through which several nerves pass to the orbit. This is the second vacuity in the side wall of the skull, the first being the one between the occipital and parietal segment, partially filled by the periotic bone.

As the occipital segment is not closed behind, so in the same way the frontal segment is open in front, the aperture being bounded by all the bones which enter into its composition—presphenoid, orbitosphenoids, and frontals. The hinder edge of the mesethmoid rising up to meet the frontals makes a median partition to this aperture (the *crista galli* of human anatomy), and it is further closed by a special ossification (*CE*) connected with the organ of smell, the *cribriform plate.*

Thus the brain-case may be described as a tube, dilated in the middle, composed of three bony rings or segments, with an aperture at each end, and a fissure or space at the sides between each of the segments.

The cranial cavity thus formed is of a general oval form, but broader behind than in front. The floor is comparatively straight; the upper surface arched. It is imperfectly divided by bony ridges into three compartments. The most posterior of these, marked off in front by a sharp ridge along the periotic bone (*Per*), extending from near the junction of the basisphenoid and basioccipital, upwards, outwards, and backwards, along the line of junction of the parietal and supraoccipital, and strongly marked by an inward shelf-like projection from the former (the ossified *tentorium cerebelli*), is called the *cerebellar fossa,* as it

lodges that division of the brain. The most anterior and
smallest compartment is marked off by a vertical ridge on
the orbitosphenoid and the frontal. Its walls are chiefly
formed by the cribriform plate. This is the *olfactory fossa*
(*rhinencephalic fossa*, Owen), for the lodgment of the olfactory lobe. Between these two is the great *cerebral fossa*, in
which the hemisphere of the cerebrum lies. This is very
imperfectly divided below into two compartments, by a slight
ridge at the hinder edge of the orbitosphenoid and continued thence outwards at the junction of the frontal and
alisphenoid. This ridge corresponds with the Sylvian fissure
of the brain ; the part of the cerebral fossa in front of it
lodges the frontal lobe of the cerebrum, that behind it the
temporal lobe.

Through the lateral parts of the floor of the cranial cavity
are various perforations, or *foramina*, either holes passing
directly through the bones, or vacuities occasioned by want
of contact, for a limited space, of contiguous bones. These
are mainly for the purpose of allowing of the exit of the
various nerves which take origin from the brain; and as
they are extremely constant in their position, and offer useful
landmarks for determining the homologies of the bones
throughout the vertebrate series, it is important that they
should be well known.

1. The most anterior is the space, before spoken of, in
front of the anterior segment, occupied by the hinder part
of the ethmoturbinal, commonly called the "cribriform
plate." The numerous perforations in this plate transmit
the olfactory nerves arising from the olfactory lobes.

2. Near the hinder border of the orbitosphenoid is a conspicuous, nearly round, hole, through which the optic nerve
passes, and hence called *optic foramen.*

3. At a very short distance behind this is a more irregular

oval opening, between the orbitosphenoid and the alisphenoid. This is the sphenoidal or orbital fissure, or *foramen lacerum anterius.* It leads into the orbit, and allows the exit of the motor nerves of the eyeball, or third, fourth, and sixth cranial nerves, and also the first division of the trigeminal or fifth nerve.

4 and 5. The alisphenoid near its base is perforated by two foramina; the anterior small and somewhat round; the posterior larger and oval: these are the *foramen rotundum* and the *foramen ovale,* and transmit respectively the second and third divisions of the fifth nerve.

6. Between the alisphenoid and the exoccipital is a large space, almost entirely filled by the bony capsule of the organ of hearing, the *periotic.* In front of the inner end of this bone is an opening (*foramen lacerum medium basis cranii*), through which the internal carotid artery enters the cranial cavity.

7. Near the middle of the inner surface of the periotic is the *meatus auditorius internus,* into which the seventh and eighth nerves enter: the former (the facial nerve) passes through the bone and emerges on the other side (by the *stylo-maxillary foramen*); the latter, the auditory, is distributed to the internal organ of hearing within the periotic bone.

A deep depression seen above the internal auditory meatus, and of nearly the same size, is not a foramen but a *fossa,* lying within the concavity of the superior semicircular canal. It lodges the flocculus, a small process of the cerebellum.

8. Between the periotic and the exoccipital an irregular space is left (the *foramen lacerum posterius*), through which the glossopharyngeal, pneumogastric, and spinal accessory nerves (the ninth, tenth, and eleventh) pass out of the cranium.

9. The exoccipital is perforated, a little in front of the condyle, by the *condylar foramen*, which gives exit to the twelfth, or hypoglossal, nerve.

10. Lastly, the large median opening, behind the bones of the posterior segment of the skull, is the *foramen magnum*, through which the spinal cord passes out.

It will be seen from the foregoing description that the three organs of special sense, situated in the walls of the cranium, have definite relations with the three osseous segments. The first, or organ of smell, is situated in front of the frontal segment; the second, or organ of sight, receives its nerves by apertures situated between the frontal and parietal segments or perforating the former; the third, or organ of hearing, is intercalated between the parietal and occipital segment.

The portion of the skull anterior to the junction of the presphenoid and the mesethmoid constitutes the face. This differs entirely from the cranial cavity, in having a complete median partition, and consists mainly of two tubular cavities placed one on each side of this partition. These are the *nasal cavities*. They are open at each end, the orifices being termed respectively anterior and posterior nares.

Each of these elongated cavities is deepest vertically in its posterior part, where it is partially divided into an upper and lower chamber: the upper one, the *olfactory chamber*, being closed behind by the cribriform plate; the lower, the *narial passage*, terminating in the posterior nares.

Each nasal cavity may be described as having an inner wall, an outer wall, a floor, and a roof.

The inner wall is formed mainly by the partially ossified mesethmoid cartilage (*ME*), but the lower part of the posterior two-thirds also by the *vomer* (*Vo*). The greater part

of this bone has the form of a trough, hollow above, embracing the inferior, thickened border of the mesethmoid
cartilage, and extending a little way behind this so as also to
underlie the anterior portion of the presphenoid; but it also
develops from its under-surface in the middle line a thin
plate, which passes vertically down to the centre of the floor
of the nasal passages, and completes the septum inferiorly.

Above, rather behind the middle of the bone, the lateral
plates of the vomer, which embrace the mesethmoid cartilage,
send out sideways a pair of wing-like processes, which join
the side walls of the nasal cavity, and form the partial horizontal partition, dividing the narial passage from the
olfactory chamber.

The outer wall of the nasal cavity is formed mainly by
four bones : (1) a somewhat quadrate, thin, nearly vertical
plate of bone (*Pt*), the *pterygoid*, attached above to the under
surface of the basisphenoid and presphenoid, supported
externally by a strong descending process of the alisphenoid, the external pterygoid plate, ending posteriorly and
inferiorly by a free border, and articulating in front with (2)
the *palatine*. This bone (*Pl*) is of much greater extent; for,
besides its vertical portion, forming the outer wall of the
nasal canal in front of the pterygoid, it sends from its upper
edge a lamina inwards to meet the horizontal plate of the
vomer, and aid in forming the roof of the hinder part of the
narial passage. It also sends a strong horizontal lamina
inwards from its lower edge, which, meeting its fellow in the
middle line, forms the posterior part of the floor of the narial
passage. In addition to these it sends a broad plate upwards
and forwards in the inner wall of the orbit.

3. In front of this is the *maxilla* (*Mx*), a still more considerable bone. It not only forms the chief part of the outer
wall of the nasal cavity, but it also sends inwards a horizontal

[*Continued on p.* 106.

(*Modified from a Diagram used by Professo*

SEGMENTS

I.
Frontal.

Nasal.
Lachrymal.

Pa

Nose. ORBITO-SPHENOID. Eye. ALI-S

ETHMO-TURBINAL.

Malar.

MESETHMOID. PRE-SPHENOID. BASI-SP

MAXILLO-TURBINAL.

Vomer.

Premaxilla. Maxilla. Palatine. Pterygoid.

Mand

The bones of which the names are printed in capital letters are d
basis, but, ossifying directly from fibrous tissue, are called *membrane bo*
Pre-sphenoid, Basi-sphenoid, and Basi-occipital, also the Vomer, the Su
The remainder are all pairs. By this it is not meant to imply that the a
the median line, but if so, these unite so early as practically to constitute
bones, as the frontals in Man, may unite across the median line at a com

Huxley, in his Hunterian Lectures, 1869.)

? THE BRAIN CASE.

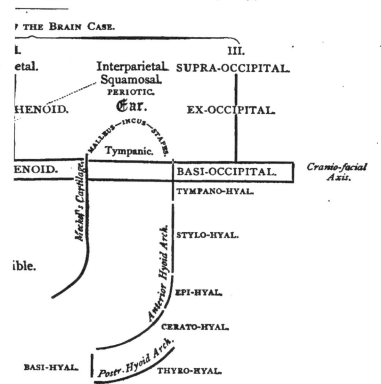

L.   III.
etal.   Interparietal. SUPRA-OCCIPITAL.
                  Squamosal.
                  PERIOTIC.
HENOID.   &ar.   EX-OCCIPITAL.
                —MALLEUS—INCUS—STAPES
                Tympanic.
ENOID.   Meckel's Cartilage   BASI-OCCIPITAL.   *Cranio-facial Axis.*
                                TYMPANO-HYAL.
                Anterior Hyoid Arch.   STYLO-HYAL.
ible.
                                EPI-HYAL.
                                CERATO-HYAL.
BASI-HYAL.   *Postr. Hyoid Arch.*   THYRO-HYAL.

le?eloped in cartilage ; the others have no primitive cartilaginous
one.. The bones of the Cranio-facial Axis, viz. the Mesethmoid,
upra-occipital, and the Interparietal, are single or azygous bones.
azygous bones may not originally ossify by nuclei on each side of
te them single bones ; while, on the other hand, some of the paired
mparatively early age.

plate, forming the middle part of its floor. At the junction of its vertical and horizontal portions is the alveolar border, in which the canine, premolar, and molar teeth are lodged.

4. The most anterior bone of this series is the *premaxilla* (*PMx*), which also has an ascending or vertical plate, forming the outer wall of the nasal cavity, and a horizontal plate forming the anterior part of its floor; at their junction its alveolar border lodges the incisor teeth. The premaxilla forms the outer and lower boundary of the anterior nares.

Besides these four, there is a small bone which enters into the outer wall of the upper part of the nasal cavity, between the ascending process of the palatine, the maxilla and the frontal. This is perforated by the duct which conveys the tears from the orbit into the nasal cavity, and is hence called *lachrymal.*

Above this a process from the frontal completes the upper and posterior part of the outer wall of the olfactory chamber.

The floor of the nasal cavity is formed, as above said, by the horizontal plates of the palatine, maxilla, and premaxilla meeting the corresponding bones of the opposite side in the middle line. The inferior surface of this same horizontal layer of bone is the roof of the mouth, or bony palate.

The roof of the nasal cavity is formed posteriorly by the continuation of the frontal forwards beyond the cerebral cavity, the "*nasal process of the frontal*," but mainly by a long narrow bone, the *nasal* bone (*Na*). The hinder extremity of this lies upon the nasal process of the frontal; its anterior end is free, and forms the upper boundary of the anterior nares; its outer side is in contact with the frontal, maxilla, and premaxilla; and its straight inner edge lies against that of the corresponding bone of the opposite side.

Within each nasal cavity are two very singular bones, each being composed of a number of delicate lamellæ folded and arranged in an exceedingly complex manner, forming a mass with so many passages and perforations that the term "spongy bones" has been applied to them.

The most posterior is the larger, and placed rather higher than the other; its anterior extremity (*ET*) overlapping it. It completely fills the proper olfactory chamber; its hinder extremity occupying the gap left in the cranial wall in front of the anterior segment of the brain-case. The various laminæ are all connected together and to the hinder end of the mesethmoid, by a plate of bone (*CE*) so full of perfora- tions of various forms and size that it is called the *cribriform* plate, and from it the name of *ethmoid* (or sieve-like) is commonly applied to all the bony structures with which it is united. On their outer side these laminæ are con- nected to a thin flat plate of bone (the so-called *os planum*) which lies against the inner wall of the maxillary, but does not ordinarily contract any union with it.

This bone results from the ossification of the complexly folded cartilage, over the surface of which the olfactory nerves are spread, the division into laminæ permitting a great increase of sensitive surface. As, although originally distinct, it subsequently unites with the mesethmoid, by means of the cribriform plate, it is considered in human anatomy as part of the same bone, under the name of "lateral mass of the ethmoid," and is described as consist- ing of the superior and middle "turbinated bones;" but the name *ethmoturbinal*, applied to it by Professor Owen, is perhaps more appropriate.

The uppermost of the lamellæ of the ethmoturbinal, lying immediately under the nasal bones, is rather distinct from the others, and extends much further forwards; and as in certain Mammals it becomes united by bone with the nasal, it is sometimes distinguished under the name of "*nasoturbinal.*"

In front, and on a rather lower level, a similar, but smaller and less complex bone (*MT*), consisting chiefly of horizontal lamellæ, is placed. This, though originally developed from the same cartilage lining the outer wall of the nasal chamber as the last, ossifies quite distinctly from it, and contracts a bony union by a horizontal lamella on its outer side with the maxilla. This is the *maxilloturbinal*, and corresponds with the inferior turbinated bone of human anatomy.

It will be observed that while the ethmoturbinal is placed high in the nasal cavity, and above the direct channel by which the air passes to the posterior nares, the maxilloturbinal, situated nearer the front of the chamber, before it has divided into an upper true olfactory chamber and a lower narial passage, nearly blocks up the whole cavity, so that air passing through in inspiration is filtered between its meshes. The moist membrane which covers its bony plates in life is supplied with nerves chiefly from the fifth pair, and not from the olfactory; so that it does not perform the function of an organ of smell like the ethmoturbinal, but rather serves to guard the entrance of the respiratory passages from foreign substances, and perhaps to warm the inspired air.

In describing the walls of the cranium, a large space was mentioned on each side, between the posterior and middle cranial segment, in which were inserted certain bones not yet noticed. These bones form a definite group by themselves, at all events locally connected, though very different in function and structure.

In a mass of cartilage, in the position just indicated, ossification takes place from several centres (three according to Professor Huxley and others in the human skull;[1] but the

---

[1] Elements of Comparative Anatomy (1864), p. 148.

process has not been accurately traced in other Mammals).
These very rapidly unite to form a single bone, which completely encloses the labyrinth or essential organ of hearing,
consisting of the vestibule, semicircular canals, and cochlea.
This bone is the *periotic* (*Per*).   It is divided into two portions : an antero-internal, which forms a somewhat angular
projection within the cranial cavity, and is of remarkable
density—the *petrous* portion ; and a postero-external, a sort
of process from the former, smaller, less dense, and forming
a small portion of the wall of the cranium, appearing externally just in front of the exoccipital—the *mastoid* portion.

The petrous is of course the more important, and has
constant characters throughout the class, while the mastoid
is very variable, and sometimes can scarcely be said to exist.
It is in no case a separate bone ; and, although a portion of it
may develop originally from a separate centre, it is always
before birth firmly united with the petrous, so that they
will be spoken of here as one bone, under the name of
periotic.

The essential characters of the petrous portion of the
periotic are, that it contains within it the internal ear ;
that it has on its inner or cranial side a foramen, through
which the facial and the auditory nerves leave the cranial
cavity, the former to pass through the bone, escaping by
the stylomastoid foramen on the outer and under surface,
the latter to be distributed on the sensitive portions of the
organ of hearing ; and that it has on its outer side two holes,
one placed above the other, the *fenestra ovalis* and the
fenestra rotunda, through which the internal ear communicates with the cavity of the tympanum, or middle-ear, which
is situated on the outer side of the petrous part of the
periotic bone.

Externally to the periotic bone are placed two bones

separately developed in fibrous tissue, which often acquire a
very close connection with the periotic, occasionally, as in
Man, becoming firmly ankylosed with it.

The upper one of these is the *squamosal* (Fig. 47, *Sq.*),
which has a broad, scale-like, vertical portion spreading out
over the side of the cranial wall, uniting with the supraoccipital behind, overlapping the lower edge of the parietal,
and the hinder part of the alisphenoid, and also appearing
for a very small space in the inner side of the cranial wall.
From near its lower border it sends a strong process outwards, which soon curves forwards, called the *zygomatic
process*. This articulates with another bone (*Ma*), the *malar*
or *jugal*, which connects it with the maxilla, and so forms
the strong, lateral, nearly horizontal, or slightly arched
osseous bridge, which passes from the face to the hinder
part of the cranium, called the *zygomatic arch*. On the
under surface of the base of the zygomatic process of the
squamosal is a laterally extended, oblong surface, concave
from before backwards, for the articulation of the condyle of
the lower jaw, called the *glenoid fossa* (*gf*), the hinder edge
of which is produced into the *postglenoid process* (*gp*).

The lower bone, on the outer side of the periotic, is the
tympanic (*Ty*). At birth this is a mere osseous ring, incomplete above, surrounding the inferior three-fourths of the membrana tympani, but it undergoes a considerable development
in the course of the first few months. The external edge of
the ring is produced horizontally outwards to form the short,
bony, external auditory meatus; while the under and inner
surface is greatly expanded, to form the conspicuous rounded
prominence, hollow within, called the auditory bulla, which
abuts against the outer edge of the basioccipital below.[1]

---

[1] The whole of the bulla is generally considered as belonging to the
tympanic bone, but its inner part is developed in a distinct cartilaginous

The space that is left among this group of bones, bounded by the periotic (the part in which the before-mentioned fenestræ are situated) within, the periotic and squamosal above, the tympanic and its bullate expansion below, behind, and in front, and by the meatus auditorius externus, closed in the natural state by the membrana tympani, to the outer side, is called the *tympanic cavity*.

It contains within it the *ossicula auditûs*, the *malleus, incus,* and *stapes,* three small bones which, articulated together, stretch across the cavity from the membrana tympani to the *fenestra ovalis*.[1] The cavity has an opening at its antero-internal angle, through which the Eustachian tube, connecting the tympanum with the pharynx, passes.

The inner side of the bulla is perforated lengthwise by a canal, which commences posteriorly within the margin of the foramen lacerum posterius (between the auditory bulla and the exoccipital), and transmits the internal carotid artery. This vessel appears again on the surface, at the anterior extremity of the bulla, close to the Eustachian orifice; then runs upwards and inwards and enters the cranium through the foramen lacerum medium.

This completes the enumeration of the bones of the cranium. Before proceeding further, it will be desirable to take a general survey of this part as a whole, pointing out the most prominent features of its various surfaces.

lamella, interposed between the lower edge of the tympanic ring and the base of the skull. Whether this ossifies from a separate nucleus, or by extension of bony deposition inwards from the true tympanic, I am unable to say. The development of this region of the skull in the Mammalia still offers an interesting field for investigation.

[1] As these bones are, in the Mammalia, completely subservient to the organ of hearing, their modifications will not be described in the present work.

The *posterior surface* is, in a general sense, a vertical
wall, somewhat triangular in form, broad below and pointed
above.   In the middle line, at its lowest border, is the nearly
round *foramen magnum*, bounded by the supraoccipital
above, the exoccipitals on each side, and the basioccipital
below.   On the sides of the foramen magnum, and
approaching each other in the middle line below, but
diverging above, are smooth eminences, the occipital
condyles.   Further outwards, and separated from these by
a deep valley, are the paroccipital processes, projecting
backwards and downwards.   Outside of the upper part or
origin of these processes, the mastoid portion of the periotic
appears on the hinder wall of the skull.   The remainder of
the region is formed by the supraoccipital, and it is distinctly marked off laterally by ridges, which, commencing
in the median line above, run downwards and outwards,
at the junction of the parietals and supraoccipital, and are
continued on the squamosal in front of the mastoid to the
upper edge of the external auditory meatus.   The ridges
of each side taken together form the *lambdoid* or *occipital
crest.*   They are far more conspicuous in old than in young
animals.

The *superior surface* of the skull (Fig. 46) may be divided
into a cranial and a facial portion.   The former is of a
somewhat oval form.   On its upper surface posteriorly, in
full-grown dogs, is a median ridge joining behind with the
superior angle of the occipital crest, and dividing anteriorly
into two less elevated ridges which curve outwards to the
superior posterior angle of the orbit.   This ridge, as long
as it is single and median, is called the *sagittal crest.*   It
bounds superiorly a large surface on the side of the skull,
limited behind by the occipital crest, and below by the
zygoma, called the "temporal fossa," from which the

temporal muscle takes its origin. In young dogs the upper boundary of the surface for the origin of this muscle is of less extent, not reaching so high as the middle line of the cranium, and is but obscurely indicated on the

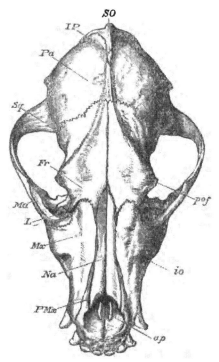

FIG. 46.—Upper surface of cranium of a Dog, ⅓. *SO* supraoccipital ; *IP* interparietal ; *Pa* parietal ; *Sq* squamosal ; *Fr* frontal ; *Ma* malar ; *L* lachrymal ; *Mx* maxilla ; *Na* nasal ; *PMx* premaxilla ; *ap* anterior palatine foramen ; *io* infraorbital foramen ; *pof* postorbital process of frontal bone.

comparative smooth surface of the skull. As the muscle increases in development its surface of origin gradually ascends until it reaches the middle line, and with advancing age a still larger space is afforded for it by the gradual growth of the sagittal crest.

These changes in the upper part of the skull during growth have been particularly noticed, because they take place in very many animals, and, without altering in the least the actual form of the brain-case, give rise to a very different external appearance of the skull, either in members of the same species, or in different but allied species.

The upper part of the skull, in front of the diverging boundary lines of the temporal fossa, is expanded and somewhat flattened, and has on each side a triangular process (*pof*), which curves somewhat downwards, and indicates the division of the temporal fossa behind from the orbit in front. This is the *postorbital process* of the frontal bone. It is connected by a ligamentous band, in the living animal, with a corresponding process arising from the zygoma; but when this is removed the orbit and temporal fossa are widely continuous, their respective limits being only indicated by the above-mentioned processes.

The face is produced considerably in front of the orbits, and not only becomes more depressed, but also more compressed laterally, and is obliquely truncated anteriorly, terminating in the rounded incisor border of the premaxilla (*PMx*); above which is placed the subcircular orifice of the anterior nares.

The upper, and a considerable portion of the lateral, surface of the cranium behind is formed by the parietal bones (*Pa*), having the narrow interparietal (*IP*) ankylosed with the supraoccipital (*SO*), extending between them for about half their length. In front of this the parietals are commonly united together by bone in old dogs.

. Anteriorly to the parietals, the upper part of the temporal fossa, the frontal plateau between the orbits, and the upper

half of the inner wall of the orbit, are formed by the frontal
bone. The remaining or lower portion of the temporal fossa
is formed by the squamosal behind and by the alisphenoid
in front. On the inner or cranial surface of the confluent
orbital and temporal fossæ, a wide groove runs obliquely
downwards and backwards, which may be considered as the
boundary line of these two regions. In the lower part of this
groove are several large foramina placed in linear series. The
highest is the optic foramen, the next (of larger size) the
sphenoidal fissure, and the third the foramen rotundum
and anterior opening of the alisphenoid canal. The orbit
has no floor except for a very short space in front; the
lower border of its inner wall passing directly into the outer
surface of the vertical ridge formed by the pterygoid, the
pterygoid process of the alisphenoid and the palatine bones,
and continuing the outer wall of the narial passage backwards beyond the bony palate. The palatine bone forms a
considerable part of the inner wall of the orbit, joining the
frontal anteriorly, though separated from it for a considerable
space posteriorly by the orbitosphenoid. The lachrymal (*L*)
appears in the anterior boundary of the orbit, the malar (*Ma*)
joins its outer boundary, and the upper surface of the hinder
end of the alveolar border of the maxilla projects backwards, so as to form a partial floor to its anterior extremity.

In front of the orbits the face is formed above by the
long narrow nasals (*Na*) pointed behind, and widening and
obliquely truncated in front to form the upper border of
the narial aperture; on each side by the maxillæ (*Mx*),
having near the middle of their surface the large *infraorbital
foramen* (*io*), through which the terminal branches of the
second division of the fifth or sensory nerve of the face pass
to be distributed to the upper lip and whiskers; and quite
anteriorly by the premaxillæ (*PMx*), which complete the

boundaries of the nares, and send up narrow processes

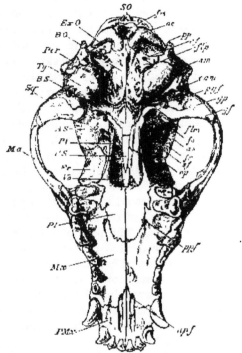

FIG. 47.—Under surface of the cranium of a Dog, ½. *SO* supraoccipital; *ExO*
exoccipital; *BO* basioccipital; *Per* mastoid portion of periotic; *Ty* tympanic
bulla; *BS* basisphenoid; *Sq* zygomatic process of squamosal; *Ma* malar; *AS*
alisphenoid; *Pt* pterygoid; *PS* presphenoid; *Fr* frontal; *Vo* vomer; *Pl* palatine;
Mx maxilla; *PMx* premaxilla; *fm* foramen magnum; *oc* occipital condyle;
pp paroccipital process; *cf* condylar foramen; *flp* foramen lacerum posterius; *sm*
stylo-mastoid foramen; *eam* external auditory meatus; *pgf* postglenoid foramen;
gp postglenoid process; *gf* glenoid fossa; *flm* foramen lacerum medium; *fo*
foramen ovale; *as* posterior opening of alisphenoid canal; *fr* foramen rotundum
and anterior opening of alisphenoid canal; *sf* sphenoidal fissure or foramen
lacerum anterius; *of* optic foramen; *ppf* posterior palatine foramen; *apf* anterior
palatine foramen.

between the nasals and maxillæ, towards, though not meeting with, similar processes which run from the frontals.

The *inferior surface* of the skull (Fig. 47) is formed anteriorly by the nearly flat, elongated surface of the palate, narrower in front than behind, composed anteriorly of the premaxillæ (*PMx*) ; then of the maxillæ (*Mx*), which diverge posteriorly and allow the palatines (*Pl*) which form the hinder border to reach in the middle line almost to the centre of the palatal surface. In front and at the sides this surface is bounded by the alveolar border of the premaxillæ and maxillæ, in which the teeth are set. Anteriorly are two considerable oval foramina (*apf*), placed longitudinally very near the middle line, formed mainly in the premaxillæ, though their boundary is completed posteriorly by the maxillæ ; these are the *anterior palatine foramina.* The naso-palatine nerve descends through them to spread over the anterior surface of the soft palate. Not far from the hinder border of the palate, and more distant from the middle line, near the suture between the maxilla and palatine, are several much smaller foramina (*posterior palatine*), also for the transmission of branches of the fifth nerve and small vessels.

The truncated median part of the hinder edge of the palate forms the lower margin of the posterior narial aperture. Laterally, the palate bones are continued backwards as vertical plates, thick and rounded below at first, but gradually becoming more compressed. These are continued still further backwards by the compressed pterygoid bones (*Pt*), ending in the backward-projecting *hamular processes,* and supported externally by the descending (pterygoid) plate of the alisphenoid. The groove between these descending lamellæ of bone continues the narial passage backwards. It has for its roof the vomer (*Vo*) in front, then the presphenoid (*PS*), and posteriorly a portion of the basisphenoid (*BS*); but the palatines and pterygoids arch over so much towards the middle line that they only leave a small strip of these bones exposed. Inferiorly, this groove is not closed by bone, but in the living animal the soft palate is stretched across it.

The base of the skull, behind this "mesopterygoid" fossa, presents in the middle a nearly flat elongated surface, consisting of the basisphenoid (*BS*) and basioccipital (*BO*); the latter roughened for the attachment of muscles, and terminating posteriorly at the inferior border of the foramen magnum (*fm*), flanked on each side by the occipital condyles (*oc*). The nearly straight lateral edges of the anterior half of the basioccipital rise up to abut against the prominent smooth rounded auditory bullæ (*Ty*), which form so conspicuous a feature in this region of the skull, and which are produced outwards into the lower wall of the external auditory meatus (*eam*). In the antero-internal angle of the bulla is seen the irregular orifice of the Eustachian canal. Close to the inner side of this is an oval aperture, which is at the same time the anterior extremity of the carotid canal and the entrance to the foramen lacerum medium (*flm*) through which the internal carotid artery enters the cranial cavity. In front, and rather to the outer side of this, is the foramen ovale (*fo*) piercing the alisphenoid, and immediately before this is a round aperture (*as*) leading to a short canal running horizontally forwards through the same bone at the root of its pterygoid process, and opening anteriorly into the foramen rotundum (*fr*). Through this the external carotid artery runs for part of its course, and it has been called the *alisphenoid canal*.[1]

In front of the outer side of the auditory bulla is the glenoid fossa for the articulation of the mandible, bordered

[1] See H. N. Turner's "Observations relating to some of the Foramina in the Base of the Skull in Mammalia, &c.," Proc. Zool. Soc. 1848, p. 63.

behind by the conspicuous curved *postglenoid process* (*gp*). Immediately behind this the root of the zygoma is pierced by a large hole, *postglenoid foramen* (*pgf*), through which a vein passes out from the lateral sinus within.

Behind the auditory bulla, to the inner side, is the large *foramen lacerum posterius* (*flp*), and, situated deeply within its recesses, the posterior opening of the internal carotid canal. On a ridge of the exoccipital, between this large foramen and the depression immediately in front of the condyle, is the small, nearly circular *condylar foramen* (*cf*), and at the outer termination of the same ridge rises the conical paroccipital process (*pp*), abutting at its base against the hinder end of the auditory bulla. Immediately behind the bulla, and to the outer side of the abutment of the paroccipital process against it, is an oval hole (*sm*), partially divided by a constriction into an inner and an outer division. In the inner division the end of a small cylindrical plug of bone, the *tympanohyal*, can generally be seen. The outer division is the *stylomastoid* foramen, through which the seventh nerve, or portio dura, makes its exit. The bone forming its outer boundary is the mastoid portion of the periotic.

Connected with the posterior lateral parts of the cranium are two appended bony parts: the lower jaw or mandible, and the hyoidean apparatus. The former forms the frame-work for the floor of the mouth, and supports the lower series of teeth; the latter gives a firm yet moveable point of attachment to the root of the tongue and to the larynx, or organ of voice. The true relation of these parts to the cranium cannot be perfectly understood without referring to their mode of development.

At a very early period, in the lamina forming the side

wall of the cervical region of the embryo, certain thicken-
ings appear, having their long axes from above downwards
or transverse to that of the general axis of the body; these
are the *visceral arches*.   Between them slit-like openings are
formed, through which there is a communication between
the external surface and the pharyngeal cavity within;
these are called the *visceral clefts*.   In the lower Vertebrata
some of these clefts remain open permanently, forming the
branchial apertures, but in the Mammalia they speedily close,
and (with the exception of the first) leave no trace of their
existence.   Permanent structures are, however, developed
in the first three of the visceral arches.

In each of the first two a rod of cartilage is formed, which
either actually meet or are closely connected above at the spot
which afterwards becomes the tympanic cavity (see Diagram,
pp. 104 and 105).   According to the best authorities the
upper end of the first rod becomes converted into the
malleus, and either from or in close connection with that of
the second the *incus*, the *stapes*, and the stapedius muscle
are developed.[1]   Whatever uncertainty may still attach to
the changes which take place in the upper ends of these
cartilaginous rods, it is generally admitted that in connection
with the lower or distal part of the one formed in the first
visceral arch (commonly called *Meckel's cartilage*), the ramus
of the mandible is developed, partly by the conversion of
the cartilage itself, but principally by the ossification of
fibrous tissue deposited around it, and that the distal part
of the rod of cartilage formed in the second visceral arch
is developed into the anterior hyoidean arch, or "anterior
cornu" of the hyoid bone.

[1] See Huxley "On the Representatives of the Malleus and the
Incus of the Mammalia in other Vertebrata," Proceedings of the
Zoological Society, 1869.

The first visceral cleft, which lies between the first and second visceral arches, becomes entirely obliterated, except at its upper end, just below the junction of the arches, where it forms the Eustachian tube, tympanic cavity, and meatus auditorius externus, which would form a canal of communication between the pharynx and the external surface but for the interposition of the delicate *membrana tympani.*

This being the essential relation of these parts as they exist in all Mammals, they may be described a little more fully as found in the Dog.

The *mandible* consists of two symmetrical elongated rami (see Fig. 45), diverging behind, and coming in contact in front at the middle line, by a roughened surface called the *symphysis (s)*; here they are firmly held together by interposed fibrous tissue, or in old animals they may become ankylosed.

Each ramus is compressed from side to side, has a thickened rounded lower border, slightly curved in the longitudinal direction, and a nearly straight upper *alveolar* border, in which the teeth are implanted. The inferior border inclines upward in front to meet the alveolar border at the front of the symphysis. Near the posterior extremity is the *condyle (cd)*, a transversely-extended projection, with its upper surface rounded in the antero-posterior direction, and which, fitting into the glenoid cavity of the squamosal bone, forms the hinge-like synovial articulation by which the lower jaw moves on the skull. The upper border, between the condyle and the hindermost tooth, rises into a high, compressed, recurved process (the *coronoid process, cp*), to which the temporal muscle is attached. The outer surface of this process gradually subsides into a considerable hollow in the side of the ramus, with prominent anterior, inferior, and posterior edges, to which the masseter, another powerful muscle for closing the jaw, is attached.

The point at which the vertical hinder edge of the ramus, descending from the condyle, meets the horizontal inferior border, is called the *angle*, which in the Dog is prolonged into a conspicuous compressed process, with an upturned and slightly inverted pointed extremity, the *angular process* (*a*). On the inner side of the ramus, a little way in front of and below the condyle, is the *inferior dental foramen* (*id*), for the admission of the inferior dental nerve (from the fifth pair) and artery. On the outer side of the ramus, near its anterior extremity, is the *mental foramen*, through which a branch of the same nerve passes out to the lower lip and surrounding structures.

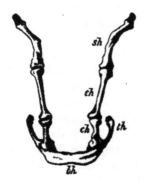

FIG. 48.—Extracranial portion of hyoidean apparatus of Dog, front view: *sh* stylohyal; *eh* epihyal; *ch* ceratohyal (these three constitute the "anterior cornu"); *bh* basihyal, or "body" of hyoid; *th* thyrohyal, or "posterior cornu."

The hyoidean apparatus (Fig. 48) consists of a median portion below, the *basihyal* (*bh*), from which two pairs of half arches, or "cornua," extend upwards and outwards. The anterior (*ch* to *sh*) is the largest, and connects it with the cranium, and is developed in the second embryonic visceral arch, as stated above. The posterior (*th*) is united externally or superiorly with the thyroid cartilage of the larynx, and is developed in the third visceral arch. In the Dog there are four distinct ossifications in the anterior arch. The first is a small cylindrical piece of bone lying in a canal between the tympanic and periotic bones, immediately to the inner and anterior side of the stylomastoid foramen, and by its upper end firmly ankylosed with the surrounding bones. It can be seen much more distinctly in some dogs' skulls than others, and is more conspicuously developed in some other Mammals. This I have called *tympanohyal*, as it is always in relation with the hinder edge of the tympanic bone, generally more or less embedded in it, and it extends upwards, embedded in, and afterwards ankylosed with, the periotic, to the hinder wall of the tympanic cavity. Its lower end is truncated and continued into a band of cartilage, which connects it with the proximal end of the bone which has been generally recognized as the uppermost of the series forming the anterior hyoidean arch, the *stylohyal* (*sh*). The two succeeding bones (*ep* and *ch*) are named by Professor Owen respectively *epihyal* and *ceratohyal*. All three are elongated, compressed, slightly curved or twisted on themselves, tipped at each end with cartilage, and connected with each other by synovial joints. The stylohyal and epihyal are nearly equal in length, the ceratohyal shorter and stouter.

The *basihyal* (*bh*) is a transversely-extended, flattened bar, with its extremities rather upturned and thickened. The posterior cornu (*th*) consists of a single, nearly straight, compressed bone, the *thyrohyal*, articulated inferiorly with the outer end of the basihyal, just below the attachment of the ceratohyal, and truncated at its superior extremity, to which the thyroid cartilage of the larynx is suspended.

Some of the changes which take place in the cranium while advancing from youth to maturity have already been noticed ; but it will be well, before proceeding to describe the modifications of the mammalian skull, to mention certain others which take place, to a greater or less degree, in all skulls.

These depend mainly on the fact that the brain, and consequently the cavity which contains it, and also the sense capsules, increase in size in a much smaller ratio than the external parts of the head, especially the jaws and prominences for the attachment of muscles. The disproportionate growth and alteration of form of these parts, concomitant with little or no change in the brain-case, is effected partly by increase in thickness of the bones, but mainly by the expansion of their walls and the development of cells within, which greatly extend the outer surface without adding to the weight of the bone.

In the Dog these cells are developed chiefly in the fore part of the frontal bones, constituting the *frontal sinuses*, and in the presphenoid, constituting the *sphenoidal sinuses*. Air passes freely into them from the nasal passages. In many animals they attain a much larger extent than in the Dog, reaching their maximum in the Elephant (see Fig. 60, p. 179), where the alteration of the external form of skull during growth, without material change in the shape or size of the cerebral cavity, is strikingly shown. At the same time the alveolar borders of the jaws gradually enlarge to adapt themselves to the increased size of the permanent teeth which they have to support, and the various ridges and tuberosities for the attachment of muscles become more prominent.

During these changes a gradual consolidation takes place in the structure of the skull generally, by the partial or complete union of certain of the bones by ankylosis. The union of the different bones generally proceeds in a certain definite order, which, however, varies much in different species. Sometimes it extends so far as to lead to complete obliteration of all the cranial sutures.

CHAPTER X.

Order PRIMATES. *Man.*—On comparing a longitudinal and vertical section of a young human skull, in which most of the sutures are still distinctly seen (Fig. 49), with that of the Dog, it will be seen to be composed of the same bones, having very nearly the same connections, and yet the whole form is greatly modified. This modification is mainly due to the immense expansion of the upper part of the middle or cerebral fossa of the brain cavity, which not only carries the roof of the cavity a great distance from the basicranial axis, but also forces, as it were, the anterior and posterior walls from the vertical nearly to the horizontal position, so that they are, roughly speaking, in the same line with the short basicranial axis, instead of being perpendicular to it. In addition to this great difference, the facial portion of the skull is deeper from above downwards, and very much shorter from before backwards.

Taking a survey of the human skull in the same order as was done with that of the Dog, we find the craniofacial axis, composed of the basioccipital bone (*BO*), terminating at the anterior border of the foramen magnum (*fm*) behind, and in this young skull still separated from the basisphenoid

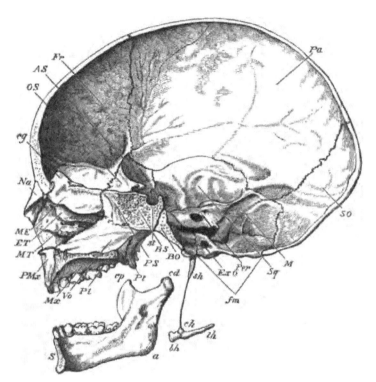

FIG. 49.—Vertical, longitudinal, median section of a young human skull, with the first dentition, ¼. As in the other sections of skulls figured, the mandible is displaced downwards, so as to show its entire form. *PMx* premaxilla ; *MT* maxillo-turbinal ; *ET* ethmo-turbinal ; *ME* ossified portion of the mesethmoid ; *Na* nasal ; *cg* crista galli of the mesethmoid ; *OS* orbitosphenoid, or lesser wing of the sphenoid ; *AS* alisphenoid, or greater wing of the sphenoid ; *Fr* frontal ; *Pa* parietal ; *SO* supraoccipital ; *M* mastoid portion of the periotic ; *Sq* squamosal ; *Per* petrous portion of the periotic ; the large foramen below the end of the line is the internal auditory meatus, the small depression above it is the nearly-obliterated floccular fossa. *ExO* exoccipital, the line points to the condylar fora-men ; *fm* foramen magnum ; *BO* basioccipital ; *BS* basisphenoid ; *st* sella turcica ; *PS* presphenoid, ankylosed with the basisphenoid, forming the "body of the sphenoid ;" *Pt* pterygoid ; *Pl* palatine ; *Vo* vomer ; *Mx* maxilla ; *s* symphysis of mandible ; *cp* coronoid process ; *cd* articular condyle ; *a* angle ; *sh* stylohyal, or "styloid process of temporal ;" *ch* ceratohyal, or lesser cornu of hyoid ; *bh* basi-hyal, or body of hyoid ; *th* thyrohyal, or greater cornu of hyoid.

in front by a vertical fissure. The *basisphenoid* (*BS*) is short
and deep, and has a strongly marked pituitary fossa or "sella
turcica" (*st*) above. It has completely united with the presphenoid (*PS*), though at birth, the line of separation (below
the spot called the *olivary process* or *tuberculum sellæ*) is still
visible. In adult age large air-cells fill the interior of this conjoined bone, which is the "body" of the so-called "sphenoid"
of human anatomy. Anteriorly the presphenoid narrows to
a sharp vertical edge, which is in contact with the mesethmoid
(*ME*) above and the vomer (*Vo*) below. The whole of the
upper part of the mesethmoid is ossified in the specimen
described, constituting the "lamina perpendicularis," but the
anterior and lower part forms the septal cartilage of the nose.
Its upper border forms a strong compressed triangular projection into the cranial cavity, called the "crista galli" (*cg*).

The posterior segment of the brain-case is completed, as
in the Dog, by the pair of exoccipitals (*ExO*), and a large
supraoccipital (*SO*).[1] The triangular upper part of the latter
may be considered to represent the interparietal, though it
very soon becomes incorporated with the rest of the supraoccipital. The middle segment is completed by large alisphenoids (*AS*), the "greater wings of the sphenoid bone,"
and enormously extended, somewhat square-shaped parietals
(*Pa*); the frontal segment by narrow triangular orbitosphenoids (*OS*), the "lesser wings of the sphenoid bone,"[2]
and by large arched frontals (*Fr*).

Of the fossæ into which the cranial cavity is divided, the
olfactory fossa is very small, rather narrow, elongated, and

[1] The "occipital bone" of human anatomy is formed by the
coalescence of the basioccipital, exoccipitals, and supraoccipital.

[2] The "sphenoid bone" of human anatomy is formed by the union of
the basisphenoid, presphenoid, alisphenoids, orbitosphenoids, and the
pterygoids. The basal portion ultimately ankyloses with the occipital.

shallow. The cribriform plate which closes it in front, instead of being vertical, as in the Dog, is_horizontal, and
almost in the same line with the basicranial axis. It is
bounded in the median line, and separated from the corresponding fossa of the other side by the prominent crista
galli of the mesethmoid. The middle fossa is, as before
said, of comparatively enormous extent; it is bounded posteriorly by the tentorial ridge, having the same relations to
bones as in the Dog, but lying more horizontally and being
far less prominent, having no osseous shelf-like inward extension. This fossa is distinctly divided into an anterior and
posterior portion, by the strongly projecting hinder ridge of
the orbitosphenoid. The floor of the anterior portion is
arched in consequence of the inward projection of the roof
of the orbit, while the floor of the posterior, or "temporal
fossa," is deeply concave. The cerebellar fossa is of moderate size, and lies entirely underneath the hinder part of
the cerebral fossa.

The "sella turcica," or depression in the basisphenoid for
the lodgment of the pituitary body of the brain, is bounded
posteriorly by an elevated transverse ridge, the corners of
which are called the "posterior clinoid processes." Corresponding processes projecting backwards from the orbitosphenoids are called "anterior clinoid processes."

The foramina in the base of the skull scarcely differ from
those of the Dog.   1. The olfactory has been already
described.   2. The optic is a large round hole close to the
inner and posterior part of the orbitosphenoid.   3. The
sphenoidal fissure is larger than in the Dog, and produced
externally into a long narrow slit.   4 and 5. The foramen
rotundum and the foramen ovale pierce the alisphenoid,
one near its anterior, the other its posterior border.   Close
behind the last-named is a small hole ("foramen spinosum"),

K

through which a branch of the external carotid artery
(middle meningeal) enters the brain-cavity. 6 and 8. The
foramen lacerum medium basis cranii and the foramen
lacerum posterius have the same functions and relation as
in the Dog. 7. Between these two the periotic has the
conspicuous meatus auditorius internus on its inner side.
The depression above this, for the lodgment of the flocculus, is distinctly seen in fœtal human skulls up to the
time of birth, but it afterwards becomes gradually obliterated. 9. The condylar foramen perforates the exoccipital,
as in the Dog; and lastly (10), the foramen magnum has
the same general subcircular form, and is bounded by the
same bones, but differs greatly in direction, its plane looking
mainly downwards instead of backwards.

The nasal cavities differ chiefly from those of the Dog in
their shortness and greater vertical height. In their inner
wall, the descending median plate of the vomer (*Vo*) is much
more developed. The pterygoids (*Pt*) are extended vertically, are narrow from before backwards, end below in a
marked "hamular" process, and soon ankylose with the pterygoid plates of the alisphenoid anteriorly, but posteriorly are
separated from them by a well-marked " pterygoid fossa."[1]
The palatines (*Pl*) and maxillæ (*Mx*) are short from before
backwards. The premaxillæ (*PMx*) are small and early
ankylosed with the maxillæ.[2] The nasals (*Na*) are short,

[1] The pterygoid, not being recognized as a distinct bone, is commonly described in works on human anatomy as "the internal pterygoid plate of the sphenoid;" the pterygoid process of the alisphenoid
being the "external pterygoid plate."

[2] The premaxilla is a distinct bone in the human fœtus, but is covered
on its external or facial aspect by a process of the maxilla, which extends
over it towards the middle line, and becomes completely fused with it
before birth, so that no trace of the maxillo-premaxillary suture is ever
seen on the outer side of the face. On the inner and palatal aspect of

and nearly vertical, broad below and narrow above. The anterior nares are also nearly vertical. The turbinal bones are comparatively little developed, and of simple structure, especially the lower or maxillo-turbinal (*MT*). The flat bony-plate on the outer side of the ethmo-turbinal or " os planum," instead of lying against the inner side of the maxilla, forms part of the outer wall of the nasal cavity and inner wall of the orbit, uniting with the frontal above, the lachrymal in front, the maxilla below, and the palatine behind.

The group of bones placed around the organ of hearing, periotic, squamosal, and tympanic, though originally distinct, become ankylosed together soon after birth, to form the so-called "temporal bone." They differ from the corresponding bones in the Dog in the following particulars. The periotic has a very much larger mastoid portion (*M*), which forms a considerable part of the wall of the cerebellar fossa. In the new-born infant its outer surface is smooth and flat, but as life advances, air-cells become developed within it, communicating with the tympanic cavity, and a strongly-marked descending projection, the "mastoid process," appears on the lower and anterior part of its outer surface. The squamosal (*Sq*) is a large flat vertical plate, forming a considerable part of the wall of the posterior cerebral fossa, behind the alisphenoid. Its zygmotic process is comparatively slender and straight. The tympanic forms a long tubular external auditory meatus, but its inner part joins the periotic, forming the floor of the tympanic cavity without being inflated into an auditory bulla. Its

the bones the suture is always evident at birth, and can often be traced even in adult skulls. See G. W. Callender " On the Formation and Early Growth of the Bones of the Human Face." (Phil. Trans. 1869, p. 163.)

under surface is produced into a rough ridge, to the inner side of which the large carotid canal perforates the base of the periotic, being directed obliquely forwards and inwards. In adult skulls the stylohyal becomes ankylosed with the tympanic and periotic, constituting the "styloid process of the temporal bone."

In examining the external aspect of the skull, the large smooth subglobular or oval brain-case, constituting by far the larger part of the whole cranium, is strikingly different from that of the Dog. The occipital surface, instead of being vertical, is nearly horizontal. The condyles, instead of being at the hindermost part of the skull, are not far from the middle of the base. The paroccipital processes of the exoccipitals are represented by mere rudiments, the so-called "jugular eminences;" on the other hand, the mastoid processes, almost obsolete in the Dog, are very greatly developed. The occipital crest is represented by a slightly raised and roughened line, the "superior curved line," and the sagittal crest is absent.

The sutures connecting the bones of the upper surface of the cranium are remarkable for their wavy or indented character, processes from one bone interlocking with those from the other in a most complex manner, at least on the external surface, for seen from within they appear comparatively straight and simple. There are very often irregular ossifications, separated from the contiguous bones, lying among the indentations of the occipito-parietal suture, called "Wormian bones." [1] The temporal fossæ are but indistinctly marked out by a curved line above, and are separated from each other by a wide expanse formed

---

[1] In works on human anatomy, the occipito-parietal suture is commonly called "lambdoid;" the interparietal, "sagittal;" and the fronto-parietal, "coronal."

by the smooth rounded upper part of the parietal and
frontal bones. The orbit is completely encircled by bone,
the outer margin being formed by a process from the malar
ascending to join the post-orbital process of the frontal ; and
it is, moreover, in great part separated from the temporal
fossa by an extension inwards of the ascending process of
the malar meeting the alisphenoid, although a communication is left between the two cavities below in the "spheno-
maxillary fissure." The axis of the orbital cavity is directed
more forwards than in the Dog. The face is altogether very
much shorter, broader, and flatter.

In the inferior surface of the skull, the palate is seen
to be much shorter and wider than that of the Dog,
especially anteriorly, where its outline forms an almost
semicircular curve. The maxillo-palatine suture is nearly
straight transversely, and so is the hinder border of the palate,
though produced backwards into an obtuse spine at the
middle line. The distance between the hinder border of the
palate and the foramen magnum is much shorter relatively,
the space between the pterygoids being particularly short
and wide. The true pterygoids and pterygoid plates of the
alisphenoid are widely separated posteriorly, leaving a considerable fossa between them ; and the latter are larger,
and project further backwards than the former. The under
surface of the tympano-periotic region is rough and irregular,
instead of being smooth and bullate, and the perforation for
the internal carotid artery is very conspicuous. There is
no alisphenoid canal, scarcely any postglenoid process, no
distinct glenoid venous foramen, a very small paroccipital,
and a very large mastoid process. By the inclination of the
occipital surface downwards, instead of backwards, an
inferior view of the skull includes nearly all this surface,
with the large foramen magnum and the condyles.

In accordance with the general form of the face the mandible is short. The two rami of which it is originally formed ankylose together at the symphysis within a year after birth. They are widely divergent behind, and approach in front at a much more obtuse angle than in the Dog. The horizontal portion of each ramus is deep and compressed, the lower margin straight or slightly concave, and produced anteriorly rather in front of the alveolar margin, so as to occasion the mental prominence, characteristic of the human lower jaw. The anterior symphysial margin (Fig. 49, *s*), therefore, instead of sloping upwards, from behind forwards, is vertical, or rather inclined in the other direction. Posteriorly, the condyle (*cd*) is more elevated than in the Dog, and is less transversely extended. The coronoid process (*cp*) is smaller and less recurved. The posterior border, between the condyle and the angle (*a*), is nearly straight and vertical, and the angle is rounded, compressed, slightly everted, and not produced into any hook-like process, as in the Dog. The depression for the masseter muscle is very faintly marked.

The hyoidean apparatus differs in several particulars from that of the Dog. The tympanohyal can generally be recognized in the skull of an infant at birth, and for a few years after, as a cylindrical piece of bone, with a truncated lower extremity, about one-twentieth of an inch in diameter, seated in a depression in the hinder border of the tympanic, immediately to the anterior and inner side of the stylo-mastoid foramen. Its upper end becomes soon ankylosed with the periotic. The tympanic is produced around it anteriorly, constituting the "vaginal process." The stylohyal (*sh*), at first a long styliform piece of cartilage, continuous with the tympanohyal, commences to ossify by a separate centre before birth, and, at a very variable period after-

wards, is usually ankylosed with the tympanohyal and surrounding cranial bones, constituting the so-called "styloid
process." This is a condition not met with in any other
Mammal. Below the stylohyal the greater part of the anterior hyoid arch is represented by a slender ligament (the
"stylohyoid" ligament), there being no ossification corresponding to the Dog's epihyal; but the ceratohyal (*ch*) to
which the ligament is attached below, is a small bony
nodule, the "lesser cornu of the hyoid" of human anatomy,
which is articulated synovially to the upper corner of the
outer extremity of the basihyal, though sometimes in old
age becoming ankylosed. The basihyal (*bh*), or "body of
the hyoid," is transversely oblong, hollowed posteriorly, and
deeper from above downwards than in the Dog. The thyrohyals (*th*) or "greater cornua of the hyoid," are elongated,
nearly straight and somewhat compressed. They usually
become ankylosed before middle life with the outer extremities of the basihyal.

The *Simiina* have the skull formed generally on the same
plan as that of Man, with certain modifications in detail.

The facial portion is enlarged and elongated as compared
with the cerebral portion, though to a very variable extent
in different members of the sub-order.

In nearly all, the brain-cavity maintains the same general
form as in Man, though it is usually of less comparative
vertical extent. With few exceptions, the middle compartment for the lodgment of the cerebrum, retains its
relative situation and superiority in size to the cerebellar
and the olfactory fossæ, completely overlying them both;
and consequently the occipital region of the skull with the
foramen magnum behind, and the cribriform plate of the
ethmoid in front, are in the same general horizontal line

with the basicranial axis as in Man, and not perpendicular to them as in the Dog.

It is remarkable that the deviations from this general rule, especially as regards the plane of the occipital surface, are not in relation to the general position of the animals in a descending series, from Man to the lowest Monkeys; for the occipital surface is nearly vertical in the anthropoid Gibbons (*Hylobates*), especially *H. syndactylus* (the Siamang), and completely so in the American Howling Monkeys (*Mycetes*), where the cerebral fossa does not project in the least degree behind the cerebellar fossa; while in the Baboons (*Cynocephalus*), among the Old World Monkeys, and still more in some of the smaller and lower forms of American Monkeys (as *Callithrix*), the posterior development of the cerebral fossa is so great as to throw the supraoccipital bone considerably more into the posteriorly prolonged base of the skull than even in Man.

The olfactory fossa is always small. It is not only very short, but, in consequence of the considerable projection inwards of the portion of the frontal forming the roof of the orbit on each side of it, is both narrow from side to side, and deep from above downwards.

In most of the *Simiina*, including the Gorilla and Chimpanzee, the frontals meet across the middle line over the presphenoid, between the mesethmoid in front and the orbitosphenoids behind; but the Orang agrees with Man in wanting this postethmoid union of the frontals, and so also do some of the *Cebidæ*.

The fossa on the inner surface of the periotic for the floccular process of the cerebellum is almost obliterated in the adult Gorilla, Chimpanzee, Orang, and Gibbons, but persistent, and often very large, in all other Monkeys.

A partial ossification of the tentorium from the inner

edge of the periotic takes place in some of the American Monkeys, as *Mycetes* and *Cebus*.

The suture between the basisphenoid and the presphenoid remains distinct in the Baboons and all the lower Monkeys, until the animal has nearly attained its full size and acquired its permanent teeth; but it is completely obliterated, and the cancellous structure of the two bones is continuous, in the Gorilla, Chimpanzee, and Orang, while the animal still retains all its milk-teeth.

The nasal cavities, with their surrounding bones, are generally longer and of less vertical extent than in Man, but, as in the case of the inclination of the occipital plane, not following any regular serial descent. Thus the proportions of these parts are more like those of Man in many of the smaller American *Cebidæ* than in the long-faced or "Dog-headed" Baboons (*Cynocephali*) of the Old World.

The vomer is generally longer, and of less vertical extent, than in Man. The turbinals have much the same general characters, their relative situation of course varying with the elongation, or otherwise, of the nasal passages. The os planum of the ethmoturbinals always forms part of the inner wall of the orbit, having the same relations as in Man.

The pterygoid plate of the alisphenoid is usually largely developed, and generally projects considerably backwards beyond the pterygoid bone (which is narrow, and has a very distinct hamular process), and there is always a wide and deep fossa between them.

The premaxilla is always distinct on the facial surface, and the suture between it and the maxilla is only obliterated in aged specimens. It generally extends upwards on the side of the anterior nares, so far as to meet the nasal and completely exclude the maxilla from taking any part in the boundary of this opening.

The lachrymal foramen is never situated externally to the orbit, although, in the lower forms, it may be close upon the margin.

As in Man the postorbital process of the frontal meets the orbital process of the malar so as completely to encircle the outer side of the orbit ; and an extension backwards and inwards of these bones joining the alisphenoid, divides the orbit from the temporal fossa.

The nasal bones vary much in length and breadth, but they present the peculiarity throughout the order of a great tendency to ankylose together in the middle line, even at a comparatively early age.

In all the smaller and middle-sized Monkeys the general surface of the calvaria is oval and smooth, but in the larger Baboons and Orangs there are well-marked supraorbital, sagittal, and occipital ridges. These attain their greatest development in the adult male Gorilla, where they completely mask the original form of the cranium. Their size, in this sex, appears to increase with age; while in the oldest females, on the other hand, they are but slightly apparent.

The paroccipital process is always rudimentary, as in Man.

The squamosal in the higher forms is developed much as in Man ; but in the lower forms it is more reduced, and takes a smaller space in the formation of the side wall of the cranium. It generally comes in contact, at its upper anterior angle, with the frontal, but not in the Orang or in the *Cebidæ*, in which animals the union of the parietal and the alisphenoid separates the frontal from the squamosal, as is usually the case with Man. The glenoid surface is flatter than in Man, and there is a well-marked postglenoid process.

The zygoma is usually narrow, horizontal, and slightly arched outwards.

The periotic generally resembles that of Man, and the mastoid portion is conspicuous on the outer side of the skull between the squamosal and the exoccipital; but its surface is smooth and rounded, without any distinct mastoid process.

In all the Old World forms, the tympanic forms an elongated inferior wall to the external auditory meatus, which has consequently a considerable bony tube; but in all the American Monkeys this bone retains more or less its primitive annular condition, and the cavity of the tympanum is close to the external wall of the cranium. This character alone will readily serve to determine to which of the two great divisions of Monkeys a skull may belong.

No auditory bulla is developed in any of the Old World Monkeys, but in all the *Cebidæ* and *Hapalidæ* the inferior surface of the ankylosed periotic and tympanic is much swollen.

The carotid canal is always very conspicuous, entering the under surface of the periotic near its hinder border. There is often a glenoid foramen, but never an alisphenoid canal.

The foramen rotundum perforates the alisphenoid, but the foramen ovale is usually a notch on its posterior border, completed by the periotic behind.

The mandible presents the same general characters as that of Man, but the horizontal portion of the ramus is usually more elongated, and the anterior border slopes upwards and forwards, there being a complete absence of mental protuberance. The condyle is extended transversely, the coronoid process well developed and recurved. The posterior or ascending portion of the ramus is broad and flat; the angle well developed, square, or more or less rounded, but without any special pointed process as in the Dog.

In the Howling Monkeys (*Mycetes*) the hinder or ascending portion of the ramus is remarkable for its extent, both vertically and antero-posteriorly, corresponding to a certain extent with the extraordinary development of the vocal organs, which it partially covers and protects.

The *Simiina* are remarkable in never having an ossified stylohyal; but on looking closely at the base of the periotic, immediately to the anterior and inner side of the stylo-mastoid foramen, a very small depression, in which there is sometimes a minute ossified tympano-hyal, can generally be seen. To this the ligament representing the stylohyal is attached.

In very few of the Old World Monkeys is there any ossification in the anterior hyoid arch (see Fig. 50); but in some *Cercopitheci* a short, bony, ceratohyal is found. This occurs also in the American Monkeys (Fig. 51), with occasionally the addition of a second piece (epihyal).

The thyrohyals are always well developed, long, narrow, nearly straight, and somewhat flattened.

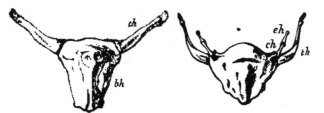

FIG. 50.—Inferior surface of hyoid bones of Baboon (*Cynocephalus porcarius*): *bh* basihyal; *th* thyrohyal.

FIG. 51.—Inferior surface of hyoid bones of an American Monkey (*Lagothrix humboldtii*): *th* thyrohyal; *ch* cerato-hyal; *eh* epihyal.

The basihyal varies much in form. In the anthropoid Apes it is broad transversely; but in nearly all the other Monkeys its antero-posterior extent exceeds its breadth, owing to a great development from the posterior border. It is generally convex below, and concave above and behind, forming a considerable cavity, in which the median laryngeal air-sac is lodged. This condition is enormously exaggerated in the American Howling Monkey (*Mycetes*), where the basi-hyal is transformed into an immense subglobular, thin-walled, bony capsule, with a large orifice posteriorly, by which the laryngeal air-sac enters, and having the straight narrow thyrohyals attached to its posterior upper angles. In this genus there are no ossifications in the anterior arch.

While, in nearly all the characters in which the skull of Man differs from that of the Dog, the *Simiina* agree with the former; the *Lemurina*, on the other hand, more resemble the lower type.

In the Common Lemur the general proportions of face to cerebral cavity, and the inclination of the occipital and olfactory planes of the cranium, are quite dog-like. The orbits, although completely surrounded behind by the junction of the postorbital processes of the frontal and the malar, are yet perfectly continuous with the temporal fossa beneath this bony bar; that extension inwards of the frontal and malar to meet the alisphenoid, and thus form a posterior external wall of the orbit, so characteristic of Man and all Monkeys, being absent. The lachrymal foramen, situated on the facial part of the bone, is altogether external to the margin of the orbit. The os planum of the ethmo-turbinal does not enter into the inner wall of the orbit, but is shut out from it by the maxilla, as in most inferior mammals. The inferior surface of the tympanic is developed into a large rounded bulla. The hyoid apparatus much resembles that of the Dog, having the stylohyal, epihyal, and ceratohyal all distinctly ossified in the anterior arch, and the basihyal in the form of a narrow transverse bar.

Some of the *Lemurina* have much shorter faces than the common species, though still possessing all the essential characters of the group. Among these, *Tarsius* is remarkable for the extraordinary size of the orbits, which are so expanded that their margins form prominent, thin, bony rings, and the interorbital part of the skull is reduced to an exceedingly delicate septum.

The general characteristics of the skull of the CARNIVORA have been described, as seen in the Dog. The more obvious modifications from this type relate to the comparative length and compression or width of the facial portion, the strength and curve of the zygomatic arch, and the extent to which the various ridges and processes for the attachment of muscles are developed. Thus the Cats have short and round skulls, with wide zygomatic arches; and in the Bears (especially the Polar Bear, *Ursus maritimus*) the whole skull is elongated, and the nasal cavities are greatly enlarged as compared with the brain-case, and the maxillo-turbinal bones are correspondingly developed.

But there are certain other modifications of the cranial bones, which, being less obviously adaptive to functional purposes, and being constantly associated with structural modifications in other parts of the body, are of considerable value in classifying the members of the group. Of these the most important are related to the form and structure of the auditory bulla, and the surrounding parts of the base of the cranium.

In the Bears, the auditory bulla is comparatively little inflated. It consists of a single bone (tympanic), readily detached from the cranium in skulls of young animals. Its form is more or less triangular, being broad and nearly straight at the inner edge, and produced outwards into a considerably elongated floor of the external auditory meatus. Its greatest prominence is along the inner border ; from this it gradually slopes away towards the meatus. The entrance of the carotid canal is a considerable circular foramen, near the hinder part of the inner edge of the bulla. In old animals it is partly concealed by the prominent lip of the basioccipital, which abuts against the inner edge of the

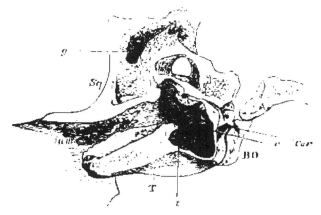

FIG. 52.—Section of the auditory bulla and surrounding bones of a Bear (*Ursus ferox*): *Sq* squamosal ; *T* tympanic ; BO basioccipital ; *am* external auditory meatus ; *t* tympanic ring ; *e* Eustachian canal ; *Car* carotid canal. (From Proc. Zool. Soc. 1869.)

bulla ; and by the growth of this, and the paroccipital process, it becomes almost included in the deep fossa leading to the foramen lacerum posterius. When a section is made through the auditory bulla (see Fig. 52) it is seen to be a simple thin-walled bony capsule, imperfect above, where it

stylohya!.
the anter
transvers

Some
common
characte
able for
expand
rings, a
an exc

The
have b
modifi
length
streng
which
of mu
round
(espec
skull
as co
bone.
Bu
bone
purp
mod
valu
the
the
the
I
infl:

... agree with
... its region of
... smaller species)
... ..lways has its
... inner border, and
... prolonged floor of
... there are often trabeculae

or partial septa passing mostly transversely across the lower part,[1] there is no distinct and definite septum dividing it into a separate outer and inner chamber. In all cases, on looking into the external auditory meatus (in the dried skull when the membrana tympani is removed) the opposite wall of the bulla can be seen; or if a probe is passed into the meatus, no obstacle will prevent its touching the inner wall.

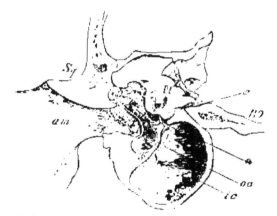

FIG. 53.—Section of the auditory bulla of the Tiger (*Felis tigris*): *Sq* squamosal; *Pi* periotic; *BO* basioccipital; *am* external auditory meatus; *oc* the outer chamber; *ic* the inner chamber; *s* the septum; * the aperture of communication between the chambers. (From Proc. Zool. Soc. 1869.)

In the Tiger, which may be taken as a type of the *Felidæ*, the auditory bulla is very prominent, rounded and smooth on the surface, rather longer from before backwards than transversely, its greatest prominence being rather to the inner side of the centre. The lower lip of the external auditory meatus is extremely short; the meatus, in fact,

---

[1] Especially developed in the Weasels (*Mustela*), in which also the entire parietes of the bulla are thickened and cancellous.

ooks like a large hole opening directly into the side of the
bulla. On looking into this hole, at a very short distance
(just beyond the tympanic ring), a wall of bone is seen quite
impeding the view, or the passage of any instrument, into
the greater part of the bulla. In the section (Fig. 53) it will
be seen that this wall is a septum (*s*), which rises from the
floor of the bulla along its outer side, and divides it almost
completely into two distinct chambers : one (*oc*), outer and
anterior, is the true tympanic chamber, and contains the
tympanic membrane and ossicula, and has at its anterior
extremity the opening of the Eustachian tube (*e*) ; while the
other (*ic*), internal and posterior, is a simple but much
larger cavity, having no aperture except a long but very
narrow fissure (*) left between the hinder part of the top
of the septum and the promontory of the periotic, which
fissure expands posteriorly, or rather at its outer end, into a
triangular space, placed just over the fenestra rotunda, so
that the opening of this fenestra is partly in the outer, and
partly in the inner chamber of the bulla. This chamber is
formed by a simple capsule of very thin but dense bone,
deficient only at a small oval space in the roof, where the
periotic projects into and fills up the gap, except such
portion of it as is left to form the aperture of communication with the outer chamber.

Not only are these two chambers thus distinct, but they
are originally developed in a totally different manner. At
birth the only ossification in the whole structure is the incomplete ring of bone supporting the membrana tympani,
and developed originally in fibrous tissue. Ossification
extends from this, so as to complete the outer chamber,
and the very limited lip of the meatus auditorius externus.
The inner chamber is formed from a distinct piece of hyaline cartilage, which at birth is a narrow slip, pointed at

each end, lying between the tympanic ring and the basi-occipital, applied closely to the surface of the already ossified periotic, and forming no distinct prominence on the under surface of the skull. Soon after birth this increases in size, and gradually assumes the bullate form of the wall of the inner chamber. In young animals, even some time after the ossification of the bulla is complete, the distinction between the two parts is clearly seen externally; not only are they marked off by a groove, but the tympanic portion has a more opaque appearance than the other. The septum is formed by an inversion of the walls of both, applied together, and ultimately perfectly fused in *Felis*, although remaining permanently distinct in some of the *Viverridæ*.

The carotid foramen in the Tiger is only represented by a minute groove deep in the recess of the foramen lacerum posterius. In the smaller Cats, this groove is more superficial, but always very minute, and apparently never converted into an actual foramen, except by the contiguous wall of the basioccipital.

The paroccipital process is flattened over the back of the bulla, being applied closely to the whole of its prominent rounded hinder end, and projecting, as a rough tubercle, slightly beyond it. From the inner side of this process a sharp ridge runs towards the occipital condyle. This forms the posterior boundary of a deep fossa, at the bottom of which is the foramen lacerum posterius, and in the hinder part of which, under cover of the aforesaid ridge, the condylar foramen opens. The mastoid process is a moderately conspicuous rough projection, not very widely separated from the paroccipital. There is no distinct glenoid foramen.

The *Viverridæ* agree with the *Felidæ* in having the auditory

bulla divided into two cavities by a bony partition, in having
the paroccipital spread over the hinder surface of the bulla,
and in having no prolonged external auditory meatus; but
the bulla is more elongated and compressed, and the inner
chamber is placed altogether behind the outer or true
tympanic chamber.

In the Hyæna this region of the skull much resembles the
same part in the Cats, but the bulla is simple and undivided.
In the Dogs there is a partial septum, and otherwise the
characters are intermediate between the two extremes of the
Bears on one side, and the Cats on the other.[1]

In nearly all the Carnivora the hyoidean apparatus is constructed on the same plan as described in the Dog, having a
narrow, transversely elongated, curved basihyal, either round,
or compressed from above downwards, a nearly straight
compressed thyrohyal, not ankylosed with the basihyal, and
a well-ossified anterior cornu, composed of three distinct
pieces of subequal length. In the Lion, Tiger, and Leopard,
however, the anterior arch is imperfectly ossified, the different bones being small, and connected together by long
ligamentous intervals; but in the Puma, Cheetah, Lynx, and
Cat, the bones are large, and in close relation with each
other.

In the Seals the brain-cavity is very broad, round, and
rather depressed. The orbits are large, and the interorbital
portion of the skull greatly compressed. The olfactory
chambers of the nasal cavities are consequently very narrow,
and the ethmoturbinals little developed; but in front of the
orbits the cavities widen, and the maxilloturbinals are very

---

[1] For the various modifications of the structure of this part of the
skull in the different genera of the order, see "On the Value of the
Characters of the Base of the Cranium in the Classification of the Order
Carnivora." (Proc. Zool. Soc., 1869, p. 5.)

large and complex. The mesethmoid is of considerable vertical extent, and its ossified portion, which is extensive, terminates anteriorly in a straight vertical line. In some forms, as *Cystophora*, this ossification extends in front of the nasals. The hyoid resembles that of the typical Carnivora, all the elements being well ossified and distinct. The *Otariidæ*, or Eared Seals, also called Sea Bears or Sea Lions, are intermediate in most of their cranial characters between the true Seals and the Bears.

The skulls of the animals composing the Order INSEC- TIVORA present great variations.

In some of the higher forms, as *Galeopithecus*, *Tupaia*, *Macroscelides*, and *Rhynchocyon*, the cranium much resembles that of the *Lemurina*, having a considerable and vaulted cerebral cavity, large orbits, nearly vertical occipital plane, large olfactory fossæ, a well-developed zygomatic arch sending up a postorbital process to meet a corresponding one from the frontal so as either partially or completely to encircle the orbit behind, and tympanics ankylosed with the other cranial bones, dilated into a bulla, and pro- duced externally into a tubular auditory meatus. The face is generally elongated, and narrow anteriorly, but in *Galeopithecus* it is broad and depressed.

In the *Macroscelidæ*, or Elephant Shrews, the auditory meatus is very large, the tympanic bulla much inflated, and there are sometimes also very large mastoid bullæ.

In *Tupaia*, the malar has a large, oval, longitudinal per- foration. There are also in this genus, as in some of the other Insectivora, vacuities in the palate, arising from defects of ossification, like those found in many Marsupials.

In the remaining Insectivora the cranial cavity is of small relative size. The orbit and temporal fossa are completely continuous, and there is often not even a trace of a post-orbital process to the frontal or malar.

In the *Erinaceidæ* (Hedgehogs) and the *Centetidæ* the tympanic is a mere ring unankylosed to the surrounding bones, but a kind of bulla is formed by a lamella projecting from the basisphenoid to join its inner and inferior edge.

In *Erinaceus* and *Gymnura* the zygomatic arch is complete, but slender, and formed chiefly by the processes of the maxilla and squamosal, which meet each other; the malar being a small splint-like bone attached to the outer and under side of the middle of the arch. In the *Centetidæ* the malar is entirely absent, and, as the zygomatic processes of both maxilla and squamosal are very short, there is no bony arch. *Centetes* (the Tenrec) has a remarkably elongated and narrow skull (both cranium and face partaking of the same character), with very prominent occipital and sagittal crests. Both in this genus and in *Erinaceus* (the Hedgehog) the mesopterygoid fossa at the base of the skull is very deep, and ends posteriorly in a hemispherical depression in the basisphenoid, between the wing-like processes which abut against the inner wall of the tympanic. Both paroccipital and mastoid processes are also well developed.

The Moles (*Talpidæ*) have an elongated and depressed cranium, broad posteriorly, and gradually narrowing to the muzzle. The occiput slopes upwards and forwards, the supraoccipital being greatly developed. The zygomatic arches are complete, but very slender, and show no distinct malar bones. There are no postorbital or parocccipital processes. A lamelliform expansion of the upper edge of the periotic (*pterotic*, Parker) forms part of the lateral wall of the cranium, as in the Echidna. The tympanic is united with the other bones of the cranium to form a flattened bulla, produced into a short meatus with a small external opening. There is a small "prenasal" ossicle in the anterior extremity of the mesethmoid cartilage, as in the Pig.

In the Cape Golden Mole (*Chrysochloris*) the cranium is conical, very broad and rounded behind, and pointed in front. There are no postorbital processes. The zygoma is complete, and tolerably strong. The tympanics ankylose with the skull, and form a completely ossified bulla.

In the Shrews (*Soricidæ*) the cranium is broad behind and tapering forwards. The facial portion is long and narrow. The occiput slopes much forwards. There is no zygoma and no postorbital process. The postglenoid process of the squamosal is remarkably large. The tympanic is ring-like, and there is a large unossified space on each side of the base of the skull.

The mandible in the Insectivora has generally an elongated and rather narrow horizontal portion, above which the transversely extended condyle is but slightly elevated, and there are well-developed coronoid and angular processes; the latter is remarkably long and slender in the Shrews.

The hyoid is formed generally like that of the Carnivora, with three complete extracranial ossifications in the anterior arch, a transversely extended basihyal, and tolerably long, stout, flattened thyrohyals, sometimes ankylosed with the basihyal.

Order CHIROPTERA.—In the large frugivorous Bats (*Pteropus*), the cranium is generally elongated, the cerebral cavity large, oval, arched above, and contracted in front; its walls formed mainly by the greatly expanded parietals both supraoccipital and frontals being small. In old individuals of some species there are well-marked sagittal and occipital crests. The base of the cranium is elongated, flat, and thin. The facial part is long and rather compressed.

The postorbital processes of the frontals are long and
pointed, and partially define the orbits behind; but
there is no corresponding ascending process from the
zygomatic arch, which is long and slender, and mainly
formed by the processes of the maxillary and squamosal,
the malar being a splint-like bone attached to their under
and outer surface. The lachrymal foramen is situated outside
the margin of the orbit. The nasals are long and narrow,
and often ankylose together in the middle line. The premaxillæ are small. The palate is elongated backwards;
the horizontal plates of the palate bones being large and
early united in the middle line, without defects of ossification. The pterygoids are small. There is no alisphenoid
canal. The glenoid fossa is broad and shallow; the postglenoid process very little developed, and with a venous
foramen behind it. The tympanics are very slightly connected with the neighbouring bones, and are consequently
nearly always lost in macerated skulls. A wedge-shaped
portion of the mastoid appears on the outside of the skull
between the squamosal and the exoccipital. The paroccipital process is long and rather slender, and directed
downwards and backwards. The periotic has a large and
deep fossa for the flocculus on its inner side.

FIG. 54.—Hyoid bones of Frugivorous Bat (*Pteropus*) from below : *bh* basihyal;
th thyrohyal; *sh* stylohyal.

The mandible has a high, broad, recurved coronoid process, a transversely extended condyle, and flattened rounded
angle, without distinct process.

The hyoid (Fig. 54) has a narrow transversely extended

basihyal, with which the elongated, laterally compressed and curved thyrohyals are commonly ankylosed. The anterior cornu contains three slender ossifications of nearly equal length.

The Insectivorous Bats generally have the skull shorter and broader than the *Pteropi.* The cranial cavity in many species is almost globular, with thin smooth walls, though sometimes sagittal and occipital crests are developed. The occipital foramen is very large. The zygoma is slender. There are no postorbital processes. The face is usually short and broad, in some (as *Mormops*) bent upwards on the cranium in a remarkable manner, so that the plane of the palate is nearly perpendicular to the basicranial axis. The premaxillæ are generally small, sometimes not meeting in the middle line, and sometimes altogether wanting. The tympanics are annular, not ankylosed to the surrounding bones, nor prolonged into a bony canal externally, though often developing a partial bulla on their inner side.

The mandible has a distinct angular process.

Order RODENTIA.—In the Rodentia the cerebral cavity is generally elongated, depressed, somewhat broad behind and narrow anteriorly. The occipital plane is more or less vertical; the cerebellar fossa altogether behind the cerebral, and the tentorial plane, or division between these fossæ, approaching the vertical. The anterior part of the cerebral fossa is contracted; the olfactory fossa is of moderate size, and situated directly in front of the cerebral.

The nasal cavities are very large, and both sets of turbinals well developed, including an upper or nasoturbinal lamella. The olfactory chambers attain their maximum of development in some of the Porcupines (*Hystrix*), where nearly all the bones of the upper part of the cranium are expanded by great air sinuses formed within their walls. In the Hare, and some others, the two optic foramina in the orbitosphenoids are confluent; and in consequence, in the dried skull, there is a direct aperture of communication between the orbits above the craniofacial axis.

The supraoccipital is more or less vertical, and does not extend far on to the upper surface of the cranium. There is often a distinct interparietal. There are generally moderately developed paroccipital processes, which in the Capybara (*Hydrochærus*) are of great length, curving forwards and compressed laterally. They are also very large in the Coypu (*Myopotamus*).

The parietals are moderate or small. The frontals, except in the Squirrels, Marmots, and Hares, have little more than a rudiment of a postorbital process, and there is never any marked corresponding process arising from the zygoma, so that the orbit is perfectly continuous with the temporal fossa. The latter is always very small.

In a very remarkable East African genus, *Lophiomys*, a broad bony lamella extends from the upper part of the parietal outwards and downwards to join a similar ascending plate from the malar, and so forming an arched covering to the temporal fossa, an arrangement unknown in any other mammal, but recalling that met with in the tortoises. The whole of the superior surface of the cranial bones of this animal are covered with miliary granulations, disposed with perfect regularity and symmetry.[1]

The nasals are both long and wide, and generally extend so far forwards as to make the anterior nares quite terminal and vertical, or even with a downward inclination. In *Hystrix* their development is enormous, but this is chiefly owing to their breadth and backward extension over the

[1] See A. Milne-Edwards, *Nouv. Archiv. du Muséum*, iii. 1867.

great nasal chambers and air sinuses.   They are narrowest
in *Bathyergus* and its allies.

The premaxillæ are large, and lodge the great curved
incisor teeth,[1] and always send a narrow prolongation backwards by the side of the nasals to join the frontals.

In the larger number of Rodents there is a great vacuity
in the anterior or maxillary root of the zygoma of varying
size and form, apparently an enormous dilatation of the
infraorbital foramen (see Fig. 55).   It is sometimes as large
as the orbit itself, with which it communicates freely posteriorly, underneath a vertical bar, formed by the maxilla
in front, and by the lachrymal and malar behind.   Its
inferior boundary is a slender zygoma-like horizontal bar,
formed by the maxilla alone.   In the Rats it is a vertical
fissure dilated superiorly.   In the Viscacha (*Lagostomus*),
the true infraorbital foramen is separated from the large
antorbital vacuity by a thin ascending bony lamella.   In
Castor, Lepus, Bathyergus, Sciurus, Arctomys, and some others,
the infraorbital foramen is of the usual size.

In the Hares, the facial surface of the maxilla is curiously
reticulated.

The zygoma is present in all, of various degrees of thickness, but always either straight or more or less curved
downwards, and usually not much arched outwards.   Its
anterior and posterior roots are formed by the maxilla
and squamosal respectively, the malar intervening.   In
many cases the last-named bone extends backwards, applied
to the under surface of the zygomatic process of the
squamosal to form the outer side of the glenoid articular
surface.   In the spotted Cavy (*Cælogenys*), the zygoma has

[1] These teeth, though first developed in the gum covering the premaxilla, have their roots, when fully developed, in the maxilla.   This
does not invalidate their determination as incisors.

an enormous vertical expansion, with a rugose or pitted outer surface, and a large fossa in the inner side of the maxillary portion, with which the cavity of the mouth communicates in the recent state.

The lachrymal bone usually presents both orbital and facial surfaces, but the orifice of the canal (lachrymal foramen) is always well within the margin of the orbit. In the Beaver, and many others, the facial portion is reduced to a mere tubercle, and in the Hare the lachrymal is entirely within the orbit.

The palate of the Rodents is usually narrow. In the long space intervening between the incisor and molar teeth, it has no definite lateral margins, but rounds off insensibly on to the sides of the face. In this region the anterior palatine foramina form very conspicuous longitudinal slits, of specially large size in the Hares. The portion of the palate situated between the molar teeth is often very narrow anteriorly, and ends posteriorly in a thickened excavated border. In the Hare it is reduced to a short transverse bridge, extending across the middle line between the pre-molar teeth. In the Capybara the alveolar border of the maxilla is very long, and presents the remarkable peculiarity of extending backwards beneath the orbit to unite with the squamosal at a level with the anterior border of the glenoid fossa. It thus forms the outer border of a large conical cavity, opening posteriorly, bounded on the inner side by the pterygoids, above by the alisphenoids, and below by the palatines.

The pterygoids are always simple subquadrate lamellæ, early ankylosed with the basisphenoids, often sending a well-marked hamular process backwards, which unites with the auditory bulla in *Hystrix, Lagostomus, Bathyergus*, &c. There are usually well-marked pterygoid fossæ, and the sides of the alisphenoids are often perforated by an alisphenoid canal. In *Hystrix* the hamular process is slightly bullate. The squamosal forms a considerable part of the outside wall of the cranium, but in consequence of the large size of the united tympano-periotic, the root of the zygomatic process is thrown very forward on the side of the skull, and the posterior part of the body of the squamosal which unites with the occipital is reduced to a long, rather narrow strip, interposed between the parietal and periotic. When the mastoid bullæ are enormously developed, as in *Pedetes* (see Fig. 55), this does not reach as far backwards as the occipital, and is a slender curved process, which clasps the outside of the bulla, and appears to hold it in its place.

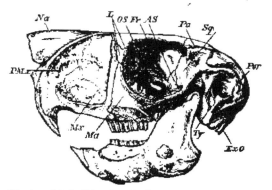

FIG. 55.—Side view of skull of Cape Jumping Hare (*Pedetes caffer*), ⅔ : *Sq* squamosal; *Pa* parietal; *AS* alisphenoid ; *Fr* frontal; *OS* orbitosphenoid; *L* lachrymal : *Na* nasal: *PMx* premaxilla ; *Mx* maxilla ; *Ma* malar; *Ty* tympanic; *ExO* ex-occipital ; *Per* points to the large supratympanic or mastoid bulla.

The glenoid fossa is situated on the under side of the posterior root of the zygoma. In its most typical form (as in the Capybara, Viscacha, Aguti, Paca, &c.) it is narrow and concave transversely, with prominent inner and outer edges, the latter being often formed, as before mentioned,

partly by the hinder end of the malar.   In the Beaver the
glenoid fossa has considerable breadth.   In the Porcupines,
Marmots, Squirrels, Rats, &c., no raised inner margin is
developed, and the fossa passes insensibly into the side of
the skull wall.   In the Hare it is a transversely oval hollow,
with a prominent rounded anterior margin.

The tympanic is ankylosed to the periotic, but not to the
squamosal; it generally develops a tubular meatus, which in
the Hare is directed upwards and backwards, in the Beaver
outwards and forwards.   In the Porcupines, as well as in
most of the smaller Rodents, the meatus is short.   In the
Capybara it is fissured below.

There is always a considerable tympanic bulla, which is
often supplemented by a bulla developed above the tympanic cavity, apparently in the periotic.   In some genera
(*Pedetes, Dipus, Chinchilla*) this attains an enormous size
(see Fig. 55, *Per*), and forms a rounded prominence on the
posterior external angle of the skull, interposed between
the squamosal, parietal and occipital.   Usually, the mastoid
portion of the periotic only appears on the surface for a
small space in front of the exoccipital.   In the Beaver, it
forms a conspicuous angular process.

The periotic is never ankylosed with any of the bones
of the cranium, other than the tympanic.   On its inner
surface the floccular fossa is nearly always wide and deep,
but it is absent, or nearly so, in the Capybara, Paca, and
Porcupine.   The place of attachment of the hyoid arch is
an inconspicuous depression in the usual situation, and the
tympanohyal is never distinct.   This is in relation with the
rudimentary condition of the anterior cornu of the hyoid.

In the mandible, the symphysial portion is narrow, curving
upwards, and rounded laterally, with a single large alveolus
on each side.   The coronoid process is never large, and is

often rudimentary or absent, in relation to the small development of the temporal fossa and muscle; while the portion adjacent to the angle is greatly developed, showing marked masseteric and pterygoid fossæ, and often with its lower edge expanded laterally, or slightly incurved. The angle is rounded in the Hares, but it is more often produced into a long backward process, more or less pointed and upturned. The coronoid process is considerably elevated, with a rounded articular surface, usually longer from before backwards than from side to side.

The hyoid has a transversely extended basihyal, a straight compressed rod-like thyrohyal, often ankylosed with the basihyal. The anterior arch is long, but mostly ligamentous, the ossification being usually confined to the lower part (cerato- and epi-hyals). In the Hares, the basihyal is deep from above downwards, and compressed, keeled, or pointed in front.

CHAPTER XI.

Order UNGULATA. Sub-order *Perissodactyla.* — In the Horse the whole skull is greatly elongated, chiefly in consequence of the immense size of the face as compared with the hinder or true cranial portion. The basal line of the skull from the lower border of the foramen magnum to the incisor border of the palate is very nearly straight. The occipital and ethmoid planes are nearly perpendicular to this line, the latter inclining slightly forwards. The tentorial plane, strongly marked by inward projecting ridges of bone, slopes obliquely backwards at an angle of 45°. The cerebral fossa is a smooth and regular oval, broad and rounded in front, and with no distinct division into anterior and posterior portions. The olfactory fossa is short, but deep from above downwards. The pituitary fossa is very shallow, and there are no distinct clinoid processes. The alisphenoid is very obliquely perforated by the foramen rotundum, but the foramen ovale is confluent with the large foramen lacerum medium behind. There are considerable frontal and sphenoidal air sinuses, but the former do not extend any great distance over the brain-cavity.

In front of the cerebral cavity, the great tubular nasal

cavities are provided with well-developed turbinal bones, and are roofed over by very large nasals, broad behind, and ending in front in a narrow decurved point. The opening of the anterior nares is prolonged backwards on each side of the face between the nasals and the elongated slender premaxillæ. The latter expand in front, and are curved downwards to form the semicircular alveolar border which supports the large incisor teeth.

The orbit is rather small in proportion to the size of the whole skull, but very distinctly marked, being completely surrounded by a strong ring of bone with prominent edges. The lachrymal occupies a considerable space on the flat surface of the cheek in front of the orbit, and below it the malar does the same. The latter sends a horizontal or slightly ascending process backwards below the orbit, to join the under surface of the zygomatic process of the squamosal, which is remarkably large, and instead of ending, as usual, behind the orbit, runs forwards to join the greatly developed postorbital process of the frontal, and even forms part of the posterior and inferior boundary of the orbit, a very exceptional arrangement (see Fig. 56).

The palate is very narrow in the interval between the incisor and molar teeth, in which are situated the large anterior palatine foramina. Between the molar teeth it is broader, but it does not extend further back than the penultimate molar and ends in a rounded excavated border. It is mainly formed by the maxillæ, as the palatines are very narrow. The pterygoids are delicate slender slips of bone attached to the hinder border of the palatines, and supported externally by, and generally ankylosed to, the rough pterygoid plates of the alisphenoid, with no pterygoid fossa between. They slope very obliquely forwards, and end in,

M

curved, compressed, hamular processes. There is a distinct
alisphenoid canal.

The base of the cranium is long and narrow. The
glenoid surface for the articulation of the mandible is
greatly extended transversely, concave from side to side,
convex from before backwards in front, and hollow behind,
and is bounded posteriorly, at its inner part, by a prominent
postglenoid process (Fig. 56, *pg*).

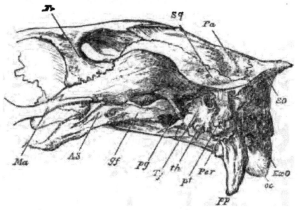

Fig. 56 —Side view of the posterior part of the skull of a Horse, ⅓. *Fr* frontal (the
line points to the postorbital process); *Sq* squamosal; *Pa* parietal; *SO* supraoccipital; *ExO* exoccipital; *oc* occipital condyle; *pp* paroccipital process; *Per*
mastoid portion of periotic; *pt* post-tympanic process of squamosal; *th* tympanohyal; *Ty* tympanic; *pg* postglenoid process of squamosal; *As* alisphenoid (the
line points to the plate of the bone which bridges over the alisphenoid canal); *Ma*
malar.

The squamosal (*Sq*) enters considerably into the formation of the temporal fossa, and besides sending the zygomatic process forwards, it sends down behind the meatus
auditorius a post-tympanic process (*pt*), which aids to
hold in place the otherwise loose tympano-periotic bone.
Behind this the exoccipital gives off a very long paroccipital
process (*pp*).

The periotic and tympanic are ankylosed together, but not with the squamosal. The former has a wide but shallow floccular fossa on its inner side, and sends backwards a considerable "pars mastoidea" which appears on the outer surface of the skull (*Per*) between the post-tympanic process of the squamosal and the exoccipital. The tympanic (*Ty*) forms a tubular meatus, directed outwards and slightly backwards. It is not dilated into a distinct bulla, but ends in front in a pointed styliform process. It completely embraces the truncated cylindrical tympanohyal (*th*), which is of great size, corresponding to the large development of the whole anterior arch of the hyoid.

The stylohyal (Fig. 57, *sh*) is of great size, compressed, and expanded at the upper end, where it sends off a triangular posterior process. Below the stylohyal, and usually becoming ankylosed with it, is a small nodular bone (epihyal), and then the arch is completed by a short cylindriform ceratohyal (*ch*). The basihyal (*bh*) is rather flattened from above downwards, arched with the concavity behind, and sends forwards a long, median, pointed, compressed "glossohyal" process. The thyrohyals (*th*) are compressed bars projecting backwards from, and in adult animals completely ankylosed to, the lateral extremities of the basihyal.

Each ramus of the mandible has a long, straight, compressed, horizontal portion, gradually narrowing towards the symphysis, where it expands laterally to form with the ankylosed opposite

Fig. 57.—Superior surface of hyoid bones of horse, ⅓. *sh* stylohyal; *ch* cerato-hyal; *bh* basihyal; *th* thyrohyal.

M 2

ramus the wide semicircular, shallow alveolar border for
the incisor teeth. The region of the angle is expanded
and compressed, with a thickened rounded border without
any process. The condyle is greatly elevated above the
alveolar border; its articular surface is very wide transversely, and narrow and convex from before backwards.
The coronoid process is slender, straight, and inclined
backwards.

The skull of the Rhinoceros resembles that of the Horse
in many essential features, but the occipital region is of
much greater extent vertically, the form of the cranial cavity
being concealed externally by large occipito-parietal air
cells. There is no postorbital process to the frontal, so
that the orbit is not divided from the temporal fossa.
There is a conspicuous rough antorbital projection on the
lachrymal bone just in front of the lachrymal foramen.
The nasals are very large and strong, early ankylosed together, arched from before backwards, and pointed anteriorly. The most elevated part of their upper surface is
roughened, and supports the great median horn which
characterizes the genus. In some species a posterior rough,
but less elevated, surface indicates the attachment of a
second horn. In some of the extinct species the mesethmoid cartilage was ossified nearly as far forwards as the extremity of the nasals, which is not the case with any existing
species. The premaxillæ are very small, and do not extend
anteriorly beyond the level of the front end of the nasals.
The hinder border of the palate is deeply excavated, the
horizontal plates of the palatines being very narrow. The
pterygoids are very slender, as in the Horse, but placed more
vertically. There is a distinct alisphenoid canal. The
squamosal sends down a very long conical, postglenoid pro-

cess parallel with, and equalling, or sometimes exceeding, in length, the paroccipital process. The meatus auditorius lies in a deep groove between the postglenoid and the post-tympanic processes of the squamosal ; the latter articulates with the exoccipital, completely excluding the mastoid from the external surface of the skull.

The tympanic and periotic are ankylosed together, but not with the squamosal. They are both very small. The under surface of the tympanic is rough, forms no distinct bulla, and is much encroached upon posteriorly by the very large tympanohyal, which presents a circular, flat, rough, inferior surface, half an inch in diameter (in an adult Sumatran Rhinoceros). Externally, the tympanic is produced into a rough, irregular, inferior wall to the auditory meatus. The periotic internally shows the internal auditory meatus near its lower part, but no distinct depression for the flocculus ; it is prolonged upwards and outwards into a small mastoid portion, which, as before said, does not appear on the outer surface of the skull.

The mandible has a very wide condylar articular surface, and slender recurved coronoid process, a rounded, somewhat incurved angle, a compressed, rather narrow, horizontal portion, and a shallow depressed symphysis.

The hyoid is much like that of the Horse, and has a glossohyal process from the middle of the basihyal.

The Tapirs present some singular modifications of the same type of skull.

As in the Rhinoceros, there is no separation between the orbit and temporal fossa, but the anterior nares are of immense size, and extend backwards above the orbits, being separated from them only by a thin plate of bone, instead of a broad, flat surface, as in the Horse and Rhinoceros.

The nasal bones are short, broad behind, pointed in front, much elevated, and supported by a tolerably well ossified mesethmoid, which spreads out laterally at its upper end.[1] The inferior lateral margins of the great narial apertures are entirely formed by the maxillæ, which extend up to meet the nasals, neither frontals nor premaxillæ taking any share in them. The ethmoturbinals are small, while the maxillo-turbinals, on the other hand, are very extensive, though their plications are comparatively simple. A conspicuous feature in the upper part of the face is a groove, which extends backwards on the side of the dilated hinder end of the nasal bone, and curves inwards to form a rounded depression over the naso-frontal suture. The form and size of this depression vary in different species. It lodges an air sinus, with cartilaginous walls extending upwards from the nasal chamber. In front of the nares, the rostrum formed by the maxillæ, with the premaxillæ in front, is produced, compressed anteriorly, and curved downwards.

The base of the cranium resembles generally that of the other *Perissodactyla*. There is an alisphenoid canal, and large postglenoid and posttympanic processes; the latter joins the paroccipital process of the exoccipital, but above their point of union a narrow slip of the mastoid appears on the surface of the skull. The periotic is not ankylosed to the squamosal or to the tympanic, which is exceedingly rudimentary, forming a small irregular floor to the tympanic cavity, with an oval lip for the attachment of the membrana tympani, and always becomes detached in macerated skulls.

The mandible is chiefly noticeable for the great rounded incurved posterior projection of the angle.

---

[1] In one species (*T. Bairdii*) the ossification of the mesethmoid extends far in advance of the nasal bones, and is clasped and supported below by ascending plates from the maxillæ.

The hyoid has a simple, elongated stylohyal without posterior process at the upper end, but one other ossification in the anterior cornu, and no glossal process to the basi-hyal.

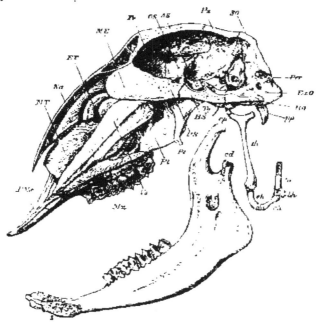

FIG. 58.—Longitudinal and vertical section of skull of a Sheep (*Ovis aries*), ½. *PMx* premaxilla; *MT* maxilloturbinal; *Na* nasal; *ET* ethmoturbinal; *ME* meseth-moid; *Fr* frontal; *OS* orbitosphenoid; *AS* alisphenoid; *Pa* parietal; *SO* supra-occipital; *Per* periotic; *ExO* exoccipital; *BO* basioccipital; *pp* paroccipital pro-cess; *Ty* styliform process of tympanic; *BS* basisphenoid; *PS* presphenoid; *Pt* pterygoid; *Pl* palatine; *Vo* vomer; *Mx* maxilla; *cp* coronoid process; *cd* condyle; *s* symphysis of mandible; *sh* stylohyal; *eh* epihyal; *ch* ceratohyal; *bh* basihyal; *th* thyrohyal.

Suborder *Artiodactyla.*—The skull of the Sheep may be first described as one of the best known and easily pro-curable examples of this group, though in some respects it is rather peculiarly modified.

On comparing the section of the cranium (Fig. 58) with that of the Dog, it will be seen that there is a great difference in the relation of the principal elements to each other, inasmuch as the face is bent downwards on the basicranial axis, so that when the latter is horizontal, the upper surface of the face looks forwards and the palate backwards. The occipital foramen is terminal posteriorly, the tentorial plane nearly vertical, so that the cerebellar fossa is altogether behind the cerebral, but the plane of the cribriform plate is horizontal, and the olfactory fossa altogether beneath the anterior portion of the cerebral fossa.

The occipital region is small and sloping forwards. There are long paroccipital processes (*pp*). In very young skulls a distinct interparietal bone is present, but in the specimen figured this has coalesced with the supraoccipital (*SO*). The two parietals (*Pa*) unite very early at the sagittal suture. The frontals (*Fr*) are large, and usually (except in some domestic races) develop from their outer surface conical, curved, bony processes, cancellous within, which are called the "horn cores," as they form the internal support of the true horns. The nasals (*Na*) are long and pointed in front. The premaxillæ (*PMx*) are slender, with a shallow alveolar border, bearing no teeth, and forming the anterior and lateral boundaries of large anterior palatine foramina. The lachrymals are large, and form a considerable portion of the side of the face in front of the orbit, but the foramen is entirely within the margin.

The olfactory chamber is large. The turbinals are greatly developed; the upper lamina of the ethmoturbinal or "naso-turbinal" is distinct, and extends over the scroll-like maxillo-turbinal (*MT*), but does not ankylose with the nasal.

The orbit is large, nearly circular, with a complete, prominent margin, formed below by the large malar, which extends considerably on the side of the face, and posteriorly sends a process upwards to meet the postorbital process of the frontal, and is continued backwards to join the zygomatic process of the squamosal.

The palate bones (*Pl*) are of moderate extent ; their horizontal plate is deeply notched posteriorly. The pterygoids (*Pt*) are broad above, but end below in a narrow lamella, with a hamular process projecting backwards. The basi-occipital (*BO*), seen from below, is square, with eminences for muscular attachments at each of its four angles. The basisphenoid (*BS*) is much contracted laterally. The posterior clinoid processes are large, and the pituitary fossa deep.

The squamosal is small, and scarcely appears in the interior of the skull. The glenoid facet is rather extensive, and slightly convex, and there is a postglenoid process and foramen. The tympanic is not ankylosed to the periotic; it forms a complete tubular external auditory meatus, and a considerable, but simple, bulla, narrowing to a sharp-pointed process anteriorly (*Ty*). The periotic (*Per*) is rather small, without any fossa for the flocculus; its mastoid portion forms a distinct, narrow, rough surface on the outer side of the skull, between the hinder border of the squamosal and the exoccipital. The tympanohyal is very large, cylindrical, curved, and almost completely embedded in the tympanic, between the inferior wall of the meatus and the outer wall of the bulla.

The extracranial portion of the hyoid consists of large compressed stylohyals (*sh*), with a prominent posterior process near the upper end, short but well-ossified epi-hyals (*eh*) and ceratohyals (*ch*), and a basihyal represented by a small rounded nodule of bone, to which the straight thyrohyals (*th*) are not ankylosed.

The mandible has a broad flat condyle (*cd*), a long

slender coronoid process (*cp*), a rounded angle, a rather
slender horizontal portion, contracted and with a sharp
upper edge in front of the molar teeth, and expanded
anteriorly for the lodgment of the incisors.

The Ox agrees generally with the Sheep in its cranial
characters. The face is bent down on the basicranial axis
almost in the same manner. The occipital surface is flat,
and terminates above in a broad transverse ridge, which
extends between the horn cores. The parietals are extremely narrow above, and placed almost entirely behind
this ridge. They unite very early with the interparietal and
supraoccipital. The intercornual ridge of the frontals is
excavated by large air-cells, communicating with those of
the horn cores, and is especially developed when the horns
are large. Unlike the parietals, the frontals are of very
great extent, and have a broad and flattened upper surface.

The tympanics are compressed and scarcely at all bullate.
They end anteriorly in long compressed styliform processes,
and become firmly ankylosed with the periotic and squamosal. The under surface of the meatus auditorius has a
compressed ridge. The large tympanohyals are entirely
embedded in the tympanic, only the rough lower surface, for
articulation with the stylohyal, being exposed.

The mandible and hyoid are like those of the Sheep, but
the basihyal is rather more developed, and has a rounded,
anterior, median projection.

Many Ruminants (especially among the *Cervidæ*) have a
vacuity of varying extent on the side wall of the face,
between the frontal, lachrymal, maxillary and nasal bones,
leading into the nasal chamber. Most of the Deer have
also a large depression on the facial surface of the lachrymal

bone, called the suborbital or *lachrymal fossa*, though it
has nothing to do with the tears, but lodges a glandular
fold of the integument, which secretes a peculiar unctuous
and odorous substance.

In the Deer the axis of the face is nearly in the same
line with that of the cranium, so that when the basicranial
axis is horizontal the nose is directed forwards instead of
downwards, as in the Sheep and Ox. The animals of this
family have no permanent horn cores, continuous with the
cranium and ensheathed by true horns, but have short processes on the frontal bones (*pedicles*), from which branching
antlers of true osseous structure are annually developed
and shed. These, as a rule, are only present in the males,
while the *horns* of the *Bovidæ* and *Antilopidæ* are usually
common to both sexes.

Among the Antelopes, the Saiga (*Saiga tartarica*) is very
remarkable for the conformation of the upper part of the
face. The anterior nares extend backwards almost to a
level with the front edge of the orbits, and have an unusual
vertical expansion. The nasal bones are very short, and
elevated in front. The turbinals are very short. The lachrymals enter largely into the side walls of the anterior nares.
The ascending processes of the premaxillæ are small, and
very widely separated from the nasals. In the living animal
the edges of these greatly expanded narial apertures are
continued forwards into a truncated, almost proboscidiform
muzzle without any bony support, giving the contour of the
face a totally different appearance from that presented by
the skull.

In the Elk (*Alces*) the nasal bones are very much shorter
than they are in ordinary ruminants.

The *Tylopoda* (Camels and Llamas) and the *Tragulina*
differ from the *Pecora*, and resemble the non-ruminating

Artiodactyles in having the tympanic bulla filled with cancellated bony tissue.

The skull of the Pig shows in section that the axis of the face is bent down upon the basicranial axis, almost as much as in the Sheep, a disposition which increases with age. Though the form of the cranial cavity is not very different from that of the Sheep, the external appearance of the hinder part of the skull is greatly changed by the elevated and backward sloping occipital crest, formed by the union of the supraoccipital (concave from side to side posteriorly) and the parietals. The latter have their outer and inner surfaces widely separated in the adult Pig by large air-cells.

The frontal is broad and flat between the orbits, and sends out a small postorbital process, which does not join the zygoma. The face is greatly elongated, tapering forwards, and compressed laterally. The nasals are long and narrow, and the apertures of the nares small and nearly terminal. The premaxillæ send up long processes on each side of the nasals, which, however, do not meet the frontals. The lachrymal has a considerable facial portion; and, as in other Ungulata, the malar encroaches considerably on the face, uniting with the lachrymal.

At the anterior extremity of the mesethmoid a peculiar ossicle (*prenasal*) is developed, which strengthens the cartilaginous snout.

The palate is long and narrow, and extends posteriorly beyond the last molar tooth. The pterygoid fossæ are well marked, being chiefly formed by the well-developed pterygoid plates of the alisphenoid; the true pterygoids are very slender. There are very long, slender, compressed paroccipital processes, curved forwards.

The squamosal and tympanic are ankylosed together; the

floor of the long, narrow, upward-directed auditory meatus is formed by the tympanic, wedged in a cleft of the squamosal, between the hinder edge of the glenoid fossa (there being no postglenoid process) and a long descending posttympanic process which articulates with the exoccipital.

Inferiorly the tympanic is dilated into a very prominent bulla, peculiarly elongated vertically, and rather compressed from side to side. The interior of this bulla is filled with cancellous bony tissue.

The periotic is small and not ankylosed to the tympanic or squamosal. The mastoid portion is quite rudimentary, being merely a short scale-like prolongation upwards and backwards, lying on the inner surface of the squamosal, and making no appearance on the external surface of the skull. The tympanohyals are very inconspicuous, being small, and situated at the bottom of a deep fossa on the outer and posterior side of the tympanic bulla.

The mandible has a high ascending portion behind, a transverse condyle, a very small coronoid process, and a flat expanded angle, rounded posteriorly.

The hyoid of the Pig is very different from that of most other Ungulata. The basihyal is very small. The thyrohyals are large, broad and flat, and ankylosed to the basihyal, but with their extremities cartilaginous even in old animals. There is a well-ossified ceratohyal, not ankylosed with the basihyal, but the greater part of the anterior arch is a long cartilaginous band, with one, or sometimes two, slender ossifications near the middle part, representing the stylohyal.

The skull of the Hippopotamus resembles that of the Pig in many essential features, although its external form is greatly modified. The brain cavity is very small, and the face immensely developed. The orbits project outwards in an almost tubular manner, and their margins are nearly, and in some cases quite, complete posteriorly. The face is contracted laterally in front of the orbits, and then expands widely into a massive truncated muzzle, which supports the great canine and upper incisor teeth.

The anterior narial orifice is nearly circular ; it is bounded by the extremities of the narrow, but greatly elongated nasals above, and laterally by the prominent rounded, rugged, and massive premaxillæ. At the anterior and lower part of the orbit, the lachrymal is dilated into a great thin-walled bony capsule, of such delicacy that it is nearly always destroyed in the skeletons preserved in museums.

The palate is long and narrow, and extends posteriorly a short distance behind the last molar teeth. The internal pterygoids end in well-marked stout hamular processes. The glenoid surface of the squamosal is very much extended, but not bounded externally by a projection from the malar, as in the Pig, and the inner half of its posterior margin is produced into a tolerably well marked postglenoid process. The paroccipital process is long and conical, but far less conspicuous than in the Pig. The tympanic bulla is proportionately smaller, and of a trihedral form, ending in an antero-inferior pointed process. Its interior is filled with cancelli, as in the Pig. As in that animal, there is a long narrow meatus auditorius, directed upwards and backwards in a fissure between the postglenoid and post-tympanic processes of the squamosal, the floor being formed by a compressed ridged prolongation of the tympanic, which is at a very early age completely fused with the squamosal. The periotic is very small, remains longer distinct, though ultimately ankylosing with the conjoined squamoso-tympanic, and has only a rudiment of a mastoid portion, which is quite confined to the interior of the cranium.

The tympanohyal is slender, ankylosed to the back of the tympanic, and in the adult skull sunk in a deep fossa, between that bone and the exoccipital, which also gives exit to the facial nerve.

The mandible is of immense size and weight. The condyles rise very little above the level of the molar teeth. The coronoid process is small and much recurved. The angle is greatly expanded and everted, rounded behind, and terminating below in a distinct process, projecting downwards and forwards. The horizontal rami are compressed in their middle portion, but widen anteriorly into a very broad and massive truncated symphysial portion, which supports the huge incisor and canine teeth.

In the hyoid apparatus, the basi- and thyro-hyals ankylose, and are something like those of the Pig. The anterior arch consists of three well-ossified pieces of subequal length.

Order HYRACOIDEA.—The skull of the Hyrax presents many affinities with that of the Perissodactyla, others with the Rodentia, and some characters peculiar to itself.

The cranium is high and truncated behind, the occiput nearly vertical, the tentorial and olfactory planes oblique, the olfactory fossa rather small.

There is a small distinct interparietal. The frontal region is broad and flat. The zygoma is tolerably strong, and formed mainly of the malar, which extends backwards so as to form the outer wall of the glenoid fossa, but it is supported anteriorly by a strong process from the maxilla. The orbit is bounded posteriorly by well-marked postorbital processes which sometimes meet, the lower one from the malar, and the upper one from the parietal (a very unusual condition). The lachrymal is small, and scarcely extends at all on to the face, but sends outwards a strong antorbital process (as in the Rhinoceros and Elephant). The face is short, and compressed laterally. The nasal bones are wide posteriorly, and anteriorly are either truncated, or more produced at their outer than their inner margins. The premaxillæ do not send up processes to meet the frontals, as in all Rodents.

The palate is not produced posteriorly beyond the middle of the last molar tooth. The palate bones are large. The pterygoids very slender. There are well-marked pterygoid fossæ, and alisphenoid canals. The paroccipital processes are long and slender. The glenoid fossa is wide transversely, and with a considerable postglenoid process. The periotic and tympanic are ankylosed together, but usually remain distinct from the squamosal. The tympanic forms a moderate-sized bulla, and a spout-like floor to the external auditory meatus, between the glenoid and post-tympanic processes of the squamosal. The periotic has a very slight floccular depression, and sends backwards no distinct mastoid process. The pituitary fossa is very shallow, without clinoid processes. The foramen rotundum and foramen ovale are distinct perforations through the alisphenoid. The optic foramen pierces the large orbitosphenoid near its hinder margin.

The mandible has a high and exceedingly broad ascending portion, its hinder margin being produced far behind the condyle, but the angle is rounded, and without any distinct process. The condyle is much extended transversely, and narrow from before backwards, especially in its inner half, for externally it is somewhat rounded. The coronoid process is small and recurved.

The hyoid apparatus of the Hyrax is unlike that of any other known Mammal. The basihyal is oval, transversely extended and flat, with a small median eminence on its anterior border, and an emarginate posterior border, only

ossified in the centre, and prolonged laterally, without any
definite segmentation, into broad, flattened, slightly curved,
cartilaginous thyrohyals. Articulated to the anterior and
external angles of the basihyal are two large, triangular,
flattened bones (ceratohyals), each with a long process
projecting forwards and meeting in the middle line, so
as to enclose (with the anterior margin of the basihyal) a
triangular space.   There is no other cartilage or bone in the
anterior arch, unless a very minute pyramidal bone, described
by Brandt as articulating with the mastoid process of the
skull, represents the stylohyal.[1]

Order PROBOSCIDIA.—The skull of the only existing
animals of this order, the Elephants, presents many very
remarkable features.   As the brain case increases but little
in size during growth, and as the exterior wall of the skull
is required to be of great superficial extent to support the
trunk and the huge and ponderous incisor teeth or tusks, and
to afford space for the attachment of muscles of sufficient
size and strength to wield the skull thus heavily weighted,
an extraordinary development of air-cells takes place in the
cancellous tissue between the outer and inner surface walls or
"tables" of nearly all the bones of the cranium, separating
them in some cases as much as twelve inches apart (see Fig.
60).   These cells are not only formed in the walls of the
cranium proper, but are also largely developed in the nasal
bone and upper part of the premaxilla and maxilla, the
bones forming the palate and the basicranial axis, and even
extend into the interior of the ossified mesethmoid and the
vomer. Where two originally distinct bones come in contact

[1] "Mém. de l'Acad. Imp. de St. Petersbourg," VII* Série, tome
xiv. No. 2, p. 68. 1869.

the cells pass freely from one to the other, and almost all the
sutures become completely obliterated in old animals.

The intercellular lamellæ in the great mass which sur-
rounds the brain cavity superiorly and laterally mostly
radiate from the inner to the outer table, but in the other
bones their direction is more irregular. Like the similar
but less developed air-cells in the skulls of many other
Mammals, they are entirely secondary to the original growth
of the bones. In the young African Elephant's skull figured
(from an animal supposed by the hunters who killed it to have
been about six months old, see Fig. 59), their formation
has scarcely commenced, and as the sutures are still quite
distinct, and the bones not distorted by these cellular dila-
tations, they are in a much better state for studying their
connections and characteristics.

When the basicranial axis is placed in a horizontal
position, it will be seen that the foramen magnum is quite
posterior, and its plane nearly vertical. The cranial cavity
is elongated and depressed (more so in the African than the
Indian Elephant), the tentorial plane nearly vertical, so that
the cerebellar fossa is altogether behind the cerebral fossa.
The latter is broad behind and contracted laterally in front.
The olfactory fossa is large, and placed altogether below
the anterior part of the cerebral fossa, the cribriform plate
being nearly horizontal. The ridge which separates the
anterior from the posterior division of the cerebral fossa is
very well marked. The pituitary fossa is very shallow, and
there are no distinct clinoid processes. The supraoccipital
(*SO*) is high, and inclines greatly forwards; so that the occipital surface looks upwards as much as backwards. In the
adult skull (Fig. 60) the lateral parts of the occipital region
(rounded smoothly off in the young state) are vastly expanded,
and leave between them a deep median depression, with a

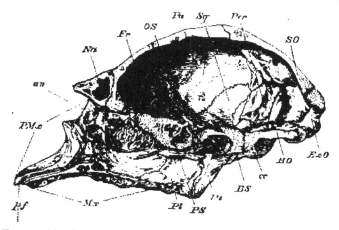

FIG. 59.—A section of the cranium of a very young African Elephant (*Elephas africanus*), taken somewhat to the right of the middle line, so that the mesethmoid and vomer are removed, ¼. The letters as in the other figures.

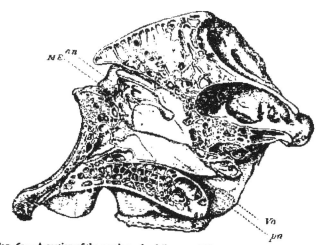

FIG. 60.—A section of the cranium of a full-grown African Elephant, taken to the left of the middle line, and including the vomer (*Vo*), and the mesethmoid (*ME*) *an* anterior, and *pn* posterior narial aperture, ⅟₁₂.

rugged floor, and a partial bony septum at the bottom, into which the ligamentum nuchæ is inserted. The median portion of the supraoccipital never becomes expanded by air-cells. The parietals (*Pa*) are very large, and form the greater part of the lateral walls of the cranium. The frontals (*Fr*) are narrow from before backwards, and produced laterally into elongate supraorbital processes, which send out small postorbital processes, not, however, completely separating the small orbit from the large and high temporal fossa.

The most remarkable feature in the face is the form and position of the anterior narial orifice (*an*). It is wide transversely, very short from above downwards, placed very high, and is directed upwards and forwards, almost as much as in the Whalebone Whales. The nasal bones (*Na*) which bound it above are very thick, short, broad behind, and conical in front, and contain large air-cavities. The inferior and lateral margins of the orifice are formed entirely by the premaxillæ (*PMx*), which send processes up to join the nasals and frontals. In front of the nares the face is prolonged into a somewhat quadrate, depressed, alveolar process, truncated in front, concave above, rounded laterally, formed by the premaxillæ above and at the sides, and by the maxillæ below. This contains the roots of the great incisor teeth or tusks.

The lachrymal is small, placed almost entirely within the margin of the orbit, and ends anteriorly in a projecting antorbital process. The zygomatic arch is slender and straight, the malar being small, and forming only the middle part of the arch, the anterior portion of which is (unlike that of all Ungulates) formed by the maxilla.

The elongated, tubular nasal cavity forms a sigmoid curve, being directed (from below) at first forwards, then upwards, then forwards. The olfactory chamber is a comparatively small fossa in the middle third of its posterior wall, filled by the complex ethmoturbinals. The maxillo-turbinals are but rudimentary, the narial passage being quite free.[1] The floor of the palate is completed posteriorly by well-developed palatines (*Pl*). The pterygoid (*Pt*) is slender and very early ankylosed with the pterygoid process of the alisphenoid, which is greatly expanded, and hollowed in front, being spread round the dilated posterior margin of the alveolar portion of the maxilla, and aiding to close the great alveolar cavity of the hindermost molar tooth.

The squamosal (*Sq*) forms a considerable part of the cranial wall, extending outside the small alisphenoid to meet the frontal, and externally sends off a broad post-tympanic process, which meeting (though not uniting with) the hinder border of the glenoid fossa in front, bounds the bony external auditory meatus, to which the tympanic contributes very little. The latter bone is, in the young specimen, completely united with the periotic, but not with the squamosal. Inferiorly it forms a large, rounded, but not very prominent auditory bulla, deeply notched on its inner side by the canal for the internal carotid artery (*ac*). The periotic (*Per*) presents a large surface within the cranium without any floccular fossa. The mastoid portion is very small, and does not appear on the surface of the cranium. There are no paroccipital or postglenoid processes. At the bottom of a deep fossa between the squamosal, exoccipital, and tympanic, the tympanohyal is distinctly seen, with the stylo-mastoid foramen to its outer side. The exoccipitals are not perforated by a condylar foramen, neither is the ali-sphenoid perforated, but it is grooved in front for the foramen rotundum, and behind for the foramen ovale.

---

[1] The elongated proboscis probably supplies their place functionally in warming the inspired air.

The mandible is of a very peculiar shape. The ascending portion of the ramus is high, and terminates in a rather small rounded condyle, wider from side to side than from before backwards. The posterior border is thick, but rounded off gradually into the inferior edge, without any projection at the angle. The coronoid process is compressed, and but very little elevated. The horizontal portion is very massive and rounded to support the great molar teeth; it unites with its fellow in front in a narrow, prolonged, spout-like symphysis.

The stylohyals are remarkable for having a long pointed process projecting downwards from near the middle of their posterior border. They have no posterior process at the upper end, as in nearly all Ungulates. The thyrohyals are long, compressed, and ankylosed to the basihyal.

CHAPTER XII.

Order CETACEA.—The animals of this order exhibit some remarkable modifications in the characters of the skull.

I will first select for description that of a young example of one of the *Odontoceti* or Toothed Whales, the common round-headed Dolphin or *Globiocephalus* of our coasts. Fig. 61 represents a vertical median section of this skull. It will be seen that the cerebral cavity is of a very unusual shape, being short and broad, but extremely high and contracted above—in fact, somewhat in the form of a truncated cone, with rounded edges. The bones of the basicranial axis are curved upwards at each extremity. They consist of the ankylosed basioccipital (*BO*) and basisphenoid (*BS*), separated by a vertical fissure from the presphenoid (*PS*) and mesethmoid (*ME*), which are also ankylosed, though their original line of separation can still be traced. The pituitary fossa scarcely forms a distinct concavity, and the clinoid processes are almost obsolete. The mesethmoid is very large, and consists of (1) a high and broad vertical plate, which closes in the vacuity between the frontals in the anterior part of the cerebral cavity, and corresponds to the cribriform plate of the ordinary Mammal, though with but few and small perforations; (2) an anterior rod-like, somewhat compressed, pointed prolongation from the lower part of this plate, which extends forwards in the groove of the vomer (*Vo*) almost to the extremity of the rostrum, and which in great part remains permanently cartilaginous. This corresponds with the septal cartilage of the nose of other Mammals, although, owing to the altered position of the nares, it has here little relation with these passages.

The cranial cavity is formed chiefly of the cerebral fossa, the cerebellar fossa being relatively small, and the olfactory fossa entirely wanting.

The optic nerve passes out through a deep notch, sometimes a foramen, in the hinder border of the orbitosphenoid. The alisphenoid is not perforated, the foramen rotundum being confluent with the large sphenoidal fissure, and the foramen ovale with a large infundibuliform opening between the alisphenoid, parietal, exoccipital, basioccipital, and basisphenoid, in the bottom of which is seen the inner surface of the periotic (*Per*), which in the Cetacea makes no projection into the cerebral cavity. The anterior part of this opening corresponds to the foramen lacerum medium with the foramen ovale, the hinder part to the foramen lacerum posterius. The squamosal (*Sq*) appears in its outer boundary for a very small space, between the parietal and the exoccipital. The condylar foramen pierces the exoccipital, near its anterior edge. The large or nearly circular carotid canal has a peculiar position, passing through the basisphenoid, near its middle, in a direction from below upwards, forwards, and inwards.

The bones forming the walls of the cranial cavity are disposed in a very remarkable manner. The occipital surface is of great size, and slopes upwards and forwards. The foramen magnum is large, and looks directly backwards; its lower lateral margins are bounded by large oval condyles, which meet in the middle line below, and are formed by the exoccipitals, with a small portion of the basioccipital. Above the foramen, the immense supraoccipital (*SO*), with which an interparietal (*IP*) is ankylosed, extends forwards beyond the vertex, to be wedged in between the frontals,

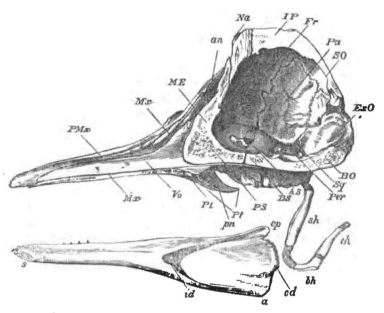

FIG. 61.—A section of the skull of a young Dolphin (*Globiocephalus melas*), ¼ : *PMx* premaxilla ; *Mx* maxilla ; *ME* ossified portion of the mesethmoid ; *an* anterior. nares ; *Na* nasal ; *IP* interparietal ; *Fr* frontal ; *Pa* parietal ; *SO* supraoccipital ; *ExO* exoccipital ; *BO* basioccipital ; *Sq* squamosal ; *Per* periotic ; *AS* alisphenoid ; *PS* presphenoid ; *Pt* pterygoid ; *pn* posterior nares ; *Pl* palatine ; *Vo* vomer ; *s* symphysis of mandible ; *id* inferior dental canal ; *cp* coronoid process ; *cd* condyle ; *a* angle ; *sh* stylohyal ; *bh* basihyal ; *th* thyrohyal.

completely excluding the parietals from the upper region of the cranium. These latter (*Pa*) form the greater part of the sides of the narrow high temporal fossæ, and are ankylosed with the supraoccipital above, although the different elements of the occipital are still distinct. The frontals (*Fr*) are broad from side to side, being prolonged outwards into the arched supraorbital plates, but are almost entirely covered by lamelliform extensions of the maxillæ, which leave but a thin strip of the frontals visible on the external surface of the cranium. The temporal fossa is bounded below and in front by a stout postorbital process of the frontal, very nearly meeting the broad zygomatic process of the squamosal. The orbit is elongated from before backwards; at its anterior extremity is a rounded antorbital prominence, formed by the junction of the maxilla, frontal and malar; below, it is bounded by a long and very slender styliform zygomatic process of the malar, which arises from near the anterior and inner angle of the body of the bone, and passes backwards, slightly curved downwards, to articulate with the extremity of the zygomatic process of the squamosal. There is no distinct lachrymal bone, or canal.

The special modification of the bones of the face has relation chiefly to the peculiar position of the nasal passages, which, instead of passing forwards above the roof of the mouth to the anterior extremity of the face, are directed upwards and somewhat backwards towards the vertex of the cranium; the external narial orifices being situated quite on the top of the head, the part which first appears above the surface of the water when the animal rises for the purpose of respiration. The whole nasal cavities are small, and they are (as far as concerns their bony walls) simple canals, entirely destitute of turbinals. Though their direction is in the main vertical, they are not straight, but curve round the anterior end of the brain cavity, both upper and lower orifices (*an* and *pn*) being directed somewhat backwards. They are compressed before backwards above, but wider and more round below. The nasal bones (*Na*), instead of being lamelliform, and roofing over the nasal passages, are reduced to nodular masses, lying in depressions in the frontals, but forming as usual the hinder boundary of the anterior narial openings.

In front of these openings, the face stretches out into an elongated, depressed, pointed beak, or *rostrum*, formed by the premaxillæ and maxillæ surrounding the vomer and mesethmoid cartilage. The premaxillæ send prolongations upwards to form the lateral boundaries of the narial orifice, and it is remarkable that these are not quite symmetrical, that of the left side being the shortest. The orifice itself, moreover, is rather inclined towards the left. Between the antorbital process of the maxilla and its rostral prolongation is a deep notch, the "antorbital notch." The upper surface of the face, near this notch, has several very large foramina for the transmission of branches of the fifth nerve.

The elongated, pointed, and convex palate is formed chiefly by the maxillæ (Fig 62, *Mx*), the premaxillæ (*PMx*) only appearing for a short space near the apex. Behind the maxillæ, the palatines (*Pl*) are somewhat wide laterally, but towards the middle line form an exceedingly narrow strip, inserted between the maxillæ and the pterygoids (*Pt*); the latter are greatly developed; besides forming the outer wall of the posterior nares, each sends a lamella inwards, which nearly (in most Dolphins, completely) meets its fellow in the middle line, and so prolongs the bony palate backwards. This process, moreover, is reflected outwards again from its inner or lower edge, and, joining with a projecting plate from the palatine, encloses a large cavity, open only behind, which contains the post-palatine air sinus. The vomer (*Vo*) is of great size, extends forwards nearly to the apex of the rostrum, embracing the mesethmoid cartilage, and posteriorly reaches for a considerable distance beneath the basisphenoid. It forms as usual the inner wall of the posterior narial apertures. Behind these apertures the base of the skull is flat in the middle line, but with pro-

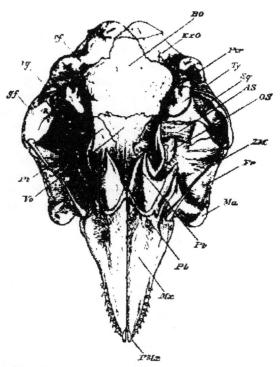

FIG. 62.—Under surface of the cranium of a young Dolphin (*Globiocephalus melas*), ⅓: *BO* basioccipital ; *ExO* exoccipital ; *Per* posterior (mastoid) process of periotic ; *Ty* tympanic ; *Sq* squamosal ; *AS* alisphenoid ; *OS* orbitosphenoid ; *ZM* zygomatic process of malar ; *Fr* supraorbital process of frontal ; *Ma* body of malar ; *Pt* pterygoid ; *Pl* palatine ; *Mx* maxilla ; *PMx* premaxilla ; *Vo* vomer ; *gf* glenoid fossa of squamosal ; *tg* deep groove on squamosal for meatus auditorius externus, leading to tympanic cavity ; *cf* condylar foramen.

minent lateral elevations formed by the basioccipital, continuing the pterygoid ridge backwards. The glenoid fossa (*gf*) is a shallow, oval facet, on the inner and under surface of the zygomatic process of the squamosal.

The periotic region of the skull differs much from that of most Mammals. On the side of the base of the cranium is a large recess, bounded below by the prominent edge of the basioccipital on the inner side, by a projecting edge of the exoccipital (paroccipital process) behind, by the base of the zygomatic process of the squamosal externally, and by a long curved process from the same bone in front, and communicating with the cranial cavity above by an irregular opening between the exoccipital and the alisphenoid. In this recess lies a bone of singular shape which, having only a ligamentous connection with the surrounding bones, is easily separated from the rest of the cranium in maceration, and is hence often wanting in specimens in museums. This is the united tympanic and periotic, ankylosed in the adult, but in young specimens still separable into its two component parts.

The tympanic (*Ty*) is a hollow, bullate bone, broad, rounded and bilobate behind, and pointed in front. It is open above, the hinder part being however in relation with the periotic; through the anterior spout-like end the Eustachian canal passes. At the upper border of the outer side, rather behind the middle, is an irregular or somewhat crescentic opening, bounded in front by a prominent lip; this is the meatus auditorius externus, closed in the living animal by the membrana tympani.

The periotic is a rounded, very dense bone, characterized as usual by having on its inner or cerebral side the large meatus auditorius internus, and on the surface turned towards the tympanic cavity the fenestra ovalis and rotunda. These two bones are separated along their inner margin by a narrow fissure, the " tympano-periotic fissure ; " but they are united externally in front of the external meatus auditorius, and more firmly posteriorly, where a tongue-shaped process (*Per*) projects backwards and outwards, fitting into a groove formed by the junction of the squamosal and exoccipital, and which is the principal point of attachment of the tympano-periotic to the rest of the skull. This process resembles in its relations the mastoid of ordinary Mammals, but in young Cetaceans it may be seen to be composed of two nearly equal parts, in close apposition with each, the inferior being derived from the tympanic, and the superior from the periotic, so that the latter alone can represent the " pars mastoidea " of other Mammals.

The mandible (Fig. 61) consists of a pair of nearly straight compressed rami, wide behind and gradually narrowing to the symphysis (*s*), where they usually become ankylosed in adult animals. The condylar articular surface (*cd*) is small, and looks almost directly backwards, being placed on the hinder edge of the ramus. The coronoid process (*cp*) is quite rudimentary. The angle is square and flat. The entrance to the dental foramen on the inner side is extremely wide and infundibuliform.

The ossified portion of the hyoid in the true Dolphins consists of a large subcylindrical, slightly curved stylohyal on each side, and a flattened crescentic median bone, composed of the ankylosed basihyal and thyrohyals. The stylohyal is connected above by a slender cartilaginous rod to a small ossified tympanohyal, which becomes ankylosed to the periotic in the usual situation, close to the stylomastoid foramen; it has also a strong ligamentous attachment to the prominent rough paroccipital process of the exoccipital. Between the stylohyal and the basihyal are one or two distinct short cartilages articulated together by synovial joints, one of which occasionally becomes ossified.

In many of the *Delphinidæ* the rostral portion of the skull is proportionally more elongated and compressed than in the species just described ; notably so in *Pontoporia*, a South American genus.   In this animal the mandible has a very long symphysial portion, the two rami being parallel and ankylosed for more than half their length, and diverging only in the posterior portion.

The Sousou, or *Platanista*, a Dolphin inhabiting the rivers of South Asia, has also a remarkably elongated and compressed rostrum and mandible, and the cranial portion of the skull presents several structural peculiarities.   The orbit is extremely small, the temporal fossa large, and the zygomatic processes of the squamosal are greatly developed.   From the outer edge of the ascending plates of the maxillæ, which lie over the frontals, great crests of bone, smooth externally, but reticulated and laminated on their inner surface, rise upwards, and, curving inwards, nearly meet in the middle line, above the upper part of the face.

The *Physeteridæ*, including the genera *Ziphius*, *Hyperoodon*, *Physeter*, and their allies, present several special modifications of the skull.   The bones of the face and cranium, meeting at the vertex, are raised so as to form a more or less elevated transverse prominence or crest behind the anterior nares, generally curved forwards at its upper edge.   The bone which corresponds to the malar in other Dolphins is usually divided into two, one of which may represent the lachrymal.   The pterygoid bones are thick, produced backwards, meeting in the middle line for a considerable space, concave on their outer side, but not involuted to form an outer wall to the post-palatine air sinus. In some of the *Ziphiinæ* the rostrum is very dense, the anterior prolongation of the mesethmoid being either partially or completely ossified, and ankylosed with the surrounding bones.

In *Hyperoodon*, the crest at the vertex is high and massive, being formed by the nasals, the ascending plates of the premaxillæ and maxillæ, the frontals and supraoccipital. Separated from this crest by a depression, there is on each maxilla, at the commencement of the rostral portion of the skull, a very thick and high longitudinal ridge.

An easy transition from this cranium leads to that of the great Sperm Whale or Cachalot (*Physeter macrocephalus*), which of all Mammals is perhaps the most modified from the ordinary type. The transverse vertical crest and the longitudinal maxillary crests are united, to form the walls of a great semicircular basin, surmounting the whole of the back part of the cranium, open only above and in front. The bones composing this wall are the same as in *Hyperoodon*, but excessively expanded and flattened. The rostrum is broad at the base, gradually narrowing to the front, and immensely elongated. The great supracranial cavity lodges the oily substance which, when refined, is known as spermaceti.

The skull of the Cachalot is remarkable for its want of symmetry, especially in the region of the anterior narial apertures, of which the left is very much larger than the right. In consequence of the small increase in the size of the brain cavity, compared with that of the external parts of the head in these enormous animals, the foramina through which the nerves pass out of the lateral parts of the base of the skull, are long channels excavated through immense bony masses. The petro-tympanic bone, which is scarcely larger than that of some of the small Dolphins, is situated at the bottom of such a channel, at the distance of fourteen inches from the inner wall of the brain cavity. In the general principle of their conformation, these bones do not differ from those of the ordinary Dolphins, but the tongue-shaped backward projection before described is greatly elongated and laminated, being composed of a large number of distinct thin plates, only held together by their common attachment to the tympanic. These fit into grooves between the squamosal and exoccipital, their extremities appearing on the outer surface of the skull, and they serve to attach the petrotympanic more firmly to the cranium than is the case with the other Toothed Whales.

The hyoid in *Physeter* and in the allied genus *Kogia* is remarkable for the great breadth and flatness of the basi- and the thyrohyals, which, moreover, do not usually become ankylosed, as in most Dolphins.

The cranium of the Whalebone Whales (suborder *Mystacoceti*) never shows that deviation from bilateral symmetry so frequent in the Toothed Whales. The cranial cavity has much the same general form, and the bones around are disposed in a somewhat similar manner, but the parietals meet at the top of the skull, although completely overlaid and concealed externally by the great supraoccipital.

The anterior nares are not directed upwards and backwards as in the Dolphins, but approach more in position to those of the ordinary mammalia, being arched over by the frontals, which are of considerable antero-posterior thickness at this part (see Fig. 63, *Fr.*), and also by moderately-developed nasals (*Na*), meeting by a flattened surface in the middle line. The nares are still near the most elevated part of the head, and the premaxillæ and maxillæ, with the vomer and mesethmoid cartilage, are produced in front of them into a long tapering rostrum, narrow, compressed, and much arched in the Right Whales (*Balæna*); broader, depressed, and nearly straight in the Rorquals (*Balænoptera*).

-o

An essential difference between the Whales and the Dolphins is the presence in the former of an olfactory organ, on the same type as in other mammals, though in a comparatively rudimentary condition. In the skull of an adult Greenland Whale (*Balæna mysticetus*), the olfactory fossa of the cerebral cavity is eight and a half inches in length, scarcely more than half an inch high, and one and a half inches wide. It runs forward from the anterior part of the floor of the cerebral fossa, through the great mass of bone formed by the union of the frontal, mesethmoid and presphenoid. In front it divides into two compartments, each somewhat oval and dilated, with a concave floor, about an inch in extent in either direction, perforated with foramina. This floor is the cribriform plate. In the hinder wall of the great narial passage is a narrow vertical slit, twelve inches in length, very near the middle line; this is the opening of the olfactory chamber of the nasal cavity, which is bounded by the under surface of the cribriform plate above, by the flat mesethmoid on the inner side, and has its outer wall raised into several longitudinal elevations of very simple character, representing the ethmoturbinal bones.

In the Rorquals (*Balænoptera*) the olfactory fossa is less elongated, the foramina of the cribriform plate larger and more numerous, and the ethmoturbinals better developed.

The supraorbital processes of the frontals are very long and narrow in the Right Whales, but broader in the Rorquals; they are not covered by plates from the maxillæ, as in the Dolphins. The orbit is small and completed below by a small curved malar, quite different from that of the Dolphins. There is a small wedge-shaped lachrymal interposed between the antorbital processes of the frontal and maxilla and the malar.

The palate is long and narrow, with a strong keel or

ridge in the middle line. The surface on each side, sloping
upwards and outwards, is perforated by many large foramina
to permit the passage of blood-vessels and nerves to the
matrix of the baleen, or "whalebone," which covers it in
the living animal. It is chiefly formed by the maxilla,
behind which are large palatines and very small and widely
separated pterygoids.

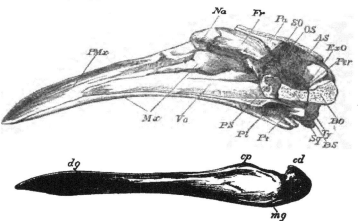

Fig. 63.—Section of the skull of a fœtal Southern Right Whale (*Balæna australis*), ½.
PMx premaxilla ; *Na* nasal ; *Fr* frontal ; *Pa* parietal ; *SO* supraoccipital ; *OS* orbitosphenoid ; *AS* alisphenoid ; *ExO* exoccipital ; *Per* periotic ; *BO* basioccipital ;
Ty tympanic ; *BS* basisphenoid ; *Sq* glenoid articular surface of squamosal ;
Pt pterygoid ; *Pl* palatine ; *PS* presphenoid ; *Vo* vomer ; *Mx* maxilla ; *cp* coronoid process of mandible ; *cd* condyle ; *dg* dental groove ; *mg* remains of groove
which lodged Meckel's cartilage.   No part of the mesethmoid is ossified.

The zygomatic process of the squamosal is an immense
trihedral pillar in *Balæna*, having the large shallow glenoid
fossa on its under surface removed considerably from the
middle of the cranium, so as to give sufficient width to the
hinder part of the capacious mouth. The periotic and
tympanic are formed much on the same principle as in the
other suborder, and in adult animals are completely excluded

by a considerable distance from the cranial cavity, owing to
the thickness of its walls. Instead of the small flattened
tongue-shaped process projecting backwards from these bones,
there is a long pyramidal tenon-like process, which fits into
a groove in the squamosal and appears on the external surface of the skull like, though more solid· than, that of the
Cachalot. In addition to this another process projects outwards and backwards, and the two together hold the bones
much more firmly in their place than in the Toothed Whale.
The tympanohyal is a large conical bony mass, with a
truncated base, with which the stylohyal is connected, and
firmly ankylosed by its apex to the periotic.

The mandible differs much from that of the Toothed
Whales. The two rami of which it is composed are not compressed and straight, but rounded and arched outwards, and
never have extensive, flat, opposed symphysial surfaces, but,
curving towards each other, meet at an angle in front, where
they are held together by strong bands of fibrous tissue.

The hyoid arch is formed essentially on the same plan as
in the other Cetacea. The basihyal has a pair of processes placed side by side on its front edge, to which
the anterior cornua are attached, the hinder edge is excavated. In *Balæna* the thyrohyals are cylindrical, and thicker
towards their free extremities. In *Balænoptera musculus* they
are cylindrical and tapering, in *B. rostrata*, flat and pointed
externally. They always ankylose with the basihyal.

Order SIRENIA.—The animals belonging to this order,
restricted at the present time to only two genera, which were
formerly, but quite erroneously, included among the Cetacea,
have skulls constructed on a very peculiar type, though with
some affinities both to the Ungulata and the Proboscidia.
Many of the special modifications are adaptations to their

aquatic mode of life, and it is in these alone that they present any resemblances to the Cetacea.

The skull of the African Manati (*Manatus senegalensis*), which may be taken as a type of the order, is remarkable

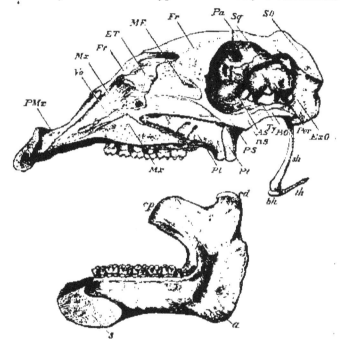

Fig. 64.—Section of the skull of an African Manati (*Manatus senegalensis*), ½: *PMx* premaxilla ; *Vo* vomer ; *Mx* maxilla ; *Fr* frontal ; *ET* ethmoturbinal ; *ME* mesethmoid ; *Fr* frontal ; *Pa* parietal ; *Sq* squamosal ; *SO* supraoccipital ; *ExO* exoccipital ; *Per* periotic ; *BO* basioccipital ; *Ty* tympanic ; *AS* alisphenoid ; *BS* basisphenoid ; *PS* presphenoid ; *Pt* pterygoid ; *Pl* palatine ; *Mx* maxilla ; *cp* coronoid process of mandible ; *cd* condyle ; *a* angle ; *s* symphysis ; *sh* stylohyal ; *bh* basihyal ; *th* thyrohyal.

for the massiveness and density of structure of the bones of which it is formed. There are no air sinuses in any part and most of the bones when cut through appear as hard and solid as ivory. This character is not peculiar to the skull, but shared with it by the ribs, and other bones, and must add much to the general specific gravity of this slow-moving animal, and aid in keeping it to the bottom of the shallow water in which it dwells, while feeding on fuci and other aquatic vegetables.

The cerebral cavity is very different from that of the Cetacea, being small as compared with the size of the animal, rather elongated and laterally compressed, truncated at each end, and with the upper surface flattened. The cerebellar fossa is large, and altogether behind the cerebral ; the olfactory fossa is distinct, but small and narrow, bounded on the inner side by a strongly-developed " crista galli" from the mesethmoid. The foramen magnum is of great size ; its plane looks backwards and downwards. The supraoccipital (*SO*) is inclined forwards, but does not extend beyond the ridge bounding the occipital region ; the roof of the cerebral fossa of the cranial cavity being formed by the parietals (*Pa*). The upper surface of the skull is very narrow, and flat, or slightly arched in the longitudinal direction ; its sides, which are parallel for a considerable distance, join at a right angle the vertical inner wall of the great temporal fossa. The squamosal has an extremely massive and long zygomatic process, flattened on the outer surface, and posteriorly it sends down a strong triangular post-tympanic process, articulating with a rough projecting edge of the exoccipital. Above this, between the squamosal, supraoccipital, and exoccipital, is a considerable vacuity in the cranial wall, partly filled by the periotic (*Per*). The lower vacuity, between the exoccipital and alisphenoid, common to all skulls, is of immense extent.

The frontals (*Fr*) are narrow, and run backwards between the parietals to the upper part of the cerebral fossa of the

brain cavity, and forwards a short distance over the nasal
cavities ; each is produced anteriorly into a long narrow
process, inclining outwards and downwards, between the
temporal fossa behind, and the great anterior narial openings
in front, forming the roof of the orbit.   This cavity has a
very prominent margin, especially below and in front, where
it is formed by the very largely developed malar.   This bone
sends upwards a conspicuous postorbital process, which
nearly (in some cases completely) meets that of the frontal,
and then is continued below the zygomatic process of the
squamosal as far as the wide shallow glenoid fossa, and
sends down from its middle a broad flattened process with a
thickened and rough inferior border.   There is a very small
scalelike and imperforate lachrymal in the usual situation at
the anterior and inner angle of the orbit.   The antorbital
foramen of the maxilla is very large.

One of the most peculiar features of the upper surface of
the face is derived from the position of the anterior nares,
which is a further modification of that met with in the Tapirs
among the Ungulata, and presents some approach to that so
characteristic of the Cetacea.   Taken together they form a
large lozenge-shaped aperture, which extends backwards
considerably behind the orbits.   Their sides are formed by
the ascending processes of the premaxillæ below, and by
the supraorbital processes of the frontals above, no trace of
nasals being found in most skulls, though these bones are
occasionally found in a most rudimentary condition attached
to the edge of the frontals, far away from the middle line,
a condition quite unique among the Mammalia, or only
approached in some of the Dolphins.   In the floor of the
great narial opening is seen the vomer (Vo), of very delicate
structure, and posteriorly the ossified portion of the mesethmoid (ME) of considerable vertical extent.   The olfac-

tory chamber of the nasal cavity is greatly compressed from
side to side, and contains a series of simple, longitudinally
placed ethmoturbinals, of which the upper one is very
much the largest. There are no maxilloturbinals in any
skulls which I have examined.

In front of the narial opening the face is prolonged into
a narrow rostrum, formed by the premaxillæ, supported
below and at the sides by the maxillæ. The under
surface of this is very rugose, and in life supports a horny
plate. There is a large, oval, single median anterior palatine
foramen. The palate is long and narrow between the two
parallel rows of numerous molar teeth. It does not extend
beyond the last of these, and is formed almost entirely by
the maxillæ, the horizontal plates of the palate bones
being very narrow. Behind each row of teeth is a massive
descending rough process, formed by the union of the
palatine, pterygoid plate of the alisphenoid, and true
pterygoid. Posteriorly this has a longitudinal groove
corresponding to the pterygoid fossa. Behind these the base
of the skull contracts in width, leaving a large opening on
each side of the basioccipital, between the alisphenoid in
front and the exoccipital behind, and only partially filled by
the tympanic and periotic.

The two last-named bones are ankylosed together, but not
to any of the other bones of the skull, and though freely
moveable in the dried skull, they are retained in their
place by the overhanging process of the squamosal.

The tympanic (*Ty*) consists of a large and very solid half-
ring, with its lower margin considerably thickened and
produced downwards; but not forming any bulla, or any
tubular meatus. It is only attached to the periotic by its
anterior extremity, so that its mode of connection as well
as its form is totally different from that of the Cetacea.

Close to the inner side of its posterior extremity is a well-marked tympanohyal ankylosed to the periotic.

The periotic (*Per*) is large, and rounded externally. It forms a very considerable part of the inner wall of the cranium. Besides the portion containing the organ of hearing, it has a large solid upper part, of somewhat kidney shape, lying in a groove in the squamosal (*Sq*). This has a large anterior prominence, to which the anterior limb of the tympanic ring is ankylosed, and a smaller rounded posterior projection, corresponding with the mastoid of other Mammals, and mentioned before as appearing on the external surface of the skull, in the vacuity between the supraoccipital, exoccipital, and squamosal.

The foramina at the base of the skull are very few and simple, as nearly all the nerves appear to pass out either by the rather small sphenoidal fissure, or by the great confluent median and posterior foramina lacera. There is a small optic foramen passing through the middle of the orbitosphenoid, but the alisphenoid is imperforate, and even the condylar foramen in the exoccipital for the hypoglossal nerve, so constant in all Mammals (except the Elephant), is represented by a groove (in some instances with a narrow bridge across it) on the anterior edge of the bone. There is no distinct carotid canal.

The mandible is exceedingly different from that of the Cetacea, and is formed of the same dense heavy bone as the rest of the skull. The rami are firmly united by a symphysis (*s*) of moderate extent in front, and diverge widely behind. The posterior border is of considerable vertical depth, the condyle (*cd*), having an obliquely placed, oval, convex articular surface, being raised high above the horizontal alveolar border. The coronoid process (*cp*) is large and directed forwards. The angle (*a*) is well marked, thickened, and somewhat inflexed, but does not form a distinct process. The lower border of the ramus is very thick, rounded from side to side, and concave from before backwards. The symphysial portion is compressed laterally, but its upper surface forms a somewhat expanded, rugose surface, concave in the middle line, to which a horny plate is attached in the living animal.

In a perfectly adult West Indian Manati (*M. australis*), in the Leyden Museum, the anterior arch of the hyoid has a single, slender, slightly curved bone (stylohyal), three inches long, cylindrical at its upper end, and laterally compressed below, attached above by a broad, short ligament, chiefly to the exoccipital, but also to the squamosal and tympanic. The basihyal is a broad, flat, reniform plate, and the thyrohyals are not ossified.

In the other existing Sirenian, the Dugong (*Halicore*), from the Indian Seas, the skull resembles that of the Manati in its essential characters, especially the form of the brain case, the condition of the tympano-periotic bones, and the form and situation of the anterior nares; but it differs mainly in the great development of the premaxillary bones, which curve downwards in front, and lodge large descending tusks. The deep, compressed symphysial portion of the mandible is bent down in a corresponding manner. The zygoma is less massive, the orbit is not closed behind, and the lachrymal bone is more developed. The nasals are absent or quite rudimentary.

CHAPTER XIII.

Order EDENTATA.—The different families of this heterogeneous group present some remarkable variations in their
cranial characters.

One of the most extremely modified forms is the Great
Anteater (*Myrmecophaga jubata*, Fig. 65). The whole skull is
very greatly elongated and narrow, its upper surface smooth
and cylindriform. The occipital plane slopes upwards and
forwards. The parietals are narrow, but the frontals much
elongated. The olfactory fossa of the cerebral cavity is very
large; the cribriform plate greatly expanded, and the ethmoturbinals much developed, and consisting of very numerous,
delicate lamellæ. Anteriorly, the face is produced into a
very long, tubular rostrum, rounded above and flattened
below, and with terminal nares. This rostrum is composed
of the mesethmoid, ossified for more than half its length,
the vomer, the maxillæ, and the long and narrow nasal
bones; the premaxillæ (*PMx*) being extremely short and
confined to the margin of the anterior nares. There are no
teeth in either jaw. The zygomatic arch is incomplete, the
styliform malar (*Ma*) only articulating with the maxilla in
front, and not reaching the very short zygomatic process of
the squamosal (*Sq*). The lachrymals (*L*) are distinct, and

have a large perforation in front of the margin of the orbit.

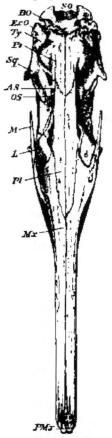

There are no postorbital processes to the frontals, or any other demarcation between the orbits and the temporal fossa.

The palate is extremely elongated, and produced backwards as far as the level of the external auditory meatus by the meeting in the middle line of the largely-developed pterygoids (*Pt*). The glenoid fossa is a shallow oval facet, with its long diameter from before backwards.

The periotic, tympanic, and squamosal are ankylosed together. A small mastoid portion appears on the outer side of the skull, forming a roughened surface between the squamosal and the exoccipital. The tympanic (*Ty*) is somewhat triangular in form, slightly bullate, and not prolonged into an auditory meatus. In front of the tympanic cavity, and freely communicating with it, is a considerable air sinus, formed

FIG. 65.—Under-surface of the cranium of the Great Anteater (*Myrmecophaga jubata*), ½ : *SO* supraoccipital ; *BO* basioccipital ; *ExO* exoccipital ; *Ty* tympanic ; *Pt* pterygoid ; *Sq* squamosal ; *AS* alisphenoid ; *OS* orbitosphenoid ; *M* malar ; *L* lachrymal ; *Pl* palatine ; *x* maxilla ; *PMx* premaxilla.

between the pterygoid (*Pt*) and the alisphenoid (*AS*), and causing an oval prominence in the side of the palate.

In another species of the same genus, *M. Tamandua*, there is a second similar but smaller sinus, anterior to this, in the side of the palatine bone.

The mandible is very long and slender, with an exceedingly short symphysis, no distinct coronoid process, and a slightly elevated, elongated, flattened, condylar articular surface.

The skull of the little Tree Anteater (*Cyclothurus didactylus*) besides being shorter, and much arched in the longitudinal direction, differs mainly from that of *Myrmecophaga* in not having the long canal of the posterior nares closed by bone below, as neither the pterygoids nor the greater part of the palatines meet in the middle line. The tympanic is more bullate. The mandible has a prominent, narrow, recurved coronoid, and a well-developed angular process; it is strongly curved downwards in front.

In the Armadillos of the restricted genus *Dasypus*, including *D. sexcinctus, villosus,* and *minutus,* the cranial portion of the skull is broad and depressed; the facial portion triangular, pointed in front, and much depressed. The anterior narial orifice is small, terminal, and directed forwards and downwards. There is a completely ossified tympanic bulla, ankylosed with the rest of the skull, perforated on the inner side by the carotid canal, and continued externally into an elongated bony meatus auditorius, with its aperture directed upwards and backwards. The zygoma is complete. The pterygoids are small, and send no horizontal plates inwards to complete the bony palate, as in the Anteater. The mandible has a well-marked ascending posterior portion, supporting a transversely extended condyle, and a high, slender coronoid process.

In all the other genera of Armadillos the tympanic is a mere half-ring, loosely connected with the surrounding bones.

The hyoid arch is strongly ossified. The anterior cornu consists of three bones. The thyrohyals ankylose with the basihyal.

In the Scaly Anteaters or Pangolins (genus *Manis*), the skull is somewhat in the form of an elongated cone, with the small end turned forwards, and very smooth and free from crests and ridges. The occipital plane slopes upwards and forwards. There is no distinction between the orbit and the temporal fossa, which together form a small oval depression near the middle of the side of the skull. There are short zygomatic processes on the maxilla and the squamosal, but the arch is incomplete, owing to the absence of the malar. There is likewise no distinct lachrymal bone. The plane of the anterior narial aperture looks forwards and upwards. The premaxilla is produced along the side of the nasals towards, but not reaching, the frontals. The palate is long and narrow. The pterygoids extend backwards as far as the tympanics, but do not meet in the middle line below. The tympanic is ankylosed to the surrounding bones, and more or less bullate, but not produced into a tubular auditory meatus. The hinder part of the squamosal is often dilated with air-cells, forming a rounded prominence at the outer posterior angle of the skull.

The mandible is very slender and straight, without any angle or coronoid process. The condyle is a slightly expanded flattened surface, not raised above the level of the rest of the ramus.

In the Cape Anteater (*Orycteropus*) the skull is moderately elongated and dilated in front of the orbits. The facial portion is subcylindrical and slightly tapering. The lachrymal forms a considerable part of the side of the face. The zygoma is complete and slender. There is a small post-orbital process. The premaxillæ are short and widely

separated from the frontals. The palate ends posteriorly in
the thickened transverse border of the palatines, and is not
continued back by the pterygoids.   The tympanic is annular,
and not ankylosed to the surrounding bones.

The mandible is slender anteriorly, but rises high posteriorly, with a slender recurved coronoid, and an ascending
pointed process on the hinder edge below the condyle ;
which is small, oval, and looks forwards as much as upwards.

The hyoid arch is completely ossified.   The basihyal
is a thin bar, narrow in the middle.   The thyrohyals are
not ankylosed to it.   The ceratohyals are thick.   There is
a small (apparently epiphysial) ossification between the epihyal and the stylohyal.

The Three-toed Sloths (genus *Bradypus*) have a high
compressed skull, and an extremely short face.   The cranial
cavity is oblong, and rather high and compressed.   There is no
fossa on the periotic for the flocculus.   The olfactory fossæ
are large.   The plane of the occiput is vertical, or sloping
slightly forwards and upwards.   The frontal region is dilated
with air sinuses.   There is a small postorbital process.
The lachrymal is very small, and the canal is external to
the margin of the orbit.   The malar is attached to the
frontal, lachrymal, and maxilla in front, curves downwards
and outwards, and then divides into a descending and a high
ascending branch ; but neither of them join the straight
zygomatic process of the squamosal.   The nasals are short
and wide.   The anterior nares are nearly vertical, or rather
inclining downwards.   The premaxillæ are exceedingly
rudimentary, only the palatal portion being present, without
any ascending process; they unite with each other across
the middle line, but not with the maxillæ, hence they are

generally lost in macerated skulls. The palate is narrow, especially posteriorly, and not produced behind the molar teeth. The pterygoids form large plates with prominent rounded borders, compressed in some, and inflated in other species. The glenoid fossa is narrow from side to side. The tympanic, squamosal, and periotic are ankylosed together. The former forms a considerable bulla, but no tubular meatus. There are large supratympanic air sinuses and a well-marked ossified tympanohyal.

The mandible has a comparatively high horizontal portion, rounded in front, with a very small median triangular process at the upper border. The coronoid process is high and slender. The condyle is small; its articular surface is convex from side to side, short and nearly straight from before backwards. The angle forms a broad compressed posterior projection, with a slightly incurved lower border.

The stylohyals are large, compressed, and curved, with a prominent posterior process near their upper end. The basihyal is small, and ankylosed with the thyrohyals, so that they form together a V-shaped bone.

The skull of the Two-toed Sloth (*Cholœpus didactylus*) though generally similar to the last, presents in some points marked deviations from it. Even in aged specimens, in which almost all the sutures are obliterated, the tympanic is a mere ring, incomplete at the upper margin, and but slightly connected with the other bones around. The premaxillæ are more developed, and become ultimately ankylosed with the maxillæ. The pterygoids are much smaller, out sometimes are bullate.

The upper margin of the mandible is produced anteriorly into a spout-like process. The condyle is scarcely above the level of the molar teeth, and is wide from side to side. The angular projection is smaller and thicker.

The hyoid (in an old specimen) has a strongly ossified anterior arch, consisting of two bones of nearly equal length, the proximal one with a stout rounded process projecting backwards and outwards from near its upper end. The second is bent at a right angle near its lower end, and may result from the ossification of two elements. The basi- and thyro-hyals are ankylosed to form a wide U-shaped bone.

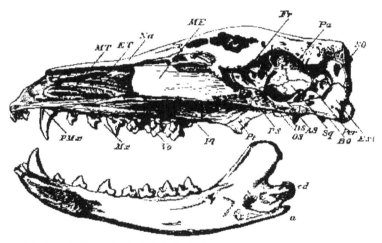

Fig. 66.—Section of the skull of the Thylacine (*Thylacinus cynocephalus*), ½ : *MT* maxilloturbinal ; *ET* ethmoturbinal ; *ME* ossified portion of mesethmoid ; *Fr* frontal ; *Pa* parietal ; *SO* supraoccipital ; *ExO* exoccipital ; *Per* periotic ; *BO* basioccipital ; *Sq* squamosal ; *AS* alisphenoid ; *BS* basisphenoid ; *OS* orbito-sphenoid ; *PS* presphenoid ; *Pt* pterygoid ; *Pl* palatine ; *Vo* vomer ; *Mx* maxilla ; *PMx* premaxilla ; *cd* condyle of mandible ; *a* angular process.

Order MARSUPIALIA.—The skull of the large carnivorous Marsupial, the Thylacine (*Thylacinus cynocephalus*), resembles so closely that of a Dog in its general aspect, that it will be well to commence an account of the peculiarities of the crania of Marsupials generally by comparing these two skulls.

P

It will be seen by the section (Fig. 66) that the brain cavity of the Thylacine is very much smaller than that of the Dog (Fig. 45) in relation to the size of the rest of the cranium, or to that of the whole animal, a sign of great inferiority of organization. This diminution affects chiefly the cerebral fossa; the cerebellar fossa is nearly equal in size, but it is placed more directly behind the cerebral, and is not in the least overlapped by it, as in the Dog. The occipital plane is vertical, or even inclining forwards above. The tentorial plane is nearly horizontal. The olfactory fossa, though smaller in vertical extent than that of the Dog, is more produced anteriorly. Thus in form, as well as in relative size, the cerebral cavity is far more reptilian than that of the Dog. The basicranial axis is very straight, and is continued forwards in the same line by the basifacial axis. The pituitary fossa forms no distinct depression, and there are no posterior clinoid processes. The ossified portion of the mesethmoid (*ME*) is extensive, and terminates anteriorly in a nearly vertical line. The vomer (*Vo*) is very shallow from above downwards. The turbinal bones resemble generally in their extent and disposition those of the Dog.

Externally the conformation of the zygomata, temporal fossæ, orbits, maxillæ, premaxillæ, and nasals are strikingly similar to those of the Dog; but the lachrymal bone of the Thylacine is larger both within and without the orbit, and it has one perforation within, and either one or two just external to the margin of the orbit. The palate has a pair 'of large oval vacuities between the molar teeth. The pterygoid plates are very thin. The glenoid fossa is rather more expanded from before backwards than in the Dog, and the malar extends so far back beneath the zygomatic process of the squamosal as to form the outer edge of the glenoid cavity. The postglenoid and paroccipital processes are developed much as in the Dog ; the former has rather greater lateral extent. A great difference is seen in the condition of the tympanic, which in the Thylacine is quite rudimentary, forms no bulla, and is not ankylosed to the other cranial bones, so that in the dried skull it is nearly always detached. On the other hand, the hinder part of the alisphenoid is dilated into an oval thin-walled capsule, which is connected with the front of the tympanic cavity. The periotic is not ankylosed to the squamosal, has a very large floccular fossa within, and a mastoid portion forming a long, narrow strip visible in the outer side of the occipital surface of the skull, between the squamosal and the exoccipital, almost exactly as in the Dog. The exoccipital is perforated by the condylar foramen ; but the carotid foramen, instead of passing through the inner edge of the tympanic bulla, perforates the basisphenoid, passing very obliquely forwards and inwards. The large alisphenoid is pierced by the foramen ovale near its posterior margin, and by the foramen rotundum near the front. The orbitosphenoid is very small, and not perforated, the optic nerve passing out through the sphenoidal fissure.

The ascending ramus of the mandible is less elevated than that of the Dog, the condyle being almost on the same level as the molar teeth. The coronoid process has a more backward inclination. The masseteric fossa has a powerful, externally projecting lower border, and the angular process is flattened from above downwards, and inclined considerably inwards.

The hyoid (Fig. 67) is constructed on a totally different type from that of the Dog. It consists of a small flat lozenge-shaped basihyal (*bh*), surmounted by flattened, triangular, imperfectly ossified ceratohyals (*ch*), partially ankylosed to the basihyal, and without any other ossifica-

tions in the anterior cornua. The thyrohyals (*th*) are tolerably long, flattened bars, meeting in the middle line at their

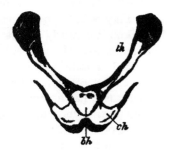

FIG. 67.—Upper surface of hyoid of Thylacine (nat. size): *bh* basihyal ; *ch* ceratohyal
(anterior cornu); *th* thyrohyal (posterior cornu).

attachment to the basihyal, and with their free, or laryngeal,
extremities expanded, but still cartilaginous in the perfectly
adult animal from which the above figure was taken.

All the other animals of the sub-class which contains
the single order Marsupialia, however their skulls may
differ in general appearance from that of the Thylacine,
agree with it in the following important particulars :—

1. The brain cavity is small, with the cerebellar fossa
entirely behind, and the olfactory fossa entirely in front
of the cerebral fossa. There are, however, degrees in
this respect, the Kangaroos representing one extreme, with
large, more vaulted cerebral fossa, and the Opossums and
Dasyures the other.

2. There is no distinct pituitary fossa, or clinoid processes.

3. The ossification of the mesethmoid is extensive, and
has an abrupt, nearly vertical, anterior termination.

4. The nasal bones are large, and the anterior nares more
or less terminal.

5. The zygoma is complete, but the orbit has not a perfect posterior boundary.

6. The malar is large, reaches the lachrymal anteriorly, and extends posteriorly beneath the zygomatic process of the squamosal, to form part of the outer wall of the glenoid fossa.

7. The perforation in the lachrymal is usually upon, and frequently external to, the anterior boundary of the orbit.

8. The ascending processes of the premaxillæ never quite reach the frontals.

9. The palate has often, but not always, large vacuities near its posterior margin.

10. The pterygoids are always small and lamelliform.

11. The alisphenoids are more or less dilated, and form the anterior wall of the tympanic cavity, which is often quite open below in the dried skull. It may be noted as a special peculiarity in the Kangaroos, that the alisphenoid extends backwards beneath the tympanic cavity to join the long paroccipital process of the exoccipital. In the larger members of the group it can scarcely be said to form a distinct bulla, but in the small *Hypsiprymni* (Rat Kangaroos) it is immensely expanded. In the Koala (*Phascolarctos*), the alisphenoid bulla is very large, elongated vertically, and compressed, having a very similar appearance in fact to the tympanic bulla of the Pig.

12. The tympanic is small, simple, and annular in some ; in others it forms a short external auditory meatus, but it is never ankylosed to any of the other bones of the cranium.

13. The periotic sends backwards a distinct mastoid, which appears as a narrow strip of bone of considerable vertical extent, between the squamosal and exoccipital, on the side of the occipital region of the skull.

14. There are almost always conspicuous paroccipital processes.

15. The internal carotid artery perforates the basisphenoid.

16. The optic foramen is confluent with the sphenoidal fissure.

17. The mandible has (*Tarsipes* excepted) an inverted border to the angle.

18. The hyoid has a small more or less lozenge-shaped basihyal, broad ceratohyals, the remainder of the anterior cornu usually unossified, and stout, somewhat compressed thyrohyals.

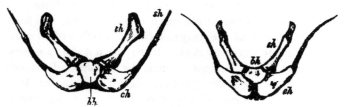

FIG. 68.—Upper surface of hyoid of Wombat (*Phascolomys latifrons*); *bh* basihyal; *ch* ceratohyal; *sh* stylohyal; *th* thyrohyal.

FIG. 69.—Hyoid of Kangaroo (*Macropus*): *eh* epihyal; *bh* basihyal; *th* thyrohyal.

Order MONOTREMATA.—Both the animals of this group present very singular modifications of the cranium.

The cerebral cavity, unlike that of the lower Marsupialia or the Reptiles, with which they have so many structural affinities, is large and hemispherical, flattened below and arched above, and about as broad as long. The broad cribriform plate of the ethmoid is nearly horizontal. The walls are very thin, and smoothly rounded externally, and the sutures become completely obliterated in adult skulls, so that it is very difficult to trace out the boundaries of the component bones. In both species, the broad occipital region slopes upwards and forwards, and the face is long and much depressed, though of very different shape in each.

In the Echidna (Fig. 70) the squamosal is large and very compressed, the zygomatic process arising very far forward ; the slender horizontal zygoma being completed by a styliform malar, confluent with the maxilla.

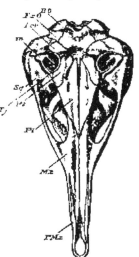

The face is produced into a long tapering rostrum, rounded above from side to side, and concave below in the same direction. The anterior nares form an oval opening on the upper surface near the apex, bounded entirely by the premaxillæ, for the nasals do not appear to reach so far forwards. The alveolar borders are narrow and rounded, without trace of teeth. The palate is produced backwards, by very large palatine bones (*Pl*), considerably beyond the glenoid fossa. The narial canals have very little extent vertically, but the true olfactory chambers are large, and provided with complex turbinals, which, in accordance with the horizontal

Fig. 70.—Under surface of cranium of Echidna (*Echidna hystrix*), ⅔: *BO* basioccipital ; *ExO* exoccipital ; *Per* periotic ; *m* malleus; *sq* squamosal ; *Ty* tympanic ; *Pt* pterygoid ; *Pl* palatine ; *Mx* maxilla ; *PMx* premaxilla.

position of the cribriform plate, are mostly placed vertically.

The pterygoids (*Pt*) are flattened, horizontal, oval plates, attached to the obliquely truncated postero-external extremities of the palatines, and form part of the floor and the inner wall of the tympanic cavity, an arrangement not met with in any other Mammal. The tympanic (*Ty*) is a very slender ring, incomplete for a small space at the upper and outer end, and does not become ankylosed to the periotic. The latter (*Per*) is large, has no fossa for the flocculus, sends out a large expansion (pterotic), forming a portion of the cranial wall between the squamosal, parietal, and occipital, the lower and hinder part at least of which corresponds with the mastoid portion.

Each ramus of the mandible is a mere slender style, without any ascending portion, and with but rudiments of coronoid process and angle. The condyle is very small, elongated from before backwards, and very narrow.

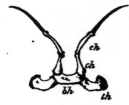

FIG. 71.—Lower surface of hyoid of Echidna (*Echidna hystrix*): *eh* epihyal; *ch* ceratohyal; *bh* basihyal; *th* thyrohyal.

The hyoid (Fig. 71) has a well-ossified, transversely extended, flattened and arched (with the concavity forwards), basihyal (*bh*). The anterior cornu has only two ossifications (*ch* and *ch*), apparently the epi- and cerato-hyal, as the upper one has a long ligamentous connection with the cranium in the situation of the stylohyal. There are broad, flattened, curved thyrohyals (*th*), expanded at their laryngeal extremities.

In the Ornithorhynchus the brain case is smaller than in the Echidna, and rather more depressed; very broad behind, and narrowing anteriorly. The olfactory fossa is compara-

tively small. There are well-marked posterior clinoid processes. The falx cerebri is largely ossified, forming a strong
median partition to the upper part of the cerebral cavity.
The zygoma is compressed, and of considerable vertical
depth, and sends up a well-marked postorbital process ; its
hinder root arises very far back on the cranium.

The glenoid fossa is wide and concave transversely. The
zygomatic process of the maxilla is widened inferiorly into
an oblong, concave, roughened surface for the attachment
of the horny plate, which takes the place of the molar
teeth.

The face is broad and much flattened. It runs out
anteriorly into two diverging processes, each formed by the
premaxilla, supported by a pointed process of the nasal on
the inner, and the maxilla on the outer, side. These bend
towards each other at their extremities, but do not meet in
the middle line. They support the partly horny, partly
membranous beak, which fills up the space between them,
and extends considerably on each side and in front. There
is a distinct median ossification in the triangular interval
between the diverging premaxillary bars, placed in, or in
front of, the anterior extremity of the mesethmoid cartilage,
and apparently corresponding to the so-called "prenasal"
of the Pig. The infraorbital foramen is very large, corresponding to the large size of the nerves distributed to the
sensitive sides of the beak. The periotic has a wide and
deep floccular fossa.

The mandible has, rather behind the middle of each
ramus, an oblong expansion for a horny tooth, corresponding to that on the maxilla. Behind this it curves
gradually upwards to the expanded and transversely extended articular surface. There is no distinct angle, the
coronoid process is small and directed much inwards, and

on the external surface there is a very deep masseteric fossa. Anteriorly the rami of the mandible have a very slight symphysial connection, in front of which their expanded, flattened terminations again diverge from each other. The apertures for the entrance and for the exit of the branches of the inferior dental nerve are remarkably large.

CHAPTER XIV.

THE SHOULDER GIRDLE.

HAVING finished the consideration of the axial portions of the skeleton, we now turn to the appendicular parts, which consist of two pairs of limbs, anterior and posterior.

The anterior limb is present, and fully developed, in all Mammals, being composed of a shoulder girdle and three segments belonging to the limb proper, viz. the upper arm or *brachium*, the fore-arm or *antibrachium*, and the hand or *manus*.

The SHOULDER GIRDLE in the large majority of Mammals is in a comparatively rudimentary, or rather modified, condition. Its true structure and its relations to the pelvic girdle can only be understood by a reference to its condition in the lower vertebrates.[1]

Each side of the girdle consists primitively of a curved rod of cartilage, placed vertically (in the horizontal position of the body), the upper or dorsal end being free, the inner side lying upon, though not united with, some of the anterior thoracic vertebræ or ribs, and the inferior or ventral end being attached to the side of the presternum.

[1] On this subject see W. K. Parker's valuable work before cited, and also Gegenbaur's "Untersuchungen zur Vergleichenden Anatomie," 2tes Heft, 1865.

postscapular fossa (*pf*), between the glenoid border and the
spine, also called "infraspinous fossa;" and (3) the *subscapular fossa*, between the coracoid and glenoid borders,
on the side of the scapula opposite to the spine.

The greater part of the scapula is ossified by *ectostosis* (as
the shaft of a long bone), from a single centre, which is
placed not far from the middle of the bone; but this ossification does not extend into a certain portion of the superior
extremity. This part (*suprascapula*) either remains cartilaginous or "is feebly ossified by one or more endosteal
patches, or by the creeping upwards of such deposit from
within the main bone" (Parker). When the spine runs
out into a projecting acromial process, more or less of its
terminal portion is ossified separately as an epiphysis.

The coracoid always ossifies from one or more separate
centres, and remains for some time suturally connected
with the scapula, though firmly ankylosing with it by the
time the animal has attained maturity. Sometimes (as in
the Sloths) it forms a considerable part of the glenoid fossa;
sometimes (as in most Carnivora and Ungulata) it is a mere
nodule, which becomes blended with the anterior margin of
the fossa.

In the *Ornithodelphia* (see Fig. 80), as in Birds and Reptiles, the coracoid is largely developed and articulates with
the presternum, and there is in addition a plate of bone in
relation with its anterior edge called *epicoracoid*. A small
plate of cartilage or bone, often found attached to the side
of the presternum in certain Rodents and Insectivores, is
considered by Parker as representing the epicoracoid of
the Ornithodelphia, and by Gegenbaur as the sternal extremity of the true coracoid, the middle part of which is
undeveloped.

The clavicular arch, when completely developed, extends

from the free acromial extremity of the spine of the scapula
to the anterior extremity of the presternum.

It consists mainly of an elongated rod of bone, ossified
usually in fibrous tissue, but at either extremity are certain
patches of true cartilage, which may become converted into
bone, or may sometimes degenerate into fibro-cartilage.
These are thus described and named by Mr. Parker.   At
the scapular extremity of the clavicle, there is often a piece
of cartilage, considered to be segmented off from the end
of the mesoscapula, and hence called *mesoscapular segment*
(Fig. 73, *mss*).   At the sternal extremity there may be two
distinct pieces, the one (*pc*) nearest the clavicle being the
supposed homologue of a displaced fragment of the *precoracoid* of the lower Vertebrates.   The one (*ost*) nearest the
sternum is called *omosternum* by Parker, and *episternum* by
Gegenbaur, who considers it homologous with the so-called
episternum (*interclavicle*, Parker) of the Ornithodelphia and
Lizards.

*Special Characters of the Shoulder Girdle in the Different
Groups of the Mammalia.*

Order PRIMATES. *Man.*—In the ordinary erect position of
the human body, the suprascapular border is directed backwards and inwards, and is commonly called the "base" or
"vertebral border" of the scapula; the glenoid cavity looks
forwards and outwards; the glenoid border, called "external" or "axillary," looks downwards and rather forwards;
and the coracoid border is "superior." The postscapular
fossa is much developed, and the suprascapular border is
long, straight, and forms an acute angle with the glenoid
border.   At the junction of the coracoid border of the
scapula with the coracoid bone, there is a more or less well-
marked notch (*coraco-scapular notch*).   The spine is well

developed, and the acromion large and curved forwards near its extremity.

The coracoid forms a well-marked hook-like process; it contributes a very small part to the glenoid fossa, and unites with the scapula at about the time of puberty.

The clavicle (Fig. 73, *cl*) is a strongly-developed sigmoid bone, remarkable for the very early age at which it com-

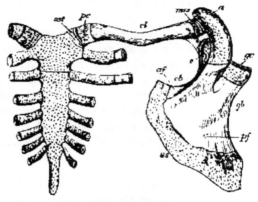

FIG. 73.—The human sternum and right shoulder girdle, at a very early period of development (from an embryo 5½ inches long) after Parker, 1½. The dotted parts are still cartilaginous; the inner surface of the sternum and clavicle, and outer surface of the scapula are represented. *ost* omosternum, afterwards developed into the interarticular fibro-cartilaginous disk; *pc* precoracoid of Parker; *cl* shaft of the clavicle; *mss* mesoscapular segment of Parker; *a* acromion; *c* coracoid; *gc* glenoid cavity of scapula; *gb* glenoid border; *cb* coracoid border; *af* anterior, or "supraspinous," fossa; *pf* posterior, or "infraspinous," fossa; *ss* suprascapular border.

mences to ossify, in fact before any other bone of the body. The outer extremity is, in the young state, tipped with cartilage (the mesoscapular segment, Parker, *mss*), which ossifies by extension of bone from the rest of the clavicle. It is connected with the acromion by a small oval, flat, synovial articulation. The inner end (*pc*) is also cartilaginous for some time, but ossifies separately by endostosis, forming an epiphysis. This extremity is attached to the presternum by synovial articulation, but with a disk-like fibro-cartilage (*ost*) interposed, which, according to Parker, is a degeneration of the " omosternal " element.

In the Gorilla the scapula is very like that of Man. In the Chimpanzee it is peculiarly elongated, the suprascapular margin being extremely oblique and long, at the expense of the greatly reduced coracoid border. The acromion and coracoid are largely developed. In the lower Monkeys the form of the scapula is quite different, the coracoid and glenoid borders being nearly equal, and the suprascapular border comparatively short and straight.

The clavicle is well developed in all, and all its correlates are present ; the omosternum being generally converted during growth into a fibro-cartilaginous intra-articular disk.

In the various members of the Order INSECTIVORA there is a great difference in the construction of the shoulder girdle.

In the Mole (*Talpa*) and its immediate allies *Scalops* and *Condylura*, the scapula is extremely high and narrow, and appears to be ossified entirely from one centre. The spine and acromion are very little developed. The bone commonly called clavicle, but which may be a combination of coracoid and clavicle, is of remarkable form, being nearly cuboid. It is formed primitively of a mass of cartilage, on the anterior aspect of which the true (membrane-developed) clavicle is engrafted. It articulates inferiorly with the presternum, and superiorly with the humerus, and is connected with the scapula only by a fibrous band. The two articulations of the upper end of the humerus, the one with the scapula, and the other with the coraco-clavicle, are separated by a strong ligamentous partition.

In the Cape Golden Mole (*Chrysochloris*) the condition of these parts is quite different. The scapula is long and

Q

narrow, but flattened.   The spine sends a flat process backwards near its middle, and a long slender "*metacromial*"
process from its extremity.   The clavicle is very long, slender,
and curved.   The "mesoscapular segment" forms a distinct,
though minute, bone between the clavicle and scapula.

In the Shrews (*Soricidæ*) the scapula (see Fig. 74) is
also long and narrow, and the slender acromion ends in
two long diverging processes, of which the anterior (*a*)
supports the clavicle, and the posterior (*ma*) is called
"metacromion."   The mesoscapular segment (*mss*) is a

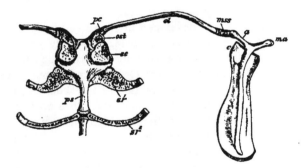

FIG. 74.—Shoulder girdle with upper end of sternum (inner surface) of Shrew (*Sorex*),
after Parker, + 7. *ps* presternum ; *sr¹* first sternal rib ; *sr²* second sternal rib ;
ec partially ossified "epicoracoid" of Parker, or rudiment of the sternal extremity
of the coracoid ; *ost* omosternum ; *pc* rudiment of precoracoid (Parker) ; *cl* clavicle ;
mss ossified "mesoscapular segment ;" *a* acromion ; *ma* metacromial process ;
c coracoid.

distinct bone.   The clavicle (*cl*) is long and slender.   It has
a small piece of cartilage (*pc*) attached to its inner end.
The omosternum (*ost*) is cartilaginous or partially ossified,
and there is a considerable triangular flattened rudiment
of the inner end of the coracoid (*ec*) attached to the presternum.

In the other Insectivora the general form of the scapula

is more normal. In *Galeopithecus* the coracoid is greatly developed and bifurcated.

All known members of the order have large clavicles, with the exception of *Potamogale*, a rare aquatic form from West Africa.

In the CHIROPTERA the scapula is large, of an oval form, and chiefly formed by the postscapular fossa, the anterior fossa being extremely small. The former is divided into two or three subfossæ by ridges. The spine is short and moderately high, with a large and simple acromion. The coracoid is long and curved, often simple (as in *Pteropus*) sometimes forked (as in *Pipistrellus*).

The clavicle is very long and curved. The " mesoscapular segment " is soon lost on the outer end, but the precoracoid ossifies separately. The omosternum is reduced to a cuneiform fibro-cartilage. A rudiment of the sternal end of the coracoid is often present as "a flat, reniform flap of cartilage, feebly ossified by endostosis, wedged in between the clavicle and the first rib " (Parker).

The RODENTIA offer great diversities in the condition of the shoulder girdle. The scapula is generally high and narrow, and the acromion long. Sometimes the acromio-scapular notch is so deep, that the actual spine only occupies a short space near the supra-scapular border, and it is completed by a very long and slender acromion (as in the Coypu, *Myopotamus*). There is often a long metacromion, as in the Hare ; but in others, as the Beaver, there is no such process. The coracoid is always a small blunt hook.

In a few forms the clavicle is altogether absent, in some it is well developed, and various intermediate stages between these two extremes are met with. In some species, as the Guinea Pig and Rabbit, although no trace of this bone is found at birth, it becomes developed at a later period. In

both of these it is very short, and is suspended by long
ligaments between the scapula and the sternum. (See Fig.
75.) In many species, as in the Porcupines, in which the
clavicular arch is more complete, the true clavicle is connected with the presternum by a long cartilaginous omosternum. In others, as the Beaver, this is replaced by a
ligamentous band. Rudiments of the sternal end of the
coracoid are often present, sometimes cartilaginous, sometimes ossified.

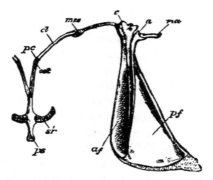

FIG. 75.—Shoulder girdle, with upper end of sternum (inner surface), of a young
Rabbit (*Lepus cuniculus*), after Parker, ⅔. *ps* presternum ; *sr* first sternal rib ;
ost omosternal cartilage ; *pc* precoracoid cartilage ; *cl* ossified clavicle ; *mss* cartilaginous mesoscapular segment ; *c* coracoid ; *a* acromion ; *ma* metacromion ; *af*
anterior fossa ; *pf* posterior fossa.

In the CARNIVORA the anterior and posterior fossæ of
the scapula are nearly equal in area. (See Fig. 72, p. 221.)
The spine and acromion are fairly developed, the latter
often with a broad metacromial process. The coracoid is
much reduced. According to Parker a portion of the
scapula, near the coracoid border, ossifies from an independent centre. The clavicle is sometimes absent, and when
present varies much in its development, but is always
rudimentary and suspended in the muscles, never reaching

either the acromion or sternum. In the *Felidæ* it is slender
and curved, being longer than in any other members of the
order. In the *Canidæ* it is very short, and rather broad and
flat. In the *Ursidæ* it is absent.

In the Seals both acromion and coracoid are much reduced, but the latter is a distinct bone in young animals,
and forms a considerable part of the glenoid cavity. The
whole scapula is much curved backwards, being almost
sickle-shaped, and the suprascapular epiphysis is very large
and slowly ossified.

In the Eared Seals (*Otaria*) the scapula has a different
form, the prescapular fossa being very much larger than the
posterior, and with a strong vertical ridge, parallel to the spine.

None of the Pinnipedia have clavicles.

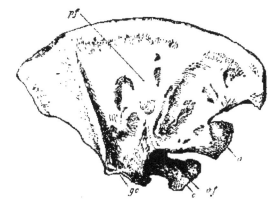

FIG. 76.—Right scapula of Dolphin (*Delphinus tursio*), ⅓. *gc* glenoid cavity ; *a*
acromion ; *c* coracoid ; *pf* postscapular fossa ; *af* prescapular fossa.

Order CETACEA.—In the true Dolphins and nearly all the
Odontoceti the scapula is usually very broad and flat, or fan-
shaped. (See Fig. 76.) The prescapular fossa (*af*) is extremely reduced ; the acromion (*a*) is a long flat process,

with a very narrow base of attachment, projecting forwards ; the coracoid (*c*) is rather long, flattened, and parallel
with the acromion.

In the Cachalots (*Physeter*) the scapula is formed on the
same general plan, but is comparatively high and narrow.
The postscapular fossa is very concave, and the subscapular fossa convex. The Gangetic Fresh-water Dolphin
(*Platanista*) has a flat flabelliform scapula, with the prescapular fossa entirely absent, and the acromion placed on
the anterior edge, the spine and the coracoid border having
coalesced.

Among the Whalebone Whales, *Balænoptera* has a broad
fan-shaped scapula, like that of the true Dolphins, with
long parallel acromion and coracoid processes, and a suprascapular border which remains permanently in a cartilaginous
condition. In the Right Whales (*Balæna*) the scapula is
more massive and not so broad, and the coracoid is much
reduced. In *Megaptera* the scapula is triangular, and neither
the coracoid nor the acromion forms a distinct process.

None of the Cetacea possess clavicles.

The scapula of the SIRENIA is formed on quite a different
plan, being rather like that of the Seals in shape, narrow,
and curved backwards. The anterior fossa is nearly as
large as the posterior. The spine is moderately developed,
and the slender acromion points downwards. The coracoid
forms a moderate-sized conical process. There are no
clavicles.

In the UNGULATA the scapula is always high and rather
narrow. The prescapular and postscapular fossæ are often
subequal. The acromion and coracoid are never much
developed. The clavicle is always absent.

The *Pecora* (see Fig. 77) have all a very large and very
slowly and imperfectly ossified suprascapular region (*ss*) ;

when this is removed, as is almost always the case with
macerated bones, the upper border of the scapula is very
straight.   The acromion usually forms a distinct process,
but is quite absent in the Giraffe, which has the longest and
narrowest scapula of the group.

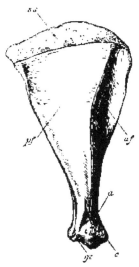

FIG. 77.—Right scapula of Red Deer (*Cervus elaphus*), ⅓. *ss* partially ossified suprascapular border; *pf* postscapular fossa; *af* anterior or prescapular fossa; *a*
acromion; *c* coracoid; *gc* glenoid cavity.

In the Horse the scapula is long and slender, the suprascapular border is rounded, and slowly and imperfectly
ossified.   The spine is very slightly developed; rather above
the middle its edge is thickened and somewhat turned backwards; it gradually subsides at the lower extremity without
forming any acromial process. The coracoid is a prominent
rounded nodule.

In the other Perissodactyles, and in the Pigs and Peccaris,
there is a strongly-marked retroverted triangular process

on the middle of the edge of the spine, and no true acromion; but in the Hippopotamus there is a small acromion and no distinct mid-spinous process. In this animal the coracoid is rather long and upturned.

In the Tapir the coraco-scapular notch is remarkably deep.

The Hyrax manifests its affinity with the Ungulata in the form of the scapula, which is generally triangular, with a small spine, most prominent and with a retroverted edge near the middle, and gradually subsiding at each extremity, so that there is no trace of an acromial process.

The Elephant has a largely developed postscapular fossa and a narrow anterior fossa. The glenoid border is short, and forms a very prominent angle posteriorly with the unusually long suprascapular border. The spine is prominent, and has a very strongly marked process projecting backwards from near the middle and a moderate-sized acromion. The coracoid is small and rounded.

The EDENTATA present some very interesting conditions of the shoulder girdle.

In the Cape Anteater (*Orycteropus*) the scapula is of the most normal form, with well-developed acromion and coracoid. The middle of the border of the spine is thickened and retroverted, and there is a well-marked metacromion. The clavicle is strong, curved, and dilated at its sternal end.

In the Pangolins (*Manis*) the scapula is broad, and rounded above, the anterior margin gently passing into the superior. The prescapular fossa is broader than the postscapular. The suprascapular region remains cartilaginous. The acromion is very small. The coracoid is extremely rudimentary, but with a separate ossific nucleus. There are no clavicles.

In the Anteaters (*Myrmecophaga*) the scapula is also broad

and rounded, so that there is no distinct angle between the anterior and superior margin. The anterior margin is produced, to meet the large adze-shaped coracoid, over the coraco-scapular notch, converting it into a foramen. The spine has a triangular process in the middle, and a long slender acromion, without distinct metacromion. The post-scapular fossa is nearly equally divided by a second spine.

There are no clavicles in this genus, but the small climbing *Cyclothurus didactylus* has moderate, gently curved clavicles.

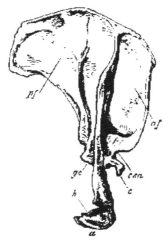

FIG. 78.—Right scapula of Great Armadillo (*Priodontes gigas*), ¼. *pf* postscapular fossa ; *af* prescapular fossa ; *gc* glenoid cavity ; *csn* coraco-scapular notch ; *c* coracoid ; *a* acromion ; *h* articular surface for humerus.

In the Armadillos (*Dasypodidæ*) the scapula is rather varied in form. The acromion is always very long and curved ; in many cases it has a distinct articular facet on its inner surface for the upper end of the humerus. (See Fig. 78, *h*.) There is a second spine on the postscapular fossa, and always a well-developed clavicle.

In the Sloths (*Bradypodidæ,* Fig. 79) the prescapular region (*af*) is larger than the postscapular (*pf*). The spine arises from little more than the middle third of the bone, vertically. In the young of both genera of this family the acromion is a long strip of cartilage connecting the spine with the end of the coracoid, while the coracoid border of the scapula and the coracoid bone join each other in front, converting the coraco-scapular notch into a small oval foramen (*csf*). This condition remains in the Two-toed Sloth (*Cholæpus*) and the extinct *Megatherium;* but in *Bradypus* the acromion gradually becomes reduced in size, losing its connection with the coracoid, and finally remains a mere styliform, or slightly flattened process.

FIG. 79.—Right scapula and clavicle of Two-toed Sloth (*Cholæpus hoffmanni*), ⅔. *af* prescapular fossa ; *pf* postscapular fossa ; *gc* glenoid cavity ; *a* acromion ; *c* coracoid ; *csf* coraco-scapular foramen ; *cl* clavicle.

The coracoid in both forms is unusually large, ossifies ectosteally, according to Parker, and has an epiphysis on its free hook-like extremity.

The clavicle (*cl*) of *Cholœpus* is well developed, attached
externally to the loop of bone on the scapula, formed by the
united extremities of the acromion (*a*) and coracoid (*c*),
and internally by the intervention of a long fibro-cartilaginous "omosternum" (degenerating into a mere ligament
in the adult) to the presternum. In *Bradypus* the clavicle
is very small, and separated by a long interval from the
sternum. It originally articulates at its scapular end, as in
Cholœpus; but in consequence of the atrophy of the acromion, it is left attached to the end of the coracoid, in which
unusual situation it remains through adult life.

In the MARSUPIALIA the scapula is tolerably uniform in
shape. The acromion is long, and the coracoid small, of a
somewhat hooked form, and thick at the base. It ossifies
by a separate endosteal nucleus.

The clavicle is present in all known Marsupials except
the Bandicoots (*Peramelidæ*). It has always a "mesoscapular segment" at its outer end, and a "precoracoid segment" at its sternal end; these are, however, not ossified.
Most generally it is attached to the acromion by a rather
strong ligament, but in the Wombat by a synovial articulation. It is usually connected to the presternum by omosternal cartilages of varying length, best developed in the
Didelphidæ.

The shoulder girdle of the MONOTREMATA (see Fig. 80)
differs widely, in many points, from that of any other
Mammal, and far more resembles that of the Lizards.

The scapula is rather long and narrow, and (especially in
the Ornithorhynchus) curved backward and pointed, sickle-
like, at its upper end. Instead of three it presents but two
distinct borders and two surfaces; but the more convex
border (*s*), which is turned forwards and outwards in its
natural position, has a small projection (*a*) near its lower

end, which affords attachment to the clavicle, and is evidently the acromion ; and the whole border may be considered to represent the spine. Following the indications afforded by the attachment of the muscles, it appears probable that the whole inner surface represents the prescapular fossa of the ordinary Mammalian scapula, and that the anterior portion of the outer surface (*pf*) is the postscapular fossa, and the posterior portion of the same surface (*ssf*) the subscapular

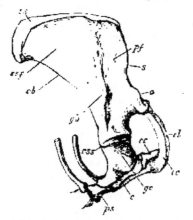

FIG. 80.—Side view of right shoulder girdle of young Echidna (*Echidna hystrix*), ⅔. *ss* suprascapular epiphysis ; *ssf* subscapular fossa ; *pf* postscapular fossa ; *cb* coracoid border ; *gb* glenoid border ; *s* spine ; *a* acromion ; *css* coraco-scapular suture ; *gc* glenoid cavity ; *c* coracoid ; *ec* epicoracoid ; *cl* clavicle ; *ic* interclavicle ; *ps* presternum.

fossa, these two being divided below by a slight ridge (*gb*), which runs to the edge of the glenoid cavity, and from which the long head of the triceps muscle takes origin. This ridge then answers to the posterior or glenoid border of the ordinary Mammal, and the hinder border of the Monotreme's scapula (*cb*) would correspond to the anterior or coracoid border. If this is really the case, the scapula of the Mono-treme and that of the Cetacean offer the widest contrast, the supposed primitive trihedral rod being flattened in opposite directions.   In the Cetacean scapula there are two nearly parallel surfaces, the postscapular and the subscapular fossæ; while the third, the prescapular fossa, is reduced to the smallest possible width—quite obsolete, in fact—in *Platanista*.   In the Monotreme the last-named fossa is so expanded that the other two, instead of being parallel to each other on opposite sides of the bone, are brought almost into one plane, which is parallel and opposite to the subscapular fossa.

The coracoid (*c*) is a stout subcylindrical bone, expanded at its extremities, taking at its upper end a considerable share in the formation of the glenoid cavity, and becoming firmly ankylosed with the scapula.   At its lower end it articulates to the side of the presternum, just in front of the first rib.

Placed in front of the inner end of the coracoid is a broad, flat, shield-like plate of bone (*epicoracoid, ec*), the rounded inner border of which passes beyond the median line, overlapping the corresponding bone of the opposite side.   In the Echidna the left lies in front of the right, while in the Ornithorhynchus this disposition is reversed.

Upon the front end of the presternum, lying below its anterior continuation (*proosteon*, see p. 84) and also below the epicoracoids, is a large azygous T-shaped bone (*ic*, see also Fig. 43, p. 83), which has no homologue in any other Mammal, called *interclavicle*.   Its lower end is broad, and rests on the expanded straight upper margin of the presternum; it contracts somewhat above, before dividing into a pair of nearly horizontal, slightly curved arms, which extend outwards towards, though not quite reaching, the acromion. This bone differs from the presternum, and the small proosteal plate behind its lower extremity, as well as the coracoids and epicoracoids, in being developed in membrane.

The clavicles (*cl*) are simple, elongated, slightly curved, thin, splint-like bones, resting upon the anterior surface of the arms of the interclavicle, pointed and not quite meeting internally, and dilated and articulating directly with the acromion at their outer end.

CHAPTER XV.

IN the upper segment of the limb proper there is always one bone, the *Humerus;* in the second segment, two bones placed side by side, the *Radius* and the *Ulna.*

The *Humerus* (except in some of its extreme modifications) is more or less elongated and cylindrical. It is described as having a shaft, and two extremities. The upper or proximal extremity has a smooth, convex, generally more or less rounded *head* (Fig. 81, *h*), the axis of which is directed upwards and backwards.[1] This, in the living animal, is covered with a thin layer of cartilage, and articulates by a synovial joint with the glenoid cavity of the shoulder girdle. The head is marked off from the shaft very indistinctly by a constriction called the *neck,* immediately below which, upon the anterior surface of the bone, are two rough prominences (*t* and *t*) for the attachment of muscles, called *tuberosities,* separated from each other by a groove (*bg*) called the *bicipital groove,* as the tendon of the biceps muscles runs in it after arising from the margin of the glenoid fossa. The tuberosities are generally distinguished

---

[1] The terms of relative position here used are those which the bone assumes in the ordinary attitude of a quadruped while standing or walking.

as *great* (*t*) and *small* (*t'*) from their relative size in Man and most Mammals ; the former is also called *external,* and the latter *internal,* from their relative situation in the most usual position of the bone ; *radial* and *ulnar* are also terms applied to them in relation to their situation, one on the side of the humerus with which the radius, and the other on the side with which the ulna, is connected below.

FIG. 81.—Anterior surface of right humerus of Wombat (*Phascolomys vombatus*), ½. *h* head ; *bg* bicipital groove ; *t* great or radial tuberosity ; *t'* small or ulnar tuberosity ; *dr* deltoid ridge ; *sr* supinator ridge ; *cf* supra-condylar foramen ; *ec* external condyle ; *ic* internal condyle ; *ar* articular surface for radius ; *au* articular surface for ulna.

The lower or distal extremity of the humerus is somewhat flattened, and usually has a broad, semi-cylindrical articular surface, which is received into a corresponding concavity on the upper end of the bones of the fore-arm. This is called the *trochlea* (*ar* and *au*). On each side, and rather above this surface, is a prominence called the *condyle,* one of which is *external,* or *radial* (*ec*), the other *internal,* or *ulnar* (*ic*). The latter is usually the most prominent. In the middle of the lower end, between the condyles, and above the thickened articular border, the bone is very thin, having a hollow both in front and behind. The latter, which is the deepest, is called the *anconeal fossa*, as it receives a projecting part of the anconeal process, or olecranon, of the ulna, when the fore-arm is fully extended. It often happens that these two fossæ are so deep that they meet, and that there is in consequence a vacuity in the bone or *supratrochlear foramen*. There is often a prominent ridge running upwards for some distance on the shaft from the external condyle, called the *ectocondylar* or *supinator ridge* (*sr*), which affords a wide surface of origin for the supinator muscles of the fore-arm. When much developed this ridge terminates above at the groove for the passage of the musculo-spinal nerve. When the edge of the bone above the inner condyle is much developed, it is sometimes grooved, but more often obliquely perforated from above, downwards and forwards, by a *supracondylar foramen* (*cf*), through which the median nerve and brachial artery pass. Lastly, somewhere towards the anterior surface of the middle of the shaft, on the outer or postaxial side, there is usually a roughened, elevated, longitudinal ridge (*dr*), sometimes developed into a tuberosity, for the insertion of the deltoid muscle, and hence called the *deltoid ridge*. The lower end of this ridge is separated from the upper end of the supinator ridge by a wide and shallow groove, winding in a spiral manner downwards and forwards round the outer side of the shaft of the bone, and indicating the course of the musculo-spinal nerve.

The whole of the shaft of the humerus is developed ectosteally from a single centre of ossification, but at each extremity there is a large epiphysis : the upper one includes the head and both tuberosities, and is usually formed

R

by the coalescence of two distinct endosteal nuclei; the
lower one includes the whole inferior articular surface with
the condyles, and is formed of three or four originally dis
tinct centres of ossification. The lower epiphysis unites to
the shaft before the upper one.

The skeleton of the second segment of the upper limb, the
fore-arm or *antibrachium*, consists of two bones called *radius*
and *ulna*, placed side by side, articulating with the humerus
at their proximal, and with the hand at their distal, extremity.

In their primitive or unmodified condition, these bones
may be considered as placed one on each border of the
limb, the radius being preaxial, and the ulna postaxial.[1]
The radius articulates above with the preaxial (external)
side of the humerus, the ulna with the postaxial (internal)
side of the humerus.

This position is best illustrated in the fore-limb of the
Cetacea (see Fig. 99, p. 271), where the two bones are fixed
side by side and parallel to each other, the preaxial border
being external, and the postaxial border internal, in their
whole extent.

In the greater number of Mammals, the bones assume a
very modified and adaptive position (as will be explained
more fully in the chapter on the comparison of the fore and
hind limbs), usually crossing each other in the fore-arm, the
radius in front of the ulna, so that the preaxial bone
(radius), though external (in the ordinary position of the
limb) at the upper end, is internal at the lower end; and
the hand being mainly fixed to the radius, also has its pre-

[1] So termed (by Prof. Huxley) in relation to the central axis of the
limb, when it is extended out from the body in its primitive embryonic
position, the extensor surface of the arm and back of the hand being
upwards or dorsal, and the flexor surface of the arm and palm of the
hand being downwards or ventral.

axial border internal. In the large majority of Mammals, the bones are fixed in this position; but in some few, as in Man, a free movement of crossing and uncrossing, or *pronation* and *supination*, as it is termed, is allowed between them, so that they can be placed in their primitive parallel condition, when the hand (which moves with the radius) is said to be *supine*, or they may be crossed, when the hand is said to be *prone*.

In most Mammals which walk on four limbs, and in which the hand is permanently prone, the ulna is much reduced in size, and the radius increased, especially at the upper end ; and the articular surface of the latter, instead of being confined to the external side of the trochlea of the humerus, extends all across its anterior surface, and the two bones, instead of being external and internal, are anterior and posterior (see Figs. 82, 83, and 84, p. 246).

The ulna is always characterized by a conspicuous, more or less compressed prolongation, extending upwards beyond the excavated humeral articular surface (sigmoid notch), and serving as the point of attachment to the extensor muscles of the fore-arm, called the *olecranon* or *anconeal process*.

Each of the bones of the fore-arm has commonly a principal centre of ossification for the shaft, and an epiphysis at either end.

Special Characters of the Bones of the Arm and Fore-arm in the different Groups.

Order PRIMATES.—In Man the humerus is long, slender, and straight, with a large globular head. Neither the tuberosities, nor the deltoid and supinator ridges, are much developed. The internal condyle is prominent, but there is no supracondylar foramen as a normal condition. The anconeal fossa is wide and deep, and sometimes, though not usually, perforated. The lower articular surface is divided by a groove into a pulley-like internal portion (*trochlea*) for the ulna, and a smaller rounded portion (*capitellum*), confined to the front side of the bone, for the radius.

The whole bone is somewhat twisted on its longitudinal axis. Supposing it is so placed that a line drawn horizontally through the axis of the head passes directly backwards, another line drawn through the condyles would not cross this at a right angle, as in most of the inferior Mammals, but its outer end would be directed forwards.

The radius has the head or proximal end expanded, disk-shaped, and cupped at its extremity, which is applied to the capitellum of the humerus (see Fig. 82). Below this expanded head the bone is comparatively slender, but increases in size as it approaches the lower end, which is wide from side to side; the surface next the ulna being hollowed to receive the lower end of that bone, while the opposite side is produced into the *radial styloid process*. The inferior surface is hollowed for articulation with the carpus. The whole bone is slightly curved. Not far below the head is a rough prominence, into which the tendon of the biceps flexor muscle is inserted.

The ulna has a large sigmoid excavation above for articulation with the trochlea of the humerus; the pointed elevated anterior edge of this is called the *coronoid process*. The olecranon is not produced upwards beyond the hinder edge of the articular surface. Below this, on the radial side, is a smaller excavation, in which the edge of the disk-like head of the radius plays, being held in its place in the living state by a strong annular ligament, which encircles it. The ulna is straighter than the radius, and gradually diminishes in size to the lower end, where it terminates in a rounded surface, which articulates with the hollow in the lower end of the radius; and also, though not very directly, with the upper surface of the carpus. By the side of this is a small conical process, the *ulnar styloid process.*

The movement of these bones upon the humerus at the elbow-joint is simply that of a hinge, formed mainly by the articular surface of the ulna. In pronation and supination, which is more free and complete than in any other Mammal, the ulna is stationary, and the radius moves, the upper end only on its own axis, being fixed to the side of the ulna by the annular ligament, but the lower end rotates round the lower end of the ulna, carrying the hand with it.

The higher Apes have the axis of the humerus almost as much twisted on itself as in Man; and they also, almost alone among Mammals, resemble Man in not having the olecranon process of the ulna prolonged upwards beyond the sigmoid notch. Even in the Baboons these special anthropoid characters are lost. The humerus has no supra-condylar perforation in any of the Old World *Simiina*, nor in *Ateles, Mycetes* or *Hapale* among the American Monkeys; but in the remaining genera of *Cebidæ*, and in most of the Lemurs, such a perforation is found. In the Aye-Aye (*Chiromys*) the supinator ridge is remarkably developed. The radius and ulna are distinct in all; in the higher forms (especially the Gorilla) greatly curved, leaving a large space between them in the middle of the fore-arm. The power of supination and pronation, which in the higher forms almost equals that enjoyed by Man, is much reduced in the inferior types of the order, although never entirely lost.

In the CARNIVORA the head of the humerus has no longer that hemispherical form, so well marked in the higher Primates. The tuberosities are strong and rough, and project upwards beyond the level of the head. The shaft is much curved forwards. The deltoid ridge is strong, and

extends far down on the bone, especially in the Bears.
The inner condyle is prominent. The anconeal fossa is
deep. A supracondylar foramen exists in the *Felidæ*, and in
most of the *Viverridæ*, *Mustelidæ*, and *Procyonidæ*, but not
in the *Canidæ*, *Hyænidæ*, or *Ursidæ*.

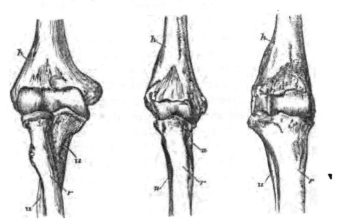

FIG. 82.   FIG. 83.   FIG. 84.

Anterior aspect of the bones forming the right elbow-joint of Man (Fig. 82); of the
Dog (Fig. 83); of the Red Deer (Fig. 84); all ½. *h* humerus; *r* radius; *u* ulna.

The radius differs from that of Man, inasmuch as its
upper end is broad, flattened, and extends further across the
front of the humeral articular surface, forming part of the
hinge (see Fig. 83); and, although it is never ankylosed with
the ulna, scarcely any appreciable amount of movement is
allowed between them. The ulna has a large compressed
olecranon, and a shaft gradually tapering to the lower
extremity.

In the *Pinnipedia* the bones of the anterior limb are very
short and stout. The humerus has a remarkably prominent
deltoid ridge, and no supracondylar foramen. The upper

end of the ulna, and conversely the lower end of the radius, are much expanded.

In most of the INSECTIVORA the bones of the arm generally resemble those of the Carnivora. In the Hedgehog (*Erinaceus*) there is no supracondylar foramen in the humerus, but a large supratrochlear perforation. In *Centetes*, *Rhynchocyon*, and nearly all the other genera, there is a supracondylar foramen.

The radius and ulna are generally completely developed and distinct; but in *Galeopithecus*, *Macroscelides* and *Petrodromus*, they are fused together inferiorly.

The Mole (*Talpa*) and its allies have a humerus of extraordinary form, being very short, and extremely broad and flattened at both extremities, though contracted in the middle. In addition to the narrow oval head for articulation with the glenoid cavity of the scapula, there is a larger saddle-shaped surface, which articulates by a separate synovial joint with the outer end of the coraco-clavicle. The deltoid ridge is very prominent, joining the inner tuberosity above. From each condyle a slender bony process extends upwards. There is a supracondylar foramen. The ulna has a greatly developed olecranon, with a narrow keel behind, and expanded laterally at the extremity.

In the Cape Golden Mole (*Chrysochloris*) the humerus is much more slender generally than in the true Moles, but the inner condyle is extremely elongated. The olecranon is long, narrow, and incurved. The fore-arm has a third bone, extending from the palmar surface of the carpus almost to the elbow, where it has a free termination. This appears to be an ossification in one of the flexor tendons.

The CHIROPTERA have a long slender humerus, having a slight sigmoid curve. The ulnar tuberosity is large. There is no supracondylar perforation. The ulna is extremely

reduced, only the upper third being present, and that ankylosed with the radius, which forms almost the whole of the
lower articular surface of the elbow-joint.   There is a
detached sesamoid ossicle on the olecranon.

In the RODENTIA the humerus varies much in its characters.   It is long, slender, and straight, with a very slight
deltoid ridge, a narrow and laterally compressed inferior
end, and without prominent condyles in the Hares and
Agutis.   But in the Beaver the deltoid and supinator ridges,
and the inner condyle, are strongly developed.   All intermediate conditions occur in different genera.   As a general
rule there is a large supratrochlear perforation, but no
supracondylar foramen.   In the Coypu (*Myopotamus*) the
deltoid ridge is an extremely salient, compressed, and
everted tuberosity.

In the fore-arm the two bones are nearly always distinct, though closely applied to each other.   The breadth
of the upper end of the radius, and the amount of rotation permitted upon the ulna, vary much in different
genera.

In the great order UNGULATA the humerus is stout and
rather short.   The outer tuberosity is very large, and generally sends a strong curved process inwards, overhanging the
bicipital groove (not, however, in the Horse and Camel).
The deltoid ridge is usually not strongly marked, and placed
rather high on the bone ; but in the Rhinoceros it is a very
salient ridge.   The lower end is always particularly straight
and flat on the inner side, (see Fig. 84, p. 246) the condyle
forming no prominence, and there is never a supracondylar
foramen.   The outer condyle and the ridge above it are
rather more developed.

The radius is large at both ends, and superiorly extends
across the whole of the humeral trochlear surface (see Fig.

84). The ulna is a complete and distinct bone in the Pig, Hippopotamus, Tapir, and Rhinoceros. In the Ruminants it is more or less rudimentary and fixed behind the radius. In the Camel the two bones become completely coalesced. In the Horse the olecranon and upper part of the shaft alone remain, firmly ankylosed to the radius. .

In the PROBOSCIDIA the humerus is remarkable for the great development of the supinator ridge. The ulna and radius are quite distinct, and permanently crossed. The upper end of the latter is small, while the ulna not only contributes the principal part of the articular surface for the humerus, but has its lower end actually larger than that of the radius, a condition almost unique among Mammals.

In Hyrax the humerus is straight, with a very prominent outer tuberosity, moderate deltoid ridge, rather compressed inferior extremity, large supratrochlear, but no supracondylar, perforation. The ulna and radius are complete and subequal, often ankylosing together in old animals.

In the CETACEA, the bones of the arm and fore-arm are usually very short, broad, and simple in their characters (see Fig. 99). The humerus has a large globular head, which moves freely in the glenoid cavity of the scapula, the tuberosities are fused into one, the bicipital groove being absent; the lower end is broad and flattened, and its inferior surface is divided into two nearly equal flat surfaces placed side by side (one external, the other internal) and meeting at a very obtuse angle. The equally flat upper surfaces of the radius and ulna are applied to these and so united that scarcely any motion is permitted between them, and often in old animals ankylosis takes place at the joint.

The ulna and radius are parallel to each other without any indication of crossing: the former has a tolerably well-developed olecranon process projecting directly outwards from the shaft of the bone; the radius is extremely simple in form, wider below than above.

In the Rorquals (*Balænoptera* and *Megaptera*) these bones are considerably elongated.

In the SIRENIA the bones of the fore-limb are formed on a different type, as there is a distinct, though small and simple, trochlear articulation at the elbow-joint. In the Dugong, the humerus is small in the middle of the shaft, and expanded at each end. The tuberosities are very prominent, especially the outer one, and the bicipital groove is distinct. The internal condyle is prominent, the anconeal fossa small, and there is no supracondylar perforation. In the humerus of the Manati the bicipital groove is obsolete, the two tuberosities coalescing, as in the Cetacea. In other respects it resembles that of the Dugong.

The two bones of the fore-arm are, in both genera, about equally developed, and generally ankylose together at both extremities.

Order EDENTATA.—In the Sloths the humerus is long and straight, slender and cylindrical in the greater part, but flattened and laterally expanded at the lower end. The head is hemispherical, the tuberosities moderately developed, and subequal in size, the deltoid ridge very indistinct. In the Two-toed Sloths (*Cholæpus*) the humerus is shorter and broader than in *Bradypus*, and has a large supracondylar perforation, which is wanting in the latter genus.

The radius and ulna somewhat recall those of the Primates in their form, and they are capable of a considerable amount of pronation and supination. The olecranon process scarcely projects beyond the sigmoid articular surface.

The humerus in all the remaining Edentates is stout and broad, and remarkable for the great development of the points of muscular attachment, as the tuberosities, deltoid and supinator ridges, and internal condyle. These all reach their maximum of development in the Armadillos, animals which make great use of their fore-limbs in scratching and burrowing. The supracondylar foramen is present in all.

The radius and ulna are also well developed and distinct in all, but with no great amount of motion permitted between them. The olecranon is always long and strong.

Order MARSUPIALIA.—In the burrowing Wombat (*Phasco-lomys*) the humerus is stout, very broad at the lower end, and with strongly developed deltoid and supinator ridges (See Fig. 81, p. 240.) These characters prevail generally throughout the order, though in a less marked degree. The supracondylar foramen is almost always present, some of the Dasyures being exceptions.

The radius and ulna are always distinct and well-developed bones. The upper end of the radius is small and rounded, and more or less rotation is permitted between the bones, even in the carnivorous forms.

In both the genera of animals constituting the order MONOTREMATA, the humerus is something like that of the Mole, short and extremely broad at both extremities, with greatly produced inner and outer condyles, though contracted at the middle of the shaft.

The radius and ulna are stout, and rather flattened at the lower end, where they are of about equal size, and closely applied together. The upper end of the olecranon is widely expanded laterally.

CHAPTER XVI.

THE MANUS.

THE terminal segment of the anterior limb is the hand or *manus*.[1] Its skeleton consists of three divisions: (1) The *carpus*, a group of small, more or less rounded or angular bones, with flattened surfaces applied to one another, and, though articulating by synovial joints, having scarcely any motion between them; (2) the *metacarpus*, a series of elongated bones placed side by side, with their proximal ends articulating by almost immoveable joints with the carpus; (3) the *phalanges*, or bones of the digits, usually three in number to each, articulating with one another by freely moveable hinge-joints, the first being connected in like manner to the distal end of the corresponding meta-carpal bone.

To understand thoroughly the arrangement of the bones of the carpus in Mammals, it is necessary to study their

[1] "On account of the ambiguity arising from the as yet unsettled con-notation of the terms 'hand' and 'foot,' I think it better, in a scientific treatise, to disuse them altogether, and . . . to adopt for the anterior extremity (the carpus and all beyond it) the term *manus*, and for the homotypal posterior segment the term *pes*. The all but necessity for distinct *homological* terms for such parts is obvious."—MIVART, *On the Appendicular Skeleton of the Primates*, Phil. Trans. 1867.

condition in some of the lower vertebrates.[1] Fig. 85 represents the manus in one of its most complete, and at the same time most generalized, forms, as seen in one of the Water Tortoises (*Chelydra serpentina*).

The carpus consists of two principal rows of bones, an upper or proximal row, containing three bones, to which Gegenbaur has applied the terms *radiale* (*r*), *intermedium* (*i*), and *ulnare* (*u*), the first being on the radial or preaxial side

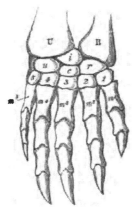

FIG. 85.—Dorsal surface of the right manus of a Water Tortoise (*Chelydra serpentina*), after Gegenbaur : U ulna ; R radius ; *u* ulnare ; *i* intermedium ; *r* radiale : *c* centrale ; 1—5 the five bones of the distal row of the carpus ; *m*1—*m*5 the five metacarpals.

of the limb. The lower, or distal, row contains five bones, called *carpale* 1, 2, 3, 4, and 5 respectively, commencing on the radial side. Between these two rows, in the middle of the carpus, is a single bone, the *centrale* (*c*).

In this very symmetrical carpus, it will be observed that the *radiale* supports on its distal side two bones, *carpale* 1 and 2 ; the *intermedium* is in a line with the *centrale* and

---

[1] See Gegenbaur, " Untersuchungen zur Vergleichenden Anatomie," 1tes Heft, Carpus und Tarsus. 1864.

carpale 3, which together form a median axis of the hand, while the *ulnare* has also two bones articulated with its distal end, viz. *carpale* 4 and 5. Each of the carpals of the distal row supports a metacarpal.

In the carpus of the Mammalia, there are usually two additional bones developed in the tendons of the flexor muscles, one on each side of the carpus, which may be called the radial and ulnar sesamoid bones; the latter is most constant and generally largest, and is commonly known as the *pisiform* bone. The fourth and fifth carpals of the distal row are always united into a single bone, and the *centrale* is often absent. As a general rule all the other bones are present and distinct, though it not unfrequently happens that one or more may have coalesced to form a single bone, or may be altogether suppressed.

The table below shows the principal names in use for the various carpal bones. Those in the second column, being most generally employed by English anatomists, will be adopted in the following pages :—

Radiale	= Scaphoid	= *Naviculare.*
Intermedium	= Lunar	= *Semilunare, Lunatum.*
Ulnare	= Cuneiform	= *Triquetrum, Pyramidale.*
Centrale	= Central	= *Intermedium* (Cuvier).
Carpale 1	= Trapezium	= *Multangulum majus.*
Carpale 2	= Trapezoid	= *Multangulum minus.*
Carpale 3	= Magnum	= *Capitatum.*
Carpale 4 } *Carpale* 5 }	= Unciform	= *Hamatum, Uncinatum.*

The metacarpal bones, with the digits which they support, never exceed five in number, and are distinguished by numerals, counted from the radial towards the ulnar side. The digits are also sometimes named (I) *pollex*, (II) *index*, (III) *medius*, (IV) *annularis*, and (V) *minimus*. One or more may be in a very rudimentary condition, or altogether suppressed. If one is absent, it is most commonly the first.

Excepting the Cetacea, no Mammals have more than three phalanges to each digit, but they may occasionally have fewer by suppression or ankylosis.

The first or radial digit (also called *pollex*) is an exception to the usual rule, one of its parts being constantly absent, for while each of the other digits has commonly a metacarpal and three phalanges, it has only three bones altogether. Whether the missing one is the metacarpal or one of the phalanges, is a subject which has occasioned much discussion, but has not yet been satisfactorily decided.   In accordance with the most usual custom, the proximal bone of this digit will here be treated of as a metacarpal.

The terminal phalanges of the digits are often specially modified to support the nail, claw or hoof, and are called " ungual phalanges."

Very frequently a pair of small sesamoid bones are developed in connection with the tendons passing over the palmar surface of the articular heads of the metacarpals and phalanges, and occasionally (as in the Armadillos) a larger bone of similar nature is met with in the middle of the same surface of the carpus and metacarpus.   More rarely similar bones occur on the dorsal surface of the phalangeal articulations.

Each of the carpal bones ossifies from a single nucleus. The metacarpals and phalanges have each a main nucleus for the greater part of the bone, and usually an epiphysis at one end only, this being the distal end of the metacarpals (except the first), and the proximal end of the first metacarpal and of all the phalanges. In many of the Cetacea epiphyses are found at both ends of the bones, and the same takes place regularly in the Elephant Seal (*Morunga proboscidea,*) and occasionally in some other Mammals.

In Man the carpus (see Fig. 86) is short and broad.   Its
upper border, by which it articulates with the radius, forms a
regular curve, with the convexity upwards.   It has the three
bones of the proximal row—the scaphoid (s), lunar (l), and
cuneiform (c)—distinct; also the usual four bones of the
distal row, but no central.   There is a well-developed rounded
ulnar sesamoid (the pisiform bone, p) which articulates by a
smooth facet with the cuneiform, but no radial sesamoid.
The trapezium (tm) has a saddle-like articular surface for the
moveable first metacarpal.   The magnum (m), as its name

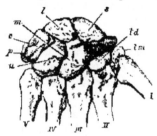

Fig. 86.—Bones of the right human carpus, ½. s scaphoid ; l lunar ; c cuneiform ;
tm trapezium ; td trapezoid ; m magnum ; u unciform ; p pisiform ; I—V the
metacarpals.

implies, is the largest bone—rather an exceptional condition
among Mammals; it has a large rounded part or head
projecting upwards and fitting into a concavity in the distal
surface of the bones of the proximal row.   The unciform
(u) has a strong hook-like process from its palmar surface
curved towards the radial side.

The first metacarpal is shorter, though somewhat broader
than any of the others.   It is articulated in a different plane
from them, its palmar surface facing towards the ulnar side
of the hand, and it is capable of a considerable range of
movement.   The other four metacarpals are nearly equally
developed, diminishing slightly from the radial to the ulnar

side; their shafts are slender and rather compressed, especially towards the palmar aspect, but they enlarge at each extremity, particularly at the rounded distal end or head. They are so articulated with the carpus as to allow of very little motion. The phalanges are of the normal number to each digit, all broad, convex on their dorsal, and flattened or slightly hollowed on their palmar, side. The proximal is the largest, and the ungual the smallest. The latter is flattened and slightly expanded or spatulate at its terminal portion. Those of the first digit or thumb are stouter than any of the others, those of the fifth digit (little finger) are the most slender. The third digit is the longest, the second and fourth somewhat shorter and nearly equal, the fifth considerably shorter, and the first still more so. Sesamoid bones are only developed behind the metacarpo-phalangeal joint of the pollex.

In the other PRIMATES, the manus is generally longer and narrower than in Man, and as a general rule the first digit or

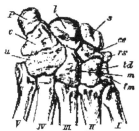

FIG. 87.—Bones of the carpus of a Baboon (*Cynocephalus anubis*), ⅔. *s* scaphoid; *l* lunar; *c* cuneiform; *p* pisiform; *ce* central; *rs* radial sesamoid; *tm* trapezium; *td* trapezoid; *m* magnum; *u* unciform; I—V the metacarpals.

thumb is less developed and less freely moveable. In the genera *Troglodytes* and *Simia*, as in Man, the proximal surface of the carpus articulates with the radius alone, in all others it articulates also with the ulna. The scaphoid and lunar bones are always distinct. An additional bone (*os centrale*, Gegenbaur, Fig. 87, *ce*) is present in all, except in the Gorilla and Chimpanzee, and in the *Indrisinæ* among the Lemurs. This is considered by some anatomists to be a dismemberment of the scaphoid. The pisiform is present in all, and generally of a more elongated form, and more salient than in Man; and there is usually a small rounded radial sesamoid (*rs*) articulating moveably to the border of the scaphoid and trapezium, and connected with the tendon of the flexor carpi radialis.

In the Potto (*Perodicticus*) there is an additional bone in the palmar side of the carpus, an ossification in the ligament connecting the posterior processes of the trapezium and unciform bones, and forming with these processes a complete bony ring, through which the flexor tendons pass.[1]

The metacarpals and phalanges are of the complete and normal number in all, with the following exceptions. In the African genus of long-tailed Monkeys *Colobus*, and also in the American Spider Monkeys (*Ateles*), the thumb is rudimentary, having usually but one very minute phalanx, in addition to the metacarpal. In the Potto (*Perodicticus*) and some allied *Lemurinæ*, the second (or index) digit is very much shorter than the others, and has but two rudimentary phalanges.

The phalanges are generally more curved than in Man, most notably so in the Orang. The hand of the Madagascar Aye-Aye (*Chiromys*) is remarkable for the extreme attenuation of the bones of the third digit.

In the CARNIVORA, the scaphoid and lunar bones always coalesce into a single *scapho-lunar* bone (Fig. 88, *sl*). There is never a centrale. The radial accessory ossicle or

---

[1] Mivart, "On the Appendicular Skeleton of the Primates;" Phil. Trans., 1867.

sesamoid (*rs*) is generally present. All have five digits, with the complete complement of phalanges, except the Hyæna, in which genus the pollex is represented only by a rudimentary metacarpal. This digit is usually much reduced in size, and often, as in the Dog, does not reach the ground in walking. It is best developed in the Bears and allied forms. The first metacarpal is never more freely moveable than any of the others. As a general rule the middle digit

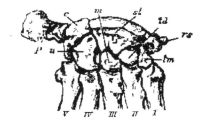

Fɪɢ. 88.—Bones of the carpus of a Bear (*Ursus americanus*), ⅓. *sl* scapho-lunar bone ; *c* cuneiform ; *p* pisiform ; *u* unciform ; *m* magnum ; *td* trapezoid ; *tm* trapezium ; *rs* radial sesamoid ; ɪ—v the metacarpals.

is somewhat the longest, the second and fourth nearly equal to it, the fifth shorter, and the first the shortest.[1]

As the toes are nearly always armed with large, strong, curved, and sharp claws (see Fig. 89), the ungual phalanges

---

[1] The fissiped Carnivora have been divided into two groups, according to the position of the feet in walking—the Plantigrade, or those that place the whole of the palmar and plantar surface to the ground ; and the Digitigrade, or those that walk only upon the phalanges, the metacarpals and metatarsals being vertical and in a line with the fore-arm or leg. This distinction, however, is quite an artificial one, and every intermediate condition exists between the extreme typical plantigrade gait of the bears and the true digitigrade action of the cats and dogs. In fact, the greater number of the Carnivora belong to neither of these groups, but may be called "subplantigrade," often, when at rest, applying the whole of the sole to the ground, but keeping the heel raised to a greater or less extent when walking.

(ph^3 a) are large, strongly compressed, and pointed, and they develop from their base a broad thin lamina of bone (b), which is reflected over the root of the horny claw, and holds it more firmly in its place. In those genera, as *Felis*, in

FIG. 83.—The phalanges of the middle digit of the manus of the Lion (*Felis leo*), ½. ph^1 proximal phalanx; ph^2 middle phalanx; ph^3 ungual phalanx; *a* the central portion forming the internal support to the horny claw; *b* the bony lamina reflected around the base of the claw.

which the claws are retractile, the middle phalanx (ph^2) is deeply hollowed on its ulnar side to receive the ungual phalanx when folded back upon it, in the quiescent state of the foot.

In the *Pinnipedia*, the manus is broader and flatter than in the terrestrial Carnivora. The scaphoid and lunar coalesce. The ulnar side of the carpus is much reduced, the unciform being especially small, and consequently the fifth metacarpal articulates partly with the cuneiform of the proximal row of the carpus. The pisiform is small. The first digit is nearly as long as the second; the remainder gradually diminish in length to the fifth. The ungual phalanges in the ordinary Seals are slender, pointed, slightly curved, and not much compressed. In the *Otariidæ* they are prolonged beyond the part which bears the very small claw, and flattened and truncated at the ends, being continued onwards in the living animal as cartilaginous rays, which support lobed expansions of the skin.

Among the INSECTIVORA, the scaphoid and lunar coalesce

in *Galeopithecus, Tupaia, Centetes, Solenodon, Erinaceus,* and *Gymnura,* but in most of the other forms these bones are distinct. A distinct os centrale is found in all except in *Galeopithecus, Potamogale, Chrysochloris,* and *Sorex.*

There are nearly always five digits, but *Rhynchocyon* and *Chrysochloris* have but four. The whole hand is generally of moderate size, with pointed, conical, slightly curved, ungual phalanges.

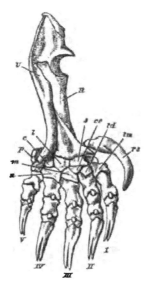

FIG. 90.—Bones of fore-arm and manus of Mole (*Talpa europæa*), × 2.   *R* radius: *U* ulna ; *s* scaphoid ; *l* lunar ; *c* cuneiform ; *p* pisiform ; *u* unciform ; *m* magnum ; *td* trapezoid ; *tm* trapezium ; *ce* central ; *rs* radial sesamoid (falciform) ; I—V the digits.

In common with every segment of the anterior extremity, the manus of the Mole (*Talpa*) and its immediate allies is extremely modified to suit its fossorial habits (see Fig. 90). It is extremely broad and strong, its breadth being increased by the great development of the radial sesamoid (*rs*), which, being sickle-shaped, has received the special name of *os falciforme*. The ungual phalanges are very large, and cleft at their extremities.

In the CHIROPTERA, the hand is especially modified in a totally different manner, constituting the organ of flight.

In the carpus the scaphoid and lunar are united, and in some genera (as *Pteropus*) the cuneiform is joined with them, so that the proximal row contains but a single bone. There is no centrale. The pisiform is very small.

The pollex is short, divaricated from the other digits, not enveloped, as they are, in a cutaneous expansion, and armed with a curved claw. The other digits are extremely long and slender.

In the Frugivorous Bats (*Pteropus*) the second digit has a short ungual phalanx and claw, but in each of the other digits the middle phalanx is elongated, and gradually tapers to the termination, the ungual phalanx being absent.

In the Insectivorous Bats, the pollex alone has a claw, and the elongation of the other digits is chiefly due to the metacarpals, the phalanges being small and very slender, and usually only two in number, except in the third digit, which generally has three.

In the RODENTIA, the scaphoid and lunar are very generally united (as in *Castor, Dasyprocta, Hydrochœrus, Capromys, Sciurus, Arctomys, Mus*, &c.), but not in all. An os centrale is present in many as *Lepus, Dasyprocta, Hydrochœrus, Capromys*, and *Castor*, while in other genera it is absent. There is very frequently an accessory ossicle on the radial side of the carpus, which is particularly large in the Beaver (Fig. 91). There are nearly always five digits, with the normal number of phalanges, though sometimes (as in *Hydrochœrus*) the pollex is rudimentary or suppressed.

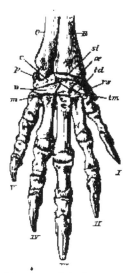

FIG. 91.—Bones of the manus of the Beaver (*Castor canadensis*), ⅓.

In the Cape Hyrax (Fig. 92, p. 264) there is an additional
carpal bone (*ce*), which appears to be an os centrale, though
in form and situation it looks as if it were a dismemberment
of the proximal part of the trapezoid (*td*). The scaphoid
and lunar are not united, and there are five digits, of which
the first is extremely small, and has only one minute
nodular phalanx. In another species, *H. dorsalis*, the pollex
is reduced to a short metacarpal; the fifth digit has but
two phalanges, and the centrale is united with the trapezoid.
The ungual phalanges of the three middle digits are small,
and somewhat conical in form.

In the Elephant the manus is short and broad, the carpal
bones are massive and square, and articulate by very flat
surfaces; they consist of scaphoid, lunar and cuneiform, a
pisiform and the usual four bones of the distal row, all

distinct, without the centrale. There are five digits, with short stout phalanges, the terminal ones being very small and rounded.

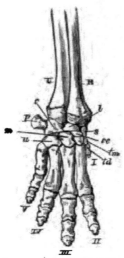

FIG. 92.—Bones of the manus of Cape Hyrax (*Hyrax capensis*), nat. size.

Order UNGULATA.—All the known animals of this order agree in the complete suppression of the pollex, in the absence of an os centrale, and in the complete separation of the scaphoid and lunar. The carpus is very compact, the bones being generally more or less square, and articulating by flat surfaces with each other, and with the radius and ulnar above. They are eminently digitigrade, the limb being entirely supported on the ungual phalanges, which are large, and encased in a hoof.

The digits are arranged according to one or the other of two distinct types, each characteristic of, and giving name to, one of the sub-orders.

1. The *Perissodactyla*, or "odd-toed" Ungulates, have the middle or third digit the longest, and symmetrical in itself, the free border of the ungual phalanx being evenly rounded. The second and fourth toes may be subequally developed, as in the Rhinoceros (Fig. 94), or they may be represented

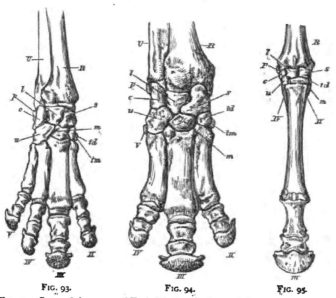

FIG. 93. FIG. 94. FIG. 95.

FIG. 93.—Bones of the manus of Tapir (*Tapirus malayanus*), ⅓.
FIG. 94.—Bones of the manus of Rhinoceros (*Rhinoceros sumatrensis*), ⅓.
FIG. 95.—Bones of the manus of a Horse (*Equus caballus*), ⅓. II and IV rudimentary metacarpals.

only by mere splint-like rudiments of their metacarpals, as in the Horse (Fig. 95). All intermediate conditions are met with in various extinct forms, as *Palæotherium, Anchitherium*, and *Hipparion*. In the Tapir (Fig. 93) there are four complete toes, in consequence of the fifth being developed, though it scarcely reaches the ground in walking. In other respects the foot resembles that of the Rhinoceros, the third toe being longest, and symmetrical in itself, and having on each side of it the nearly equal second and fourth. In the Rhinoceros there is a rudiment only of the fifth metacarpal.

In the Horse (Fig. 95), the three bones of the first row of the carpus are subequal. The second row consists of a very broad and flat magnum (*m*), supporting the great third metacarpal, having to its radial side the trapezoid (*td*), and to its ulnar side the unciform (*u*), which are both small, and articulate distally with the rudimentary second and fourth metacarpals. The pisiform is large and prominent, flattened and curved; it articulates partly to the cuneiform, and partly to the lower end of the radius. The single digit consists of a moderate-sized proximal, a very short middle, and a wide, semilunar, ungual phalanx. There is a pair of large nodular sesamoids behind the metacarpo-phalangeal articulation, and a single, transversely extended, "navicular" sesamoid behind the joint between the second and third phalanx.

2. The *Artiodactyla* have the third and fourth digits almost equally developed, and their ungual phalanges flattened on their inner or contiguous surfaces, so that each is asymmetrical in itself, but when the two are placed together they form a figure symmetrically disposed to a line drawn between them. Or, in other words, the axis or median line of the whole manus is a line drawn between the third and fourth digits, while in the Perissodactyles it is a line drawn down the centre of the third digit.

In the *Suina*, Pigs (Fig. 96), Peccaries, and Hippopotamus, the second and fifth toes are well developed, though always considerably smaller than the third and fourth, all four metacarpal bones are distinct, and the manus is comparatively broad. The second row of carpal bones in the

Pig consists of a small trapezoid, a moderate-sized magnum, and a large unciform. In the Hippopotamus there is also a trapezium.

In the ruminating sections of the sub-order (Figs. 97 and 98), the third and fourth metacarpals, though originally

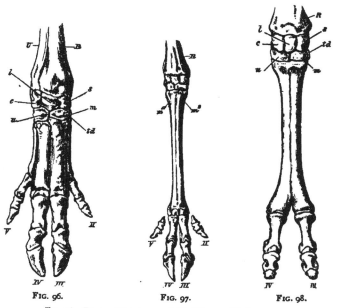

FIG. 96.   FIG. 97.   FIG. 98.

FIG. 96.—Bones of the manus of Pig (*Sus scrofa*), ⅓.
FIG. 97.—Bones of the manus of Red Deer (*Cervus elaphus*), ⅓.
FIG. 98.—Bones of the manus of Camel (*Camelus bactrianus*), ⅓.

distinct, become more or less conjoined, generally so as to form what appears externally to be a single bone, though traces of their separate origin always remain ; the two distal articular surfaces are quite distinct, each supporting a digit. The lateral (second and fifth) metacarpals and digits are generally rudimentary, sometimes completely absent. Sometimes not even the hoofs remain, as in the Giraffe and Prongbuck (*Antilocapra*); sometimes the hoofs alone, as in the Sheep and Ox, supported, it may be, by irregular nodules of bone, rudiments of the ungual phalanges. In the Deer (Fig. 97), the three phalanges are complete, sometimes with the lower end of the metacarpal, tapering above, and not directly attached to other parts of the skeleton of the foot. Rudiments of the proximal ends of the metacarpals are also often present. In the *Tragulina* alone these metacarpals are completely developed, and articulate with the carpus. In *Hyomoschus*, belonging to this section, the third and fourth metacarpals commonly remain distinct through life, so that the manus of this animal scarcely differs from that of one of the *Suina*.

The *Tylopoda*, or Camels, differ considerably from the true Ruminants in the structure of the fore-foot (see Fig. 98). In the carpus the trapezoid and magnum are distinct, as in the *Suina* and *Perissodactyla*, whereas these bones are confluent in the *Pecora* and *Tragulina*. There are no traces of any metacarpals or digits, except the third and fourth. The metacarpals of these are very long and, as in the *Pecora*, confluent throughout the greater part of their length, though separated for a considerable distance at the lower end. The distal articular surfaces, instead of being pulley-like, with deep ridges and grooves, are simple, rounded, and smooth. The proximal phalanges are expanded at their distal ends, and the wide and depressed middle phalanges are imbedded in a broad cutaneous pad, forming the sole of the foot, on which the animal rests in walking, instead of on the hoofs, as in other Ruminants. The ungual phalanges are very small and nodular, not flattened on their inner or apposed surfaces, and not completely encased in hoofs. These characters are better marked in the true Camels than in the Llamas.

In the animals constituting the order CETACEA, the manus has undergone a special modification, being converted into a simple, flattened, oval or falciform, usually pointed flipper or paddle, showing externally no signs of division into separate digits, nor any traces of nails or claws. The skeleton, however, consists, as in other Mammals, of a carpus, metacarpus, and either four, or more commonly five, digits, the great peculiarity of which is, that the number of phalanges is not limited to three, as in all other animals of the class, but may extend even to twelve or thirteen.

In the Whalebone Whales, a large portion of the skeleton of the hand remains permanently cartilaginous, and the cartilages composing the various carpal bones and phalanges are confluent or slightly separated from each other by interposed tracts of fibrous tissue, without any synovial joints. Nodules of bone are deposited in the centre of some of these cartilaginous masses, and slowly reach the surface as the animal attains maturity; there are commonly not more than five such ossifications. The phalanges appear like cylindrical or slightly flattened bony masses, with roughly truncated ends, set in a continuous rod of cartilage. In this way a certain amount of flexibility and elasticity is secured in the flipper, but beyond this there is no actual motion between the various bones of which it is composed.

The manus of the Right Whale (*Balæna mysticetus*) is comparatively short and very broad, having all five digits present, and being also extended on the ulnar side by a flattened cartilage projecting from the edge of the carpus, probably representing the pisiform bone. In an adult specimen there are only three distinct ossifications in the carpus.

The numbers in the digits are respectively I. 1, II. 4, III. 5, IV. 4, and V. 3. In the Rorquals (*Balænoptera*) the first digit is absent, and the manus is of an extremely elongated and narrow form. The carpus has five ossifications, and the number of phalanges varies somewhat in different species.

In the Odontocetes, the ossification of the skeleton of the manus is usually more complete than in the Whalebone Whales, the carpal bones generally coming in close contact at their edges, and assuming a somewhat polygonal form. The phalanges are also better ossified, often having epiphyses at each extremity, and they are connected together by imperfect synovial joints. They are always very much flattened, and their extremities being truncated and their sides nearly parallel, they are either square or oblong in form. In size they gradually decrease to the end of the digit, the last often consisting of minute nodules or granules, so irregularly or imperfectly ossified, and so easily lost in cleaning, that it is in many cases impossible, when describing the skeleton of one of these animals, to give the exact number of phalanges to each digit.

The determination of the homologies of the carpal bones of the Cetacea with those of other Mammalia is beset with difficulties, and has consequently led to some differences of opinion among those anatomists who have attempted it. Moreover every species appears liable to certain individual variations, and sometimes the different sides of the same animal are not precisely alike, either in the arrangement, or even the number of the carpal ossifications.

The pisiform is occasionally represented by a small ossification on the ulnar border of the carpus. Excluding the above, the carpus of the Odontocetes appears never to consist of more than six bones, three belonging to the proximal, and three to the distal row.

The three bones of the proximal row are constant, and may easily be identified as corresponding to the scaphoid, lunar and cuneiform of human anatomy, or the *radiale, intermedium,* and *ulnare* of Gegenbaur. The middle one is usually the largest and most thoroughly ossified.

The three bones of the distal row are generally represented by distinct ossifications (corresponding apparently with the trapezoid, magnum, and unciform) in the genera *Hyperoodon, Beluga,* and *Monodon.*

In most cases (see Fig. 99) the bones of the distal row of the carpus are reduced to two, which appear to correspond best with the trapezoid and unciform, the magnum being either absent or amalgamated with the trapezoid.[1]

The trapezium appears never to be present as a distinct bone, although the first metacarpal so often assumes the characters and position of a carpal bone, that it may easily be taken for it.

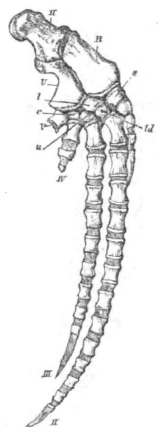

Fig. 99.—Dorsal surface of bones of right anterior limb of Round-headed Dolphin (*Globiocephalus melas*). ₁/₃. The shaded portions of the digits are cartilaginous.

[1] For the reasons for these determinations see " On the Osteology of the Sperm Whale ;" Trans. Zoological Society, vol. vi. p. 360.

The cuneiform always directly supports the fifth meta-carpal, and frequently some part of the fourth. Moreover, in those species in which the ulnar side of the carpus is greatly reduced, as *Globiocephalus*, the fifth metacarpal is even connected with the ulna.

In the Cachalot (*Physeter*) many of the carpal bones, in addition to the usual central nucleus, have epiphysial ossifications developed in the periphery of the cartilage, which ultimately unite with the central piece of bone.

All the Cetacea with teeth have five digits, though the first is usually rudimentary, and in close contact with the metacarpal of the second. In some forms, as *Physeter*, *Hyperoodon*, *Monodon*, *Beluga*, *Inia*, *Platanista*, and *Orca*, the manus is short, broad, and rounded at its distal extremity; the digits being nearly equally developed, spreading from each other, and without any excessive number of phalanges. In the Grampus (*Orca*) all the phalanges are broader than they are long.[1] In the Round-headed Dolphins (*Globiocephalus*, Fig. 9b), on the other hand, it is extremely elongated, narrow, and pointed. This elongation is mainly due to the great development of the second, and, though to a less extent, of the third digit; the fourth and fifth being quite short, and having but few phalanges. The number of phalanges (including the metacarpals) in the different digits are respectively I. 4, II. 14, III. 9, IV. 3, and V. 1.

In the common Dolphin (*Delphinus*) the manus has the same essential form, though in a less exaggerated degree, the numbers of the phalanges being I. 2, II. 10, III. 7, IV. 3, and V. 1. The digits are all in close contact.

Order SIRENIA.—Though in external form, and in being

[1] This genus is remarkable for the imperfect ossification of the carpal bones.

enclosed in an undivided integument, the terminal segment of the fore limb of the animals constituting this order much resembles that of the Cetacea, its skeleton is totally different.

The carpus is short and broad. In the genus *Manatus* the seven most usual bones of this region are all distinct, though there is no pisiform. The trapezoid is very small, and placed almost on the dorsal surface of the trapezium. The cuneiform is large, and supports the greater part of the fifth metacarpal. In *Halicore* many of the bones of the carpus usually coalesce; thus the first row may consist of two bones, a scapho-lunar and a cuneiform, and all the bones of the second row may unite together.

In both genera the digits are five in number, with moderately elongated and flattened phalanges, which are never increased in number beyond the limit usual in the Mammalia.

Among the animals constituting the Order EDENTATA there is great diversity in the structure of the fore-foot. They agree, however, in wanting an os centrale, and (with the exception of *Manis*) in the presence of distinct scaphoid and lunar bones.

In the existing Sloths the whole manus is long, very narrow, habitually curved, and terminating in two or three pointed, curved claws, in close apposition with each other, incapable, in fact, of being divaricated, so that it is reduced to the condition of a hook, by which the animal suspends itself to the boughs of the trees among which it lives.

The carpus is small, and articulates by a smooth rounded surface with the lower end of the radius. In the Three-toed Sloths (genus *Bradypus*) it consists of distinct scaphoid, lunar, and cuneiform bones in the first row, but usually of only two bones in the second row, the unciform and a connate magnum and trapezoid, the trapezium being generally

T

ankylosed to the rudimentary first metacarpal. There is a small rounded pisiform, but no radial sesamoid. The first and fifth metacarpals are present in a rudimentary condition, but have no phalanges. The three middle digits are nearly equally developed. The proximal phalanges are extremely short, and become soon ankylosed to the ends of the metacarpals, so that in adult animals one of the usual bones of the digit appears to be entirely wanting. The middle phalanges are long and compressed. The ungual phalanges are also long, much compressed, gently curved, and pointed. Bony laminæ reflected from their base encase and support the roots of the claws.

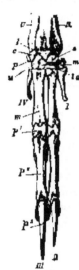

FIG. 100.—Bones of the right manus of the Two-toed Sloth (*Cholæpus didactylus*), ⅓.

In the Two-toed species (genus *Cholæpus*, Fig. 100), the magnum and trapezoid are distinct. The functional digits are the second and third, and there are rudiments of the first and fourth metacarpals, though not of the fifth. The proximal phalanges (p^1) are extremely short, as in *Bradypus*, but do not ankylose with the metacarpals. The ungual phalanges are not so long as in *Bradypus*.

In the Pangolins (*Manis*) the scaphoid and lunar are united, but all the other carpal bones are distinct. There are five digits with the complete number of phalanges, which, except in the pollex, are short and broad. The distal ends of the ungual phalanges have deep median clefts. This phalanx in the third digit is immensely developed, and considerably so in the fourth. The first, second, and fifth digits are comparatively small.

In the Cape Anteater (*Orycteropus*) the pollex is entirely

suppressed, but all the other digits are well developed, and terminate in subequal, compressed, ungual phalanges of moderate size. The second and third digits are nearly equal, the fourth and fifth shorter. A sesamoid bone is developed on the dorsal side of the metacarpo-phalangeal articulations.

In the true Anteaters (*Myrmecophaga*) all the usual carpal bones are distinct. The unciform supports the fifth, fourth, and a considerable part of the third metacarpal. The first digit is very slender, the second also slender, with compressed phalanges of nearly equal length. The third digit is immensely developed; though its proximal phalanx is extremely short, its ungual phalanx is so long that the entire length of the digit exceeds that of the second. The fourth has a long and rather slender metacarpal, and three phalanges gradually diminishing in size, the ungual phalanx being very small. The fifth has the metacarpal nearly as long, but not so stout as the fourth, and followed by two small phalanges, the last rudimentary and conical.

The little Tree Anteater (*Cyclothurus didactylus*) has a remarkably modified manus. The third digit is greatly developed at the expense of all the others; it has a stout, short metacarpal, and but two phalanges, of which the most distal is large, compressed, pointed, and much curved, bearing a very strong hook-like claw. The second digit has the same number of phalanges, and bears a claw, but is very much more slender than the third. The fourth is represented only by a styliform metacarpal, and there are no traces of either the first or fifth digits of the typical manus. The pisiform is very large.

In the Armadillos (*Dasypodidæ*), the manus is stout and broad, with strongly developed ungual phalanges, adapted for digging and scratching. The fifth metacarpal articulates

with the cuneiform as well as the unciform.   There is always
a very large palmar sesamoid.   The digits are almost always
five in number, but vary much in relative size and structure.

In the six-banded Armadillos (genus *Dasypus*), all the
digits have the normal number of phalanges (see Fig. 101).
The first digit is rather short and especially slender ; the
second is the longest, and has all the phalanges, as well as

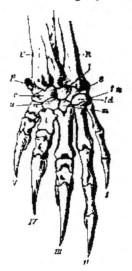
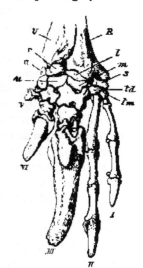

FIG. 101 —Bones of the right manus of the
Hairy Armadillo (*Dasypus villosus*), ⅓.

FIG. 102.—Bones of the manus of the
Great Armadillo (*Priodontes gigas*),
⅓. *a* an accessory carpal ossicle in
front of the pisiform, which is not seen
in the figure.

the metacarpal, of nearly equal length ; the third has a long
metacarpal, then two short broad phalanges, the first being
especially short, and a long, curved, compressed, ungual
phalanx.   The fourth and fifth are shorter, but present
the same general characters, and their metacarpals are also
reduced in length.

All the deviations from the normal type of manus observed in the common Armadillos, when greatly exaggerated, produce the curiously modified condition seen in the Cabassou (*Xenurus unicinctus*). The first and second digits are still more slender and elongated, and retain the normal number of phalanges ; but in the other three the metacarpal is short and broad, the proximal phalanx is either suppressed or incorporated with the metacarpal, as in some of the Sloths, the middle phalanx is very short, but the ungual phalanx is enormously developed, larger in the third than in the fourth and fifth digits.

A still further modification of the same type is seen in the extraordinary manus of the great Armadillo (*Priodontes gigas*), the largest existing member of the group (Fig. 102). The metacarpals of the three outer toes are still further reduced in length, the ungual phalanx of the third is increased in size, while that of the fourth, and especially the fifth, greatly diminished.

In the genus *Tolypeutes*, the manus is formed on a somewhat similar type ; but in the Nine-banded Armadillos (genus *Tatusia*) it is altogether different, the second and third toes being subequal (the third the longest), with moderate, conical, and slightly compressed ungual phalanges ; and the first and fourth also nearly equal and smaller, all with the normal number of phalanges. The fifth is absent, or (as in *T. hybrida*) represented by three very rudimentary nodular bones.

Order MARSUPIALIA.—The carpus never has a distinct os centrale. It is commonly stated that there is a scapholunar bone ; but the lunar, though always small, is distinct in *Didelphys*, *Perameles*, *Dasyurus*, *Thylacinus*, *Phalangista*, and *Hypsiprymnus* (where it is very minute) ; and its absence in *Macropus* appears to be due rather to suppression than to coalescence with the scaphoid. In *Phascolomys* a small lunar is present in some individuals, and not in others.

With the exception of the genus *Chœropus*, all known Marsupials possess the normal number of digits and phalanges, and the manus is short and rather broad, with moderately developed, compressed, curved, ungual phalanges.

FIG. 103.—Bones of manus of Bandicoot (*Perameles*), × 1½.　　FIG. 104.—Bones of manus of *Chœropus castanotis*, × 2.

The little "pig-footed" insectivorous-Marsupial *Chœropus castanotis*, belonging to the family *Peramelidœ*, has a remarkably modified manus (see Fig. 104), in which only two digits are functionally developed; and as the metacarpals are very long, and closely pressed together (though not ankylosed), and the phalanges are short, and the nails rather hoof-like, the whole manus has much general resemblance to that of the Artiodactyle Ungulates. It presents, however, the essential difference that the functional digits are the second and third of the normal series, instead of the third and fourth. This is proved by comparing it with the less modified manus of a true *Perameles* (Fig. 103). The principal changes from the typical mammalian manus observed in *Perameles* are the great reduction of the first and fifth digits; while the second, third, and fourth remain functional, with long ungual phalanges cleft mesially at their extremities. The third is longer than the second, and this longer than the fourth. In *Chæropus* the second and third remain, and retain their relative size, though comparatively longer, more slender, and with smaller ungual phalanges. The fourth digit is rudimentary, but with the normal number of phalanges; the first and fifth are entirely suppressed. The carpal bones have their normal relations, but the trapezium is exceedingly reduced.

Order MONOTREMATA.—In the Echidna the carpus is short and broad, and has a very complex articulation with the distal ends of the radius and ulna. The first row consists of a scapho-lunar and a cuneiform. There is no central. The distal row has the usual four bones. The pisiform is large, and articulates with the ulna as well as the cuneiform, and there is a small radial sesamoid, articulating with the scapho-lunar. There are two large sesamoids, sometimes united, in the palmar tendons. The digits are five in number, all with the normal number of phalanges, which are short and broad, except those that bear the long, slightly curved, broad nails, with which the animal scratches and burrows in the ground. The pollex is more slender than the other digits; it is of about the same length as the fifth, the second and fourth are nearly equal and longer, and the third slightly the longest.

In the Ornithorhynchus the manus is comparatively more slender and elongated; but the number and arrangement of the bones are the same as in the Echidna.

CHAPTER XVII.

THE PELVIC GIRDLE.

THE posterior limb consists of a pelvic girdle and three segments belonging to the limb proper, viz. the thigh, the leg, and the foot, or *pes*.

The PELVIC GIRDLE is present in some form in all Mammals, though in the Cetacea and the Sirenia it is in an exceedingly rudimentary condition.

In all Mammals, except those belonging to the two orders just named, each lateral half of the pelvic girdle consists primitively, like the corresponding part of the anterior limb, of a rod of cartilage crossing the long axis of the trunk, having an upper or dorsal, and a lower or ventral, end. The upper end diverges from that of the opposite side, but the lower end approaches, and, in most cases, meets it, forming a *symphysis*, without the intervention of any bone corresponding to the sternum.

The pelvic girdle differs from the shoulder girdle in being articulated to the vertebral column, at a point near to, but not at, the upper end of the rod.

Like the shoulder girdle, it bears on its outer side, near the middle, a cup-shaped articular cavity (*acetabulum* or *cotyloid* cavity, Fig. 105, *a*, p. 282), into which the proximal extremity of the first bone of the limb proper is received.

Like the shoulder girdle, it is divided by its mode of ossification, into an upper (*dorsal*) and a lower (*ventral*) segment, and the point of union between these is near the middle of the articular cavity.

Unlike the shoulder girdle of most Mammals, the lower segment is always largely developed, and ossifies from two

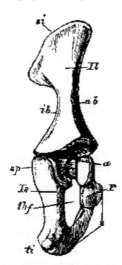

FIG. 105.—External surface of right innominate bone of a young Lamb (*Ovis aries*), ⅔. *Il* ilium (gluteal surface); *si* supra-iliac border; *ab* acetabular border; *ib* ischial border; *Is* ischium; *sp* spine; *ti* tuberosity of ischium; *P* pubis; *s* symphysis; *thf* thyroid or obturator foramen; *a* acetabulum.

separate centres, which form an anterior and a posterior bar, in contact above and below, but leaving a space between them in the middle, filled only by membrane, and called the *thyroid* or *obturator* foramen (*thf*).

The upper segment is named the *ilium* (*Il*), the anterior bar of the lower segment the *pubis* (*P*), and the posterior bar the *ischium* (*Is*). In the process of growth these three osseous pieces always coalesce into a single bone, called the *os innominatum.*

This is further completed by the addition of epiphyses ; one for the upper extremity of the ilium (corresponding to the suprascapular epiphysis of the shoulder), others for the most prominent parts of the lower or free borders of the pubis and ischium (symphysis pubis and tuber ischii), and also certain epiphysial ossifications developed in the cartilage, at the place of junction of the three main elements.

There is never any secondary osseous bar in the pelvic girdle corresponding to the clavicle of the upper extremity.

The ilium of Mammals is essentially an elongated, three-sided, or prismatic bone, though the relative size and position of the various surfaces and angles may differ greatly in different species. In the most characteristic form, one of the surfaces is internal, or directed towards the vertebral column, articulating by a flat irregular surface with the lateral " pleuropophysial " ossifications of the sacral vertebræ. This may be called the *sacral surface* (see Figs. 106 and 107, p. 285, and Fig. 108, *ss*, p. 293). Another is directed mainly forwards, and may be called anterior or *iliac* (*is*), as it gives origin to the iliacus muscle. The third is posterior or *gluteal* (*gs*), as it gives origin to the gluteal muscles.

Of the borders one is external or *acetabular* (*ab*), as it ends below at the margin of the acetabulum ; another is antero-internal or *pubic* (*pb*), and the third is postero-internal or *ischial* (*ib*), so called because they end below by joining the pubis and the ischium respectively.

The innominate bone is always placed more or less obliquely to the vertebral column, the upper or iliac end inclining forwards, and the lower or ischio-pubic end turning backwards, contrary to the usual direction of the scapular arch. In order to give still greater stability and fixity to the pelvic girdle, and to incorporate it more completely for mechanical purposes with the vertebral column, there is, in addition to the articulation between the ilium and true sacral vertebræ, a very strong double ligamentous union between the ischium and the side of the anterior caudal or pseudosacral vertebræ, constituting the greater and lesser sacro-sciatic ligaments, which are replaced in some Mammals (as most of the Edentata) by a complete bony union.[1]

The two innominate bones, together with the sacrum, constitute the *pelvis*, a complete circle of bone, or rather a short tube. This has two outlets: an anterior (sometimes called *inlet* or *brim*) bounded by the inferior surface of the first sacral vertebra above, by the pubic borders of the ilia laterally, and by the anterior borders of the converging pubic bones, meeting at the symphysis below; and a posterior outlet, bounded by the posterior part of the sacrum above, by the great sacro-sciatic ligaments laterally, and by the converging posterior borders of the ischia below. In consequence of the oblique position of the innominate bones, the plane of the anterior outlet (in the horizontal position of the body) looks downwards and forwards; that of the posterior outlet upwards and backwards; but these two planes do not exactly coincide, the long axis of the cavity being usually more or less curved.

Modifications of the Pelvic Girdle in the different Groups of Mammalia.

Order PRIMATES.—The pelvis of Man is very considerably modified from the usual form met with in Mammals.

---

[1] Practically, though not morphologically, the pelvis is a part of the trunk or axial skeleton. The functions of the hind limb in propelling and raising the body necessitate that it should be so.

The innominate bone (Fig. 106) is remarkably broad in
proportion to its length. The ilium is flattened and expanded, and has a greatly extended, almost semicircular,
supra-iliac border (*si*). The sacral surface (*ss*) is small, and
scarcely rises above the vertebral attachment. The iliac

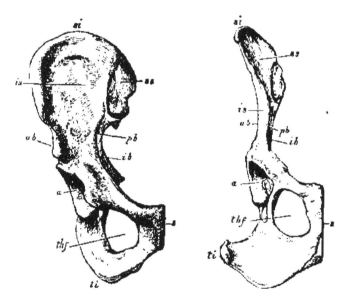

Fig. 106.—Ventral surface of right innominate bone of Man, ½.

Fig. 107.—Ventral surface of right innominate bone of Dog, ½.

si supra-iliac border or crest of the ilium ; *ss* sacral surface ; *is* iliac surface ; *ab*
   acetabular border ; *pb* pubic border ; *ib* ischial border of ilium ; *a* acetabulum ; *thf*
   thyroid foramen ; *ti* tuberosity of ischium ; *s* symphysis of pubis.

surface (*is*) is very broad and hollowed. The gluteal surface
is likewise much expanded, and, though presenting several
curves, is, in the main, convex. The acetabular border (*ab*)
is very short, and has a strong, rounded, rough prominence
for the attachment of the tendon of the *rectus* (extensor)

muscle of the leg. The pubic border (*pb*) is slightly marked, constituting the *linea arcuata interna*, or *linea ilio-pectinea* of human anatomy. The ischial border (*ib*) is short and deeply hollowed. The acetabulum (*a*) is large, circular, with very prominent borders, incomplete only for a small space on the infero-internal aspect.

The pubis and ischium are short, and widely divergent from each other, so that the thyroid foramen (*thf*) is elongated in the direction across the main axis of the bones. The symphysis (*s*) is rather short, and formed by the pubis alone. Each of the apposed surfaces of bone is capped by a plate of fibro-cartilage; these are held together by strong ligamentous fibres, while between them there is usually a more or less perfect synovial cavity. Ankylosis at this spot, so common in the lower Mammalia, very rarely takes place in Man.

The posterior and inferior border of the ischium is thickened and rounded, and distinguished as the *tuber ischii* (*ti*). Above this, on the hinder border of the same bone, is a smooth, hollowed surface, called the lesser sciatic notch, surmounted by an angular prominence called the *spine;* above the spine the edge of the ischium passes into the great concavity of the posterior or ischial border of the ilium, and which is called the great sciatic, or, more properly, ilio-ischiatic notch. The strong ligaments (sacrosciatic) which pass from the side of the pseudo-sacral and caudal vertebræ, the one to the tuber and the other to the spine of the ischium, convert these notches in the living body into foramina.

The anterior or superior (in the vertical position) outlet of the pelvis is subcircular, usually rather broader from side to side than from the vertebral to the pubic border. Its plane is not far from a right angle with the axis of the vertebral

column. The posterior outlet is also very wide. In consequence of the great curve of the sacrum, and the shortness of the symphysis, the axis of the whole pelvis is
strongly curved.

In all the *Simiina* the innominate bone, especially the
iliac portion, is more elongated than in Man; the anterior
outlet of the pelvis is longer from above downwards, narrower, and more oblique; the tuberosities of the ischia are
more everted, and the spine and sciatic notches less marked.

In the highest forms, such as the Gorilla and Chimpanzee,
the upper part of the ilium is expanded, flattened, and everted,
the iliac surface being even wider than in Man, though much
flatter; but in the Baboons and Monkeys, the whole ilium is
long and narrow, the sacral surface rises considerably above
the sacral articulation, the iliac surface is narrow, the gluteal
surface is very hollow, and the borders all approximate to
straight and parallel lines. In the Old World monkeys
the tuberosities of the ischia are greatly everted, and terminate in broad, triangular, flattened, rough surfaces, to
which the ischial cutaneous callosities are attached.

In the true Lemurs the pelvis is very wide; the ilia are
long, narrow, and have a sigmoid curve, while the pubes
approach each other at the symphysis at a very open angle,
giving an elegant lyre shape to the anterior outline of the
pelvis. On the other hand, in the genus *Loris* of the same
group (and to a less extent in *Tarsius*, *Perodicticus*, and
others) the cavity of the pelvis is remarkably narrow from
side to side; the ilia are straight slender rods, from the
lower end of which the large, flattened, and compressed
pubes project forward at a right angle, forming a prominent
keel at the symphysis.

In the CARNIVORA the pelvis is generally elongated and
narrow, the ilium and ischium being in a straight line, and

of nearly equal length. In most species the ilia are straight, flattened, and not everted above (see Fig. 107, p. 285); the iliac surface (*is*) is very narrow, and confined to the lower part of the bone, as the acetabular and pubic borders meet in front above; the gluteal surface looks directly outwards and is concave; the sacral surface (*ss*) forms a broad flat plane above the attachment to the sacrum, the crest being formed by the united edges of the sacral and gluteal surfaces, instead of the iliac and gluteal surfaces, as in Man. The symphysis is long; it includes part of both pubis and ischium, and commonly becomes completely osseous in adult animals. The thyroid foramen (*thf*) is oval, with its long axis parallel to that of the whole bone. The ischia are wide and divergent posteriorly.

In the Hyæna the pelvis is shorter and wider than in most other Carnivora, both the upper ends of the ilia and lower ends of the ischia being considerably everted.

In the Bears the ilia are short and everted above.

In the Seals the pelvis is small, and of a different form from that of the terrestrial Carnivora. The ilia are exceedingly short, and with much everted upper borders; the pubes and ischia are very long and slender, enclosing a long and narrow obturator foramen, and meeting at a symphysis of very small extent, in which the bones of the two sides are very slightly connected, and capable of being widely separated during parturition.

The pelvis of the INSECTIVORA varies considerably in form. In *Rhynchocyon*, *Macroscelides*, and *Tupaia*, the symphysis is long, as in the Carnivora, and becomes ankylosed; in *Erinaceus* it is short, though the bones of the two sides are in contact; but in many other genera the pubic bones are widely separated in the middle line below.

The Mole has an exceedingly long, narrow, and straight pelvis, the innominate bones lying almost parallel with the vertebral column. Both ilium and upper end of the ischium are firmly ankylosed with the sacrum, leaving a small sacro-sciatic foramen between them. Though the pubic bones do not quite meet in the middle line below, the brim of the pelvis is extremely contracted, and the pelvic viscera pass below and external to the cavity instead of through it. The pubes and ischia are very long and straight, and enclose a large, but narrow, oval thyroid foramen.

In the CHIROPTERA, the pelvis is small and narrow; the ilia are rod-like, the pubes and ischia are not in a line with them, but project forwards. The symphysis is often not closed. There is usually a strongly developed "pectineal" process, near the acetabular end of the anterior border of the pubis, to which the *psoas parvus* muscle is attached.

In many of the RODENTIA, as the Beaver, the ilia are markedly trihedral, with sides of nearly equal extent; but in the Hares, the outer (acetabular) border is almost obsolete, the gluteal and iliac surfaces are confluent, and both face outwards, and the internal surface is largely developed above the sacral attachment.

The pubes and ischia are always largely developed, flat, and diverging posteriorly, the obturator foramen is of considerable size, and the symphysis is long, and usually becomes osseous; in the Guinea Pig (*Cavia*), however, it remains ligamentous, and the bones are widely separated during parturition.

Order UNGULATA.—In the *Pecora* the pelvis generally is elongated. The ilium is expanded and everted at the upper extremity; but between the sacral attachment and the acetabulum it is much contracted, and its borders rounded, so that the divisions of its surfaces are no longer distinct.

There is usually a deep oval depression above the acetabulum, just within the attachment of the rectus muscle. The anterior outlet forms a regular oval with the long diameter between the sacrum and symphysis. The latter is very long, including a considerable portion of the ischia. The margins of the bones are completed by large epiphyses in this region, but ultimately coalesce across the middle line. The ischia are much developed; the tuberosities are large, and have on the middle of their outer side a well-marked conical process, directed outwards, and very characteristic of this group of animals.

In the Giraffe the pelvis is shorter than in most of the other Pecora; the upper ends of the ilia are more expanded, the thyroid foramen is nearly circular, and the supra-acetabular fossa is almost obsolete.

These characters are still more strongly marked in the Camels; while, on the other hand, in the Pigs the pelvis is elongated, and much resembles that of the Pecora, but the supra-acetabular fossa is wanting.

In the *Perissodactyla*, the ilia are widely expanded above, but much contracted on approaching the acetabulum. The ischia are less elongated than in the Pecora, and the thyroid foramen is more circular.

The Elephant has a very peculiar pelvis, the form of the ilium, and the arrangement of its surfaces, somewhat recalling those of the human pelvis. The supra-iliac border or crest is greatly extended and curves outwards and downwards. The sacral surface of the ilium is narrow, and scarcely rises above the attachment to the sacrum. The iliac and gluteal surfaces are widely expanded, especially at the upper part, and, the pelvis being set nearly vertically to the vertebral column, they face almost directly forwards and backwards. The outer or acetabular border is short and deeply hollowed.

The pubic and ischial portions are comparatively small, the latter being very little produced backwards beyond the symphysis.

In the SIRENIA, the pelvis is extremely rudimentary, being composed, in the Dugong, of two slender, elongated bones on each side, placed end to end, and commonly ankylosing together. The upper one, which represents the ilium, is connected by a ligament with the end of the transverse process of the sacral vertebra; the lower one is the ischium, or ischium and pubis combined, and approaches, though it does not meet, its fellow of the opposite side.

In the adult Manati, the innominate bone is represented by a single irregular triangular bone, connected by rather long ligaments with the vertebral column above, and with the opposite bone across the middle line.

There is no trace of an acetabulum, or of any portion of the limb proper in any of the existing Sirenia; but in the extinct *Halitherium* an acetabular depression and rudimentary femur have been discovered.

In the CETACEA the pelvis is reduced to a pair of elongated, slender bones (each of which ossifies from a single centre), placed on each side of, and rather below, the vertebral column, lying nearly parallel to its long axis (though they converge somewhat anteriorly), and opposite the spot where the chevron bones commence to be developed beneath the bodies of the vertebræ. These bones probably represent the ischia, and their principal function is to give attachment to the crura' of the penis or clitoris, as the case may be. Hence they are usually more largely developed in the male than in the female.

In the Whalebone Whales they usually have a projecting angle placed about the middle, near which, in some species, a second small bone, which probably represents the femur, is attached by ligament (see Fig. 112, p. 303). In a full-grown male Rorqual (*Balænoptera musculus*), sixty-seven feet in length, each pelvic bone was sixteen inches long. In the Greenland Whale (*Balæna mysticetus*), they are rather shorter and stouter. As might be expected, from the rudimentary character of these bones, they vary considerably in size and form in different individuals of the same species, and often on the two sides of the same animal.

In the Dolphins, they are generally smaller, and more simple than in the Whalebone Whales, and usually quite straight, though sometimes arched, or presenting a sigmoid curve.

Order EDENTATA.—In the Sloths, the pelvis is very short and wide, with tolerably broad flattened ilia, and slender pubes and ischia, enclosing a large oval thyroid foramen, the inferior boundary of which, and the extremely narrow ossified symphysis, are formed by the pubis alone. The spine of the ischium is produced backwards to unite with the transverse processes of some of the pseudosacral vertebræ, enclosing a sacro-sciatic foramen. The sacro-iliac articulation is commonly ankylosed.

In all the other Edentates the pelvis is more or less elongated, the ilia trihedral, the ischia largely developed, the pubes slender, the symphysis exceedingly short, but usually ossified, and the thyroid foramen large. In all, except *Orycteropus*, the ischia unite with the vertebral column. This union is carried to its greatest extent in the Armadillos, in which animals the broad transverse processes of as many as five pseudosacral vertebræ may coalesce with each other and with the side of the ischium, converting the pelvis into a long bony tube, the more so as the ilia are also firmly and extensively united with the true sacrum. There is usually, especially in *Orycteropus*, a strongly developed "pectineal" tubercle.

Order MARSUPIALIA.—In the American Opossums (*Didel-phys*), the ilium is a very simple, straight, three-sided rod, thicker at its upper than at its acetabular end, each side being nearly equal in extent, hollowed, and sharply defined by prominent straight borders.

In the Kangaroo (*Macropus*, Fig. 108), the three surfaces of the ilium are also well marked and nearly equal; but the whole bone is curved outwards at the upper end.

In the Thylacine and Dasyures the ilia are compressed laterally, the ace-tabular and pubic borders meeting above in front, so that the iliac surface is (as in the Carnivora) very narrow, and disappears in the upper half of the bone, the "crest" being formed by the united edges of the sacral and gluteal surfaces; whereas in the wide, depressed pelvis of the Wombat (*Phascolomys*), the flattening has taken place in the contrary direction, and the iliac surface spreads out to form with the gluteal surface behind, a wide, arching, supra-iliac border or crest.

The ischia and pubes are always largely developed, and the symphysis is long and generally ossified. In the Kangaroos the pectineal tubercle (*pt*) of the pubis is strongly developed.

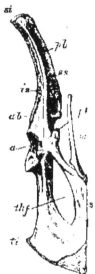

FIG. 108.—Ventral surface of innominate bone of Kangaroo (*Macropus major*), ¼. *si* supra-iliac border ; *ss* sacral surface ; *is* iliac surface ; *ab* acetabular border ; *pb* pubic border of ilium ; *pt* pectineal tubercle ; *a* acetabulum ; *thf* thyroid foramen ; *ti* tuberosity of ischium ; *s* symphysis ; *m* "marsupial" bone.

Nearly all Marsupials have a pair of elongated, flattened, slightly curved bones (Fig. 108, *m*), moveably articulated by one extremity to the anterior edge of the pubis, near the symphysis, and, passing forwards, diverging from each other, within the layers of the abdominal parietes. They are, in fact, ossifications in, or intimately connected with, the inner tendon or "pillar" of the external oblique muscle, and therefore come under the category of sesamoid bones. They vary in size and shape in different species. In *Didelphys* they are nearly as long as the ilia, while in the Kangaroo they are scarcely half the length of that bone. Though largely developed in the Dasyures, in the allied genus *Thylacinus*, they are represented only by small, unossified fibrocartilages.

These bones are commonly called "marsupial bones," though they have no special function relating to the ventral pouch of the female, being nearly equally developed in both sexes, and also in those species in which the marsupium is not present.

In the MONOTREMATA the pelvis is short and broad. The ilia are short, distinctly trihedral and everted above. The ischia are large, and prolonged into a considerable backward-directed tuberosity. The symphysis is long, and formed about equally by pubes and ischium. The thyroid foramen is round. The pectineal tubercle is greatly developed. There are large "marsupial" bones in both genera.

CHAPTER XVIII.

THE THIGH AND LEG.

THE skeleton of the first segment of the limb proper consists of an elongated, more or less cylindrical bone, the *femur*, which is described as having a shaft and two extremities.

The dorsal, or (in the ordinary position of the limb) *anterior* surface of the shaft is smooth and rounded, from side to side, and generally arched somewhat forwards from above downwards; the ventral (or *posterior*) surface is more or less compressed, and has a rough longitudinal ridge, the *linea aspera*.

At the proximal extremity is a hemispherical, smooth, articular "head" (Fig. 109, *h*, p. 296) which fits into the acetabulum of the innominate bone, and is generally more round and more distinctly separated from the rest of the bone by a constriction or "neck" (*n*) than is the corresponding part of the humerus. The axis of the head does not coincide with that of the shaft of the bone, but crosses it at an angle varying in different animals, being directed towards the preaxial[1] or (in the ordinary position of the limb) *internal* side, and slightly also towards the anterior aspect. In nearly all Mammals there is a rounded depres-

[1] See note to p. 242.

sion near the middle of the surface of the head into which the *ligamentum teres* of the hip-joint is inserted. Both ligament and depression are, however, wanting in the Orang Utan, Seals, Sea-Otter, Elephant, Sloths, and the Monotremata.

FIG. 109.—Right human femur, dorsal or anterior aspect, ½. The boundary lines of the various epiphyses are shown. *h* head; *n* neck; *gt* greater trochanter; *lt* lesser trochanter; *ec* external condyle; *ic* internal condyle.

Immediately below the neck of the femur are two tuberosities, called *trochanters*. One (*lt*) is a comparatively small, conical eminence, situated rather to the preaxial side, and called the *lesser trochanter*. The other (*gt*) is generally very prominent, projecting upwards, as high or higher than the top of the head, situated mainly on the postaxial border of the bone, but curving inwards and backwards at its extremity; this is called the *great trochanter*. To the posterior side of its base there is usually a deep depression, the *digital fossa*.

In some Mammals, as the Perissodactyle Ungulates, some Rodents and Edentates, there is a compressed ridge for muscular attachments, on the postaxial side of the shaft, a short distance below the great trochanter, distinguished as the *third trochanter*. (See Fig. 110, *t*, p. 301.)

The distal extremity of the femur is thickened, and has a large trochlear articular surface for the bones of the leg. This surface is narrow in front, and bounded by more or less prominent ridges; posteriorly it is divided by a deep median notch (*intercondylar*) into two prominent rounded eminences, called *condyles* (Fig. 109, *ec* and *ic*). The slightly elevated roughed portions of bone above the articular condyles are termed the tuberosities.

The femur has a main centre of ossification for the shaft, and epiphysial centres for the head, for each trochanter, and for the lower extremity. (See Fig. 109.) In most Mammals the great trochanter and head coalesce together before they join the shaft. The lower epiphysis is the last to become united.

The skeleton of the second segment of the limb consists of two bones, the *tibia* and *fibula*,[1] of which the former is the larger in all Mammals. These bones always lie in their primitive, unmodified position, parallel to each other, the tibia on the preaxial, and the fibula on the postaxial side, and are never either permanently crossed or capable of any considerable amount of rotation, as in the corresponding bones of the fore limb. In the ordinary walking position the tibia is internal, and the fibula external.

The tibia has an expanded proximal end, with a flattened articular surface, divided into two slightly concave facets, by a rough median eminence, to which the intra-articular or *crucial* ligaments of the knee-joint are attached. The shaft is usually more or less trihedral, with one flat surface directed backwards, and one border forwards. The upper end of this border is thickened into a rough tuberosity, into which the tendon of the great extensor muscles of the leg are inserted. The lower end is slightly expanded, and has a somewhat square articular surface to receive the proximal bone of the tarsus, or astragalus. The inner (or preaxial) side of the bone is prolonged beyond this surface, forming a process called *internal malleolus*, which is applied

---

[1] Also occasionally called *perone*, whence "peroneal," applied to structures in relation with it.

to the side of the astragalus, giving additional strength to the articulation, called " ankle-joint."

The fibula has a slender and generally compressed shaft, and is somewhat expanded at each extremity. Its upper end usually takes no part in the knee-joint, being connected, by a separate synovial joint, with the tibia just below that articulation. The lower end, however, forms the outer side of the ankle-joint, under the name of *external malleolus.*

In many Mammals the fibula is in a more or less rudimentary condition, and it often ankyloses with the tibia at one or both extremities.

As a general rule each of these bones has a principal centre of ossification for the shaft, and an epiphysis at either extremity.

In the neighbourhood of the knee-joint, certain sesamoid bones are often found in connection with the tendons which pass over the various bony prominences.

The largest and most constant is the *patella*, placed on the anterior surface of the joint, in the conjoined tendon of the four great extensor muscles of the leg, and having a smooth articular facet, which plays upon the narrow anterior part of the inferior articular surface of the femur, and forms part of the wall of the cavity of the knee-joint. This bone varies considerably in form, being in some cases broad, flattened, or lozenge-shaped, and in others, laterally compressed or oval. It is found in an ossified condition in all Mammals, with the exception of a few of the Marsupialia.

There are also very frequently smaller ossicles, one or two in number, situated behind the femoral condyles, called *fabellæ;* and occasionally there is a wedge-shaped bone within the joint, lying on the articular surface of the tibia, an ossification of the internal interarticular semilunar cartilage.

Special Characters of the Bones of the Thigh and Leg in the various Groups.

In Man, the femur (see Fig. 109, p. 296) is long and rather slender, the shaft is curved forwards, the head is large and globular, the neck elongated and narrow.

In the Gorilla, the femur is much shorter and broader; the head is smaller and less globular, the neck is shorter and set on the shaft more at a right angle. In the Chimpanzee the femur more resembles that of Man. In the Lemurs it is very slender and straight, the head is globular, and the neck very short.

The tibia and fibula are distinct, and well developed in all the Primates, and are united with each other only at their extremities. Fabellæ are wanting in the highest forms, but generally present in the others. The patella is usually broad and flat, and more or less lozenge-shaped.

In the terrestrial CARNIVORA, the femur is straight, moderately slender, and with rather a small head. The fibula is slender, and in the Dogs curved towards the tibia, the lower half being closely applied to that bone; but in the Bears, and many others, there is a considerable interval between the bones throughout, except at their articular extremities. Fabellæ are generally present.

In the Seals, the femur is exceedingly short, broad, and flattened, with a globular head and an extremely short neck. The fibula is almost as large as the tibia, especially at the distal end. These bones are commonly ankylosed together at their proximal extremities.

Among the INSECTIVORA, the Hedgehog has a strong ridge, below the great trochanter of the femur, and several other forms have a similar rudiment of a third trochanter. As a general rule the fibula is slender, and in its lower half ankylosed with the tibia, but it is complete and distinct in the genera *Galeopithecus, Tupaia, Centetes, Ericulus,* and *Solenodon.*

In the CHIROPTERA, the femur is slender and straight, with trochanters of nearly equal size, and with a small globular head, set on a very short neck, with its axis pointing almost directly to the anterior or dorsal surface of the bone. The fibula varies in condition. In *Pteropus* it is extremely slender, and the upper end is atrophied, but in many of the insectivorous Bats it is well developed.

In the RODENTIA the femur varies much. In the Hares and Squirrels it is long and slender, with a third trochanter immediately below the great trochanter. In the Beaver it is broad and flat, and has a strong ridge about the middle of the outer side of the shaft. In many other forms neither of these accessory prominences exist, but the great trochanter is usually much developed.

In some forms, as the Beaver, the fibula is distinct, strongly developed, and separated from the tibia, except at the extremities, by a wide interosseous space. In others, as the Hares, it is slender, and in its distal half united with the tibia. The patella is generally elongated, fabellæ are usually developed, and there are often wedge-shaped ossifications in the semilunar cartilages of the knee-joint.

In the UNGULATA, the femur is rather compressed, especially at the lower end. There is no distinct constriction of the neck, separating the head from the rest of the bone. The great trochanter is very large, and usually rises above the level of the head. The small trochanter is not very salient, and sometimes, as in the Rhinoceros (Fig. 110), is a mere rough ridge. The inner edge of the anterior part of the

inferior articular surface is very prominent. In all the
Perissodactyles there is a strongly marked third trochanter
(*t'*), in the form of a compressed ridge curving forwards.
This is entirely absent in all the known Artiodactyles.

FIG. 110.— Anterior aspect of right femur of Rhinoceros (*Rhinoceros indicus*), ⅓.
h head ; *t* great trochanter ; *t'* third trochanter.

The fibula is subject to great ' variations among the
different members of the order. In the Rhinoceros, Tapir,
Pig, and Hippopotamus it is complete and distinct, though
slender in proportion to the tibia. In the Horse a mere
styliform rudiment of the upper end is present.

In all *Pecora* and *Tylopoda*, a small distinct bone, having
a very definite form, articulating with the lower end of the
tibia, and forming the external malleolus, appears to
represent the distal extremity of the fibula (see Fig. 111).
There is occasionally in addition a slender styliform rudi-

ment of the proximal extremity, but the two are never united together by bone.

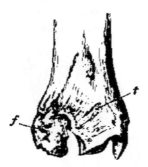

FIG. 111.—Anterior aspect of lower end of the right tibia and fibula of Red Deer (*Cervus elaphus*), ⅓. *t* tibia ; *f* fibula.

In the *Tragulina*, the fibula is long and slender, and complete, but its lower end is indistinguishably blended with the tibia.

The patella is well ossified, and usually somewhat triangular, with the broad end upwards ; but fabellæ are not commonly developed in the Ungulata.

In the Hyrax there is a slight ridge on the femur in the place of a third trochanter. The fibula is complete, thickest at its upper end, where it generally ankyloses with the tibia.

The femur of the Elephant is long and very straight ; the axis of the head is more in a line with that of the shaft than usual. The great trochanter is not much developed, and the small trochanter is nearly obsolete. The fibula is complete, distinct, and slender, though considerably enlarged at the lower end.

In the CETACEA, certain small nodular bones or cartilages attached by fibrous tissue to the outer side of the pelvic bone in some of the Whalebone Whales, are commonly regarded as rudimentary and functionless representatives of the skeleton of the hind limb. In the Greenland Whale (Fig. 112), there is a proximal, somewhat pear-shaped, bone (*f*), about eight inches in length, and a smaller conical distal bone (*t*), which may represent the femur and tibia respectively, as suggested by their disccverer, Professor Reinhardt.[1]

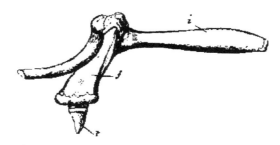

FIG. 112.—Side view of bones of posterior extremity of Greenland Right Whale (*Balæna mysticetus*), ⅓, from Eschricht and Reinhardt. *i* ischium ; *f* femur ; *t* accessory ossicle, probably representing the tibia.

In *Megaptera longimana* there is but one such bone, and in an adult Fin Whale (*Balænoptera musculus*), sixty-seven feet long, this was found to be only represented by an oval nodule of cartilage about the size of a walnut. Even this is wanting in some species of the group, as *B. rostrata*.

No trace of any structure representing the skeleton of the hind limb, beyond the pelvis, has yet been detected in any of the Odontocetes.

In none of the existing SIRENIA are there any rudiments of the hind limb proper, but the extinct *Halitherium* had an ossified femur, articulated to a well-defined acetabulum in the pelvis.

In the terrestrial and fossorial EDENTATA, the femur is generally short and broad. There is a third trochanter in

[1] See "Recent Memoirs on the Cetacea ;" Ray Society, 1866, p. 134.

the Armadillos and *Orycteropus*, and a sharp ridge along the whole external border in *Myrmecophaga*. The fibula is as long as the tibia; in the Armadillos these bones are commonly ankylosed together at each extremity, but curve away from each other at the middle, leaving a wide interosseous space. In the Anteaters they are both nearly straight and parallel.

In the Sloths the femur is long, slender, and flattened from before backwards. There is no third trochanter; the head is large and globular, and placed near the middle of the proximal end of the shaft, with the axis of which it more nearly coincides than in most Mammals. The tibia and fibula are complete, and more nearly equal in size than in most Mammals. They are both curved, so as to be separated considerably in the middle part of the leg. The lower end of the fibula has a conical prominence which turns inwards, and fits into a depression on the outer side of the articular surface of the astragalus, as a pivot into a socket.

In none of the MARSUPIALIA is a third trochanter present on the femur. The fibula is always well developed, and its upper extremity is often produced into a well-marked process, to the top of which a sesamoid bone is not unfrequently attached. In the climbing Australian Phalangers and Koalas, which have broad hind feet, with an opposable hallux, there is a greater freedom of movement between the fibula and tibia than in other Mammals, approaching in some degree to the rotation often permitted between the radius and ulna.

In the MONOTREMATA the femur (Fig. 113, *f*), is of very remarkable form, being short, flattened from before backwards, narrow in the middle of the shaft, and very broad at each end; the trochanters are nearly equal in size, and

The head placed between them on a very short neck, and with its axis directed quite towards the anterior or dorsal aspect of the bone. The fibula (f') is large and straight; it has a broad flattened process, completed by an epiphysis, pro-

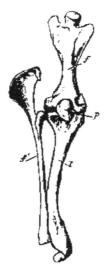

FIG. 113.—Anterior aspect of bones of right leg of *Ornithorhynchus paradoxus,* ½. *f* femur; *t* tibia; *f'* fibula; *p* patella.

jecting from the upper extremity above the point of articulation with the tibia, much resembling the olecranon of the fore limb. The tibia (t) is strongly curved.

CHAPTER XIX.

THE terminal segment of the hind limb is the foot or *pes*. Its skeleton presents in many particulars a close resemblance to that of the manus, being divisible into three parts :—(1) a group of short, more or less rounded or square-shaped bones, constituting the *tarsus*; (2) a series of long bones placed side by side, forming the *metatarsus*; and (3) the phalanges of the digits or toes (see Fig. 114, p. 308).

The metatarsal bones never exceed five in number, and the phalanges follow the same numerical rule as in the manus, never exceeding three in each digit. Moreover, the first digit (counting from the tibial side), or *hallux*, resembles the pollex of the hand in always having one segment less than the other digits.

The bones of the tarsus in many of the lower Vertebrata closely resemble both in number and arrangement those of the carpus, as shown in Fig. 85, p. 253. They have been described in their most generalized condition by Gegenbaur under the names expressed in the first column of the following table.[1] The names in the second column are those by which they are most generally known in this

[1] "Untersuchungen zur Vergleichenden Anatomie." Carpus und Tarsus. 1864.

country, and which will be used in the present work, while
in the third column some synonyms, occasionally employed,
are added.

Tibiale			
Intermedium	= Astragalus	=	*Talus.*
Fibulare	= Calcaneum	=	*Os calcis.*
Centrale	= Navicular	=	*Scaphoideum.*
Tarsale 1	= Internal Cuneiform	=	*Entocuneiforme.*
Tarsale 2	= Middle Cuneiform	=	*Mesocuneiforme.*
Tarsale 3	= External Cuneiform	=	*Ectocuneiforme.*
Tarsale 4			
Tarsale 5	Cuboid.		

The bones of the tarsus of Mammals present fewer diversities of number and arrangement than those of the carpus.
The proximal row (see Fig. 114) always consists of two
bones, the *astragalus* (*a*, which according to Gegenbaur's
view represents the coalesced scaphoid and lunar of the
hand) and the *calcaneum* (*c*). The former is placed more
to the dorsal side of the foot than the latter, and almost
exclusively furnishes the tarsal part of the tibio-tarsal or
ankle-joint. It has a rounded anterior or distal projection
called the " head." The calcaneum, placed more to the
ventral or "plantar" side of the foot, is elongated backwards to form a more or less prominent tuberosity, the *tuber
calcis*, to which the tendon of the great extensor muscles of
the foot is attached. The *navicular* bone (*n*) is interposed
between the proximal and distal row on the inner or tibial
side of the foot, but on the outer side the bones of the two
rows come into contact. The distal row, when complete,
consists of four bones, which, beginning on the inner side,
are the three *cuneiform* bones, internal (c^1), middle (c^2), and
external (c^3), articulated to the distal surface of the navicular,
and the *cuboid* (*cb*) articulated with the calcaneum. Of these

the middle cuneiform is usually the smallest in animals in
which all five digits are developed; but when the hallux is
wanting, the internal cuneiform may be rudimentary or
altogether absent.

FIG. 114.—Bones of a right human foot, showing the epiphyses, ⅓. *T* tarsus: *M*
metatarsus; *Ph* phalanges; *c* calcaneum; *a* astragalus: *cb* cuboid; *n* navicular;
c¹ internal cuneiform; *c²* middle cuneiform; *c³* external cuneiform; the digits are
indicated by Roman numerals, counting from the tibial to the fibular side.

The three cuneiform bones support the first, second, and
third metatarsals respectively, the cuboid supports the fourth
and fifth; they thus exactly correspond with the four bones
of the distal row of the carpus.

In addition to these constant tarsal bones, there may
be supplemental or sesamoid bones; one situated near the
middle of the tibial side of the tarsus, largely developed in
many Carnivora and Rodents; another, less frequent, on the

fibular side ; and a third often developed in the tendons of the plantar surface of the tarsus. There is also usually a pair of sesamoid bones opposite each metatarso-phalangeal articulation, on its plantar aspect.

The development of the bones of the foot corresponds in the main with that of the bones of the manus. Each tarsal bone is ossified from a single centre, but the calcaneum has in addition an epiphysis for the most projecting part or tuberosity. The four outer metatarsals have each one centre from which the shaft and proximal end is ossified, and a large epiphysis at the distal end ; the first metatarsal (if it should be so called) and all the phalanges have an epiphysis only at the proximal extremity. This rule is almost universal, the most notable exception being found in the Seals, in which animals (see Fig. 116, p. 313) each of the metatarsals and all the bones of the toes, except the terminal phalanges, have epiphyses at both ends of the shaft.

Order PRIMATES.—In Man (see Fig. 114) the foot is broad, and in the ordinary standing position the whole length of the plantar surface (at least its outer edge) rests on the ground, the main axis of the foot being at a right angle with that of the leg. The inner or tibial side of the foot is arched before backwards, each extremity only resting on the ground.

The tarsus is longer than the metatarsus, and the latter is longer than the digits, but the forms and relations of the tarsal bones are quite characteristic of the general Mammalian type, and the five digits are present with the complete number of phalanges. The hallux is much stouter than any of the others, though usually not quite so long as the second toe. Its metatarsal is articulated to a nearly flat surface on

the internal cuneiform, directed distally, so that it is placed
in the same plane as the other toes, and cannot be freely
separated from, or opposed to, them. There are no supplementary tarsal bones, and sesamoids are developed under
the metatarso-phalangeal joint of the hallux only. The
phalanges are much smaller, shorter, and more compressed
than are those of the manus. The ungual phalanges are
very small, depressed, and somewhat spatulate.

The principal distinction of the foot of the *Simiina* from
that of Man is that it is more or less modified into a grasping
organ. The tarsal and metatarsal bones and phalanges are
the same in number and relative position, but the articular
surface of the internal cuneiform for the hallux is saddle-
shaped, and is directed obliquely towards the inner or
tibial side of the foot. The consequence is that the hallux
is not only somewhat separated from the other digits, but
is also set in a different plane, so that when it is flexed it
turns towards the sole of the foot, and becomes opposed to
the others, much as the thumb does in the human hand. It
is this peculiarity of the pes which has given rise to the term
quadrumanous, or "four-handed," often applied to this
group of animals.

The hallux is usually relatively shorter than it is in Man.
In the Orang (*Simia satyrus*) it is particularly short, and
often wants the terminal phalanx, while the metacarpals and
the phalanges of the other digits are long and curved, the
proportions of the three segments of the foot being exactly
the reverse of those of Man, as the tarsal segment is
shortest, and the phalangeal the longest.

The form of the articular surface of the astragalus, and
especially the free mobility of the navicular and cuboid
bones on the astragalus and calcaneum cause the foot of
the Orang to be set very obliquely on the leg, so that when

placed on a level surface the fibular border only rests on the
ground, and the sole is directed inwards. This position suits
well for grasping vertically-placed boughs of trees, but is ill
adapted for standing or walking on the ground.   A similar
disposition is seen in a varying degree in most of the
Monkeys, but in none so markedly as the Orang, in which
animal all the peculiarities by which the simian is dis-

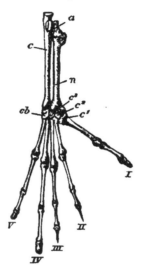

FIG. 115.—Right pes of *Tarsius spectrum* (nat. size). *a* astragalus ; *c* calcaneum
n navicular ; *c'* internal cuneiform ; *c²* middle cuneiform ; *c³* external cuneiform
cb cuboid ; I. to v. the digits.

tinguished from the human foot, are most strikingly
displayed.

   There are usually two sesamoid bones behind each
metatarso-phalangeal joint, and a single one behind the
cuboid in the tendon of the peroneus longus muscle.

   The structure of the foot of the *Lemurina* resembles
generally that of the *Simiina*, and is in fact one of the

principal bonds of union between these groups. The hallux is large and opposable, with a flattened ungual phalanx. The second digit in *Lemur* has a narrow, pointed, ungual phalanx, while that of the other digits is flat and spatulate, as in the *Simiina*. In *Chiromys* all the ungual phalanges, except that of the hallux, are compressed, curved, and pointed.

In *Perodicticus* there is a supplemental ossicle in the transverse ligament of the plantar surface of the tarsus, corresponding to that met with in the carpus (see p. 258).

A remarkable elongation of the tarsal segment of the pes occurs in the Galagos (*Otolicnus*), owing to the modification of two bones, the calcaneum and the navicular; the distal portion of the former, and the whole of the latter, having the form of nearly cylindrical rods placed side by side, while the other bones retain nearly their normal form and proportions. A precisely similar modification is carried to a still greater extent in the genus *Tarsius* (see Fig. 115, p. 311).

All the terrestrial CARNIVORA have the normal number of tarsal bones, with very little deviation from their normal form and relations.

The hallux is present and well developed, though shorter than the other toes in the *Ursidæ, Procyonidæ, Mustelidæ,* and most of the *Viverridæ.* In the *Canidæ, Hyænidæ,* and *Felidæ,* it is only represented by a rudimentary metacarpal. The other four metacarpals and digits are always well developed and subequal. The ungual phalanges in the *Felidæ* present the same characters as those of the fore limb (see p. 260).

In the Bears, the foot is flat, broad, and plantigrade. In the Dogs and Cats, it is longer and narrower, and the heel is raised from the ground in walking.

In the Sea Otter (*Enhydris*), the hind foot approximates to that of the Seals. It is very large and flattened, almost fin-like, and much everted; but the hallux is still shorter than any of the other digits, and the two outer toes are the longest.

In the Seals the pes is completely modified for a special purpose. It has no longer any function as an organ of

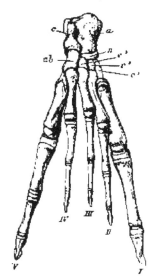

Fig. 116.—Dorsal surface of right pes of young Elephant Seal (*Morunga proboscidea*), ⅓, showing the epiphyses. The letters as before.

support or progression on land, and is habitually directed backwards, with the dorsal surface outwards, and the plantar surface in contact with the corresponding part of the opposite limb. The calcaneum is very short, its tuberosity being almost obsolete. The two lateral digits (first and fifth) are both longer and much stouter than the others;

the middle digit is the shortest. In the Elephant Seal (*Morunga proboscidea*), all the phalanges (except the terminal ones) have epiphyses at both ends of the shaft (see Fig. 116, p. 313).

In the *Otariidæ*, or Eared Seals, and the Walrus, which use the hind feet in walking, these modifications from the ordinary type are not so marked, the calcaneum having a greater backward projection, and all the digits being of nearly equal length. In both there is a large sesamoid on the tibial side of the tarsus.

In the greater number of the animals of the order IN-SECTIVORA, the tarsus is quite normal, and there are five digits, all with curved, pointed, moderately developed, ungual phalanges, the hallux being the shortest. In the Mole, the pes is narrow, having none of the modifications of structure observed in the manus, except that there is an unusually large slender sesamoid on the tibial side of the tarsus, corresponding to the falciform bone of the fore limb. In the Water Moles (*Myogale*), the pes is remarkably large and almost fin-like.

In the African genera *Petrodromus* and *Rhynchocyon*, the hallux is only represented by a rudimentary metatarsal. The last-named animal has a remarkably elongated pes, produced partly by the length of the metatarsals, and partly by a peculiar elongation of all the bones of the distal row of the tarsus, the cuboid, and three cuneiform bones. Contrary to what occurs in the Galagos, the navicular and calcaneum are of normal proportions.

Order CHIROPTERA.—The tarsus is very short; the tuber calcanii a slender curved process; the metacarpals are equal and rather short; the phalanges elongated and subequal in length, the hallux being rather the shortest; the ungual phalanges are long, curved, compressed, and pointed.

Order RODENTIA.—The structure of the pes varies much
in different members of this order.   In the Beaver, as in
most swimming quadrupeds, it is disproportionately large and
flat.   The five digits are well developed, but the third and
fourth are considerably longer and stouter than the others.
The head of the fifth metacarpal is articulated to the outer
side of the fourth· metacarpal, and not directly to the
cuboid.   The middle cuneiform is very small.   There is a
large sesamoid bone on the tibial side of the tarsus, articulating with the astragalus, navicular, and
internal cuneiform.   The tuberosity of
the calcaneum is long and obliquely
compressed.

FIG. 117.—Bones of right
     pes of Jerboa (*Dipus
     ægyptius*), ⅓.

The functional digits in other Rodents may be five, as in the Rats, Porcupines, and Squirrels; or the hallux
may be suppressed, as in the Hares;
and occasionally the fifth digit is also
wanting, reducing the number to three,
as in the Capybara, Viscacha, and
Aguti.   The last-named animal has the
three metatarsals elongated and closely
pressed together, and all the digits with
short subequal phalanges. A still further
modification of the same type leads to
the singular condition of pes met with in
the Jerboas (genus *Dipus*, see Fig. 117),
which at first sight much resembles that
of a bird.   The three metatarsals are
ankylosed together to form a single bone, which supports
the three separate short digits, each with three phalanges.
These alone are applied to the ground, the tarsus and long
metatarsal segment being raised almost vertically.   The

hallux is wanting or rudimentary, but in some species there is a small fifth digit.

All the animals of the order UNGULATA are digitigrade, the heel being raised from the ground, and the metatarsal segment usually much elongated. There is never any trace of a hallux. As in the corresponding segment of the fore limb, the pes is formed upon one or other of two distinct types, each characteristic of one of the sub-orders.

In the *Perissodactyla*, the third digit is the largest, in the centre of the foot, and symmetrical in itself; the second and fourth are smaller, and nearly equal in length, but sometimes quite rudimentary. A line drawn through the centre of the foot passes through the axis of the third digit, and the middle of the external cuneiform, navicular, and astragalus. The distal surface of the astragalus has a large articular surface for the navicular, and a very small one for the cuboid, which is of comparatively less importance than in the Artiodactyla.

The Rhinoceros (Fig. 118) and Tapir have all the usual bones of the tarsus well developed. The internal cuneiform has a curved process projecting backwards. The middle cuneiform (c^2) is very small. The whole foot is comparatively short and broad. The second and fourth toes are well developed, being nearly as long as the middle toe. The phalanges resemble those of the fore limb. In the Tapir the pes differs from the manus in wanting the fifth digit.

In the Horse (Fig. 119), the middle toe is greatly enlarged, and the second and fourth reduced to slender styliform metacarpals, about three-fourths the length of the second, but supporting no phalanges. The navicular (n) and the external cuneiform (c^3) are very broad and flat. The cuboid (cb) is small, and the internal and middle cuneiform bones are small and united together.

Various gradational stages between the complete tri-
dactyle foot of the Rhinoceros and the monodactyle foot of
the Horse are met with in extinct species of the Perissodactyla.

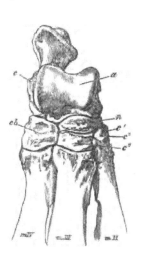
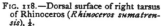
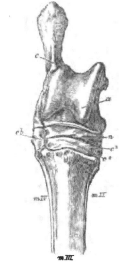

Fig. 118.—Dorsal surface of right tarsus
of Rhinoceros (*Rhinoceros sumatrensis*), ¼.

Fig. 119.—Dorsal surface of right tarsus
of Horse (*Equus caballus*), ⅓.

In the *Artiodactyla* the third and fourth digits are nearly
equally developed, and their ungual phalanges are flattened
on their contiguous sides, so that together they constitute a
symmetrical form. The second and fifth toes, when present,
are also equal, but smaller than the others. A line drawn
through the centre of the foot has on its tibial side, the
third digit and metacarpal, the external cuneiform, the
navicular, and half the astragalus; and on its fibular side,
the fourth digit and metacarpal, the cuboid and the other
half of the astragalus. The distal articular surface of the

astragalus is divided into two nearly equal facets, one for the navicular and one for the cuboid.

In the *Suina* (Fig. 120) all the tarsal bones are distinct. The four toes are well developed, and the metatarsals are usually distinct. The foot is relatively shortest and broadest in the Hippopotamus, the outer toes being nearly as long as the others, and the ungual phalanges very short, broad, and rounded in front. The Peccaries show a transition towards the ruminating sections of the order in the reduc-

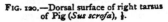
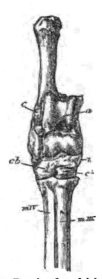

FIG. 120.—Dorsal surface of right tarsus of Pig (*Sus scrofa*), ⅓.   FIG. 121.—Dorsal surface of right tarsus of Red Deer (*Cervus elaphus*), ⅓.

tion of the size of the outer toes and the confluence of the third and fourth metacarpals.

In the *Tylopoda* the cuboid and navicular are distinct. There is no internal cuneiform. The second and fifth digits are entirely absent. The metatarsals of the third and fourth are united except at their lower extremity. The phalanges resemble those of the fore-foot.

In the *Tragulina* the cuboid and navicular are united to form a single bone. The internal cuneiform is wanting. The third and fourth metatarsals are confluent. The second and fifth are complete, extending from the small digits up to the tarsus, but are very slender.

In all the *Pecora* (Fig. 121) the cuboid (*cb*) and navicular (*n*) are united, and the first cuneiform is wanting. The second is very small. The third and fourth metatarsals (*m* III. and *m* IV.) are united in the same manner as the metacarpals, and the phalanges of the digits are very similar to those of the manus. The second and fifth metatarsals are always wanting; the bones of the corresponding digits are absent in the Giraffe and most of the Oxen Sheep, and Antelopes. In the Deer there are usually three small phalanges to each of these digits, not directly articulated with the rest of the skeleton. A large, oval sesamoid is commonly present in the plantar surface of the tarsus.

The pes of the Hyrax closely resembles that of the Rhinoceros, but the ungual phalanx of the second digit is cleft almost to its base.

The PROBOSCIDIA have a very short, broad pes, with all the usual tarsal bones distinct, and all five digits with the normal number of phalanges developed. The ungual phalanges are very small and rounded.

Order EDENTATA.—In the Sloths, the pes much resembles the manus in its general characters, being long, very narrow, and curved, terminating in strong, compressed, pointed ungual phalanges, supporting hook-like claws. The tarsus is short; the astragalus has a deep, cup-shaped cavity on its outer side, into which a conical projection of the lower end of the fibula is received.

The appellation "Two-toed" applied to the genus *Cholœpus* refers only to the anterior limb, for in the pes the three middle toes are functionally developed, and of nearly equal size in both the genera of the family.

In *Bradypus* the tuber calcis is long, compressed, and widened at the extremity. The tarsal bones have a great tendency to ankylosis. The first and fifth metatarsals are very rudimentary, and support no phalanges. The proximal phalanges of the three middle digits are very short, and coalesce very early with the metatarsals, as in the corresponding part of the upper extremity.

In *Cholœpus*, the tuberosity of the calcaneum is very small. The tarsal bones remain distinct from one another. The proximal phalanges of the three middle digits are extremely short, but not ankylosed with the metatarsals. The first and fifth metatarsals are about three-fourths of the length of the others, flattened, and gradually diminishing in size to their free ends.

In nearly all the members of the Entomophagous section of the Edentata, the pes is much more normal in type, and adapted for plantigrade progression on the ground. It does not even present any modifications corresponding to those observed in the manus of the same animals. The normal number of tarsal bones, and the complete number of phalanges, are always present in each digit. Of these the second and third are usually the longest, the fourth next, and the first and fifth shortest.

The little prehensile-tailed Tree Anteater (*Cyclothurus didactylus*) has the pes modified into a climbing organ. The hallux is rudimentary, but the four other toes are subequal and much curved, with long, pointed, compressed, ungual phalanges. The tuber calcis is very short, but the sesamoid ossicle on the tibial side of the foot is exceedingly long and slender, and projects backwards far behind the other bones of the tarsus.

In the MARSUPIALIA, the hind foot is subject to great modifications, some of the genera presenting very striking deviations from the typical condition.

·The seven bones usually found in the Mammalian tarsus are always present and distinct from each other, but the astragalus is relatively smaller and more flattened than in Placental Mammals. In the climbing Marsupials especially, the articular surface for the fibula, instead of being perpendicular to that for the lower end of the tibia, is almost in the same plane with it; and in all, the "head," or portion of the bone which projects forwards to articulate with the navicular, is very slightly developed.

In the American Opossums (*Didelphidæ*), the foot is short and broad; the hallux is stout, placed at right angles with, and opposable to, the other four digits; it has a short, rounded terminal phalanx, which bears no nail. The other digits are subequal, and have compressed, pointed, curved, ungual phalanges.

In the *Dasyuridæ*, the foot is comparatively narrow; the second, third, fourth and fifth toes subequal; the hallux is either very small, and placed close to the others, or completely suppressed, as in the Thylacine.

In the Wombats (*Phascolomyidæ*), the foot is short and broad; the hallux is very short, with only one rounded phalanx, and divaricated from the other toes. These are nearly equal in length; the fourth and fifth are stouter than the second and third, thus showing a slight tendency towards the condition met with in the next group.

In all the remaining Marsupials a peculiar condition of the pes, called syndactylism, prevails. Whatever the condition of the other toes, or whatever the general form or

function of the foot may be, the second and third metacarpals and digits are very slender, and enclosed nearly to
their extremities in a common integument, so that they look
externally like one small toe with two claws.

In the Kangaroo (*Macropus*) the whole foot (Fig. 122) is
very long and narrow, and rests entirely on the ground in
the ordinary position of the animal. The tarsal segment is

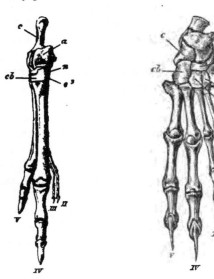

FIG. 122.—Bones of right pes of Kan-   FIG. 123.—Bones of right foot of Pha-
garoo (*Macropus bennettii*), ⅓.   langer (*Phalangista vulpina*), ⅓.

short, the metatarsus very long. The cuboid is greatly
developed, the navicular and the three cuneiform bones
exceedingly small, in conformity with the condition of the
digits they respectively support. There is a sesamoid on
the plantar surface of the tarsus. The fourth metatarsal
and digit are enormously developed, the fifth moderately

so ; the second and third nearly as long as the fifth, but excessively attenuated. There is no rudiment of a hallux. The ungual phalanges are conical, pointed, slightly curved above, and flattened on the under surface. The whole foot is much compressed laterally, especially at its hinder part, so that the proximal ends of the second and third are thrown behind that of the great fourth metatarsal, and entirely concealed in a view of the dorsal surface of the foot.

The Tree-Kangaroos of New Guinea (*Dendrolagus*), which habitually live among the boughs of large trees, have the feet constructed on the same type, but shorter, and more laterally extended.

In the leaf-eating, climbing Australian Opossums (*Phalangista*, Fig. 123) and Koalas (*Phascolarctos*) the second and third toes are also very slender, but the fourth and fifth are more equal, especially in length, the foot is broad, and there is a strongly developed prehensile and opposable, though nailless, hallux.

The insect- and root-eating, ground-dwelling Bandicoots (*Peramelidæ*) differing in many other respects from the Kangaroos, have their hind-foot constructed on exactly the same type as in

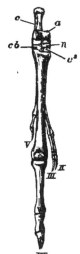

Fig. 124.—Bones of right foot of *Chæropus castanotis* (nat. size.)

Macropus, even to the relative length of the different digits, though there is often a rudiment of the metatarsal of the hallux. In one remarkable genus (*Chæropus*), already mentioned on account of the peculiar structure of the manus (see Fig. 104, p. 278), the same type is carried to a great extreme,

Y 2

the fourth toe (see Fig. 124) remaining of a prodigious size and the fifth being reduced to even smaller dimensions than the second or third.

MONOTREMATA.—In both species the seven usual bones of the tarsus are complete and distinct,[1] and the five digits have the normal number of phalanges.

In the Ornithorhynchus the proximal articular surface of the astragalus is divided by a deep groove into two distinct heads, one for the tibia, and the other for the fibula, the latter being the larger of the two ; the inner side has a cup-shaped socket, into which fits an incurved conical process from the lower end of the tibia. The tuberosity of the calcaneum is broad and bifid at the extremity, and directed not backwards, but towards the tibial side of the foot. In the male there is an additional, large, flat, curved ossicle, on the hinder and tibial side of the palmar aspect of the tarsus, articulated chiefly to the tibia, which supports the peculiar perforated horny spur characteristic of this sex, the function of which has not been discovered. There is also a small, rounded, supplementary ossicle, below the tibial edge of the tarsus, near the articulation between the astragalus and scaphoid. The metacarpals increase in length from the first to the fifth. The phalanges are all rather long and slender. The four outer toes are nearly equal ; the hallux is somewhat shorter. The ungual phalanges are compressed, slightly curved, and very sharp pointed.

In the Echidna the astragalus is large, with an irregular, broad, rounded, proximal articular surface, not divided by a groove, and with a much less distinct fossa, for the in-

---

[1] It has been stated that the cuboid in the Ornithorhynchus is divided into two bones, as in some reptiles, one for the fourth and the other for the fifth metatarsal; but this is not the case in any specimen which I have examined.

ternal malleolus. The tuber calcanei is directed forwards, it is also bifid, and its external process is much longer than the other and curved towards the plantar surface of the foot. The spur of the male, and the ossicle which supports it, are much smaller than in the Ornithorhynchus. The metacarpals are shorter and broader; they increase in length from the first to the fifth. The hallux is very short, and has a flattened, conical, ungual phalanx. The proximal and middle phalanges are all very short and broad. The ungual phalanx of the second digit is extremely long and falcate, the others gradually diminish to the fifth. The ends of the toes are turned outwards and backwards in the ordinary position of the animal.

The ungual phalanges of both extremities in the Monotremata have a deep median groove, near the base of the under surface, leading at its distal extremity into a foramen.

CHAPTER XX.

THAT a general correspondence exists in the plan of construction of the anterior and posterior extremity cannot fail
to strike the most superficial observer, though to follow out
this correspondence into all its details has severely exercised
the ingenuity of many an anatomist.

It would be quite beside the character of the present
work to give an historical account of the numerous and
very various views which have been held upon this subject,[1] but I propose to lay before the student in a con-
densed form such portions of the general outcome of these
researches as appear to be most satisfactorily established,
premising, however, that all the statements hereinafter to
be made have not yet met with universal assent.

In the first place, it is perfectly obvious that the fore and
hind limbs have each a similar division into four main segments, the shoulder girdle, the arm, the fore-arm, and the

---

[1] For the bibliography of this question, see Mivart, "On some
Points in the Anatomy of Echidna Hystrix" (Linn. Soc. Trans. xxv.
1866); and Rolleston "On the Homologies of certain Muscles connected with the Shoulder Joint" (Ibid. xxvi. 1869).

manus of the one representing respectively the pelvic girdle, the thigh, the leg, and the pes of the other.

To proceed to further details, it is necessary to place the limbs (at least in imagination) in an exactly corresponding position—one, in fact, which is often impossible in the adult animal on account of the modifications of the articular surfaces to suit the posture best adapted for the habits and mode of life of the individual, but which is the position of all limbs when they first appear as bud-like processes from the side of the body of the embryo. In this position the limbs are extended at right angles to the axis of the trunk and parallel to each other, as in Fig. 125, A and B. There is then to each limb a superior or dorsal surface (turned towards the observer in the figure), an inferior or ventral surface, and an anterior and a posterior edge. These last are called by Professor Huxley *preaxial* and *postaxial* (in reference to the axis of the limb itself) to avoid the confusion with *anterior* and *posterior* in the modified positions they assume in Man and various animals. In the figures the preaxial side is left light, and the postaxial side is shaded.

The dorsal surface of the anterior extremity includes the back of the hand and the extensor surface of the fore-arm and arm. The dorsal surface of the posterior extremity includes the dorsum of the foot, front of the leg, and the extensor surface of the thigh. The preaxial border of the anterior extremity has in it the pollex, the radius, the condyle commonly called "external," and the greater tuberosity. The preaxial border of the posterior extremity includes the hallux, the tibia, the condyle commonly called "internal," and the lesser trochanter. All these parts, then, should be regarded as serially homologous.

Leaving for the present the shoulder and pelvic girdles out of consideration, we will next consider the adaptive

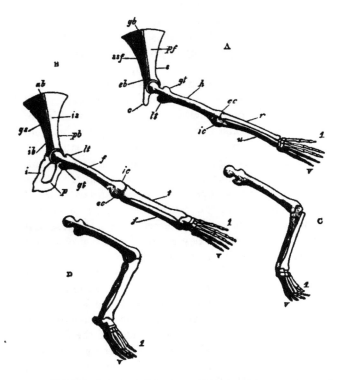

FIG. 125.—Diagrammatic representation of the positions of the limbs of Mammalia.
The preaxial border is left light, the postaxial border shaded, in all the figures.
Limbs of the right side are represented in all cases. A dorsal aspect of the anterior extremity in its primitive unmodified position ; *gb* glenoid border of the
scapula ; *s* spine ; *cb* coracoid border ; *ssf* subscapular fossa ; *pf* postscapular (in-
fraspinal) fossa ; *c* coracoid ; *h* humerus ; *gt* greater, radial, or preaxial tuberosity ;
lt lesser, ulnar, or postaxial tuberosity ; *ec* external (in the modified position), radial,
or preaxial condyle ; *ic* internal, ulnar, or postaxial condyle ; *r* radius ; *u* ulna ;
I pollex ; v fifth digit. B dorsal aspect of the posterior extremity in the same
position ; *ab* acetabular border of the ilium ; *pb* pubic border ; *ib* ischial border ;
gs gluteal surface ; *is* iliac surface ; *i* ischium ; *p* pubis ; *f* femur ; *lt* lesser, tibial,
or preaxial trochanter ; *gt* greater, fibular, or postaxial trochanter ; *ic* internal
(in the modified position), tibial, or preaxial condyle ; *ec* external, fibular, or postaxial condyle ; *t* tibia ; *f* fibula ; I hallux ; v fifth digit ; c the anterior extremity,
with the humerus in the same position, but the elbow- and wrist-joints bent ; D
the posterior extremity in the same position.

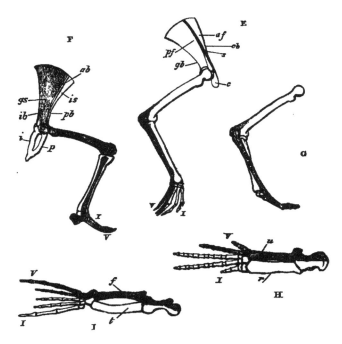

FIG. 126.—Diagrammatic representation of the positions of the limbs of Mammalia continued. E the anterior extremity with the same flexures as in C, but with the whole limb rotated backwards. The preaxial side is external. The letters as before. F the posterior extremity, with the joints bent, and the whole limb rotated forwards, as in the ordinary position of quadruped Mammals. The postaxial side is external. G the humerus in the same position as in B, but the fore-arm rotated, as in the ordinary position of quadruped Mammals. Whilst the preaxial side of the humerus remains external, the postaxial side of the manus is now external. H the anterior extremity of a Cetacean (*Hyperoodon*), dorsal surface. I the posterior extremity of a Seal, dorsal surface.

changes which take place in the segments of the limb proper in various animals. These will be best understood by dividing them into stages (all of which are represented in the diagram), though it is not meant to imply that the limbs actually go through so many distinct phases in the course of development, as all the various modifications from the primitive to the most adaptive positions may take place gradually and even simultaneously.

In what may be considered the first stage of modification (Figs. C and D), each segment of the limb is simply bent upon the one above it. The proximal segments (humerus and femur) remain unchanged in position, the dorsal surface still looking upwards, and the ventral surface downwards; the middle segment is bent downwards, so that its ventral surface faces inwards and its dorsal surface outwards; and the joints between these segments (elbow and knee) form prominent angular projections. The third segment being bent to a greater or less degree in the opposite direction to the middle one, retains much of its primitive position, the dorsal surface being directed upwards and the ends of the digits pointing outwards. The relations of the preaxial and postaxial borders of the limb are unchanged. No Mammal habitually carries its limbs in this position, although the climbing *Galeopithecus* and the Sloths are not far from it. It is, however, very nearly the normal position of some Reptiles, especially the Tortoises, though it is ill adapted for anything but a very slow and clumsy mode of progression.

The next change, and one which takes place at a very early period in embryonic life, and which is one of the most essential in giving the characteristic conformation of the extremities of the higher Vertebrates, is a rotation of the whole limb from the proximal end, though in opposite directions in each case.

The anterior extremity (see Fig. E) is rotated from the shoulder, through nearly a quarter of a circle, *backwards*, so that the humerus, instead of being at a right angle to the axis of the trunk, is nearly parallel with it, the elbow points backwards, the preaxial side is outwards, and the postaxial side towards the middle line of the body, and as long as the radius and ulna retain their primitive parallel position, the manus is placed with the ends of the digits directed backwards, the preaxial side being external.

The hind limb (see Fig. F) is, at the same time, rotated from the hip to the same extent *forwards*, so that the femur is also nearly parallel to the axis of the body, but with the knee projecting forwards; the preaxial side is inwards and the postaxial side outwards; the tibia and fibula are parallel, the former internal and the latter external; the foot has the ends of the digits directed forwards, the hallux or preaxial digit is on the inner, and the fifth or most postaxial digit is on the outer, side.

In this position the hind limb remains, subject only to minor modifications, in nearly all terrestrial Mammals; but the Walrus, and to a certain extent the Sea-Lions, alone carry the fore limb as described above without further modification.

The next stage, affecting the fore limb alone, consists in the rotation of the lower end of the radius around the ulna, which brings the distal extremity of the manus round from the back to the front of the limb (see Fig. G).. In most Mammals the limb is permanently fixed in this position, and the bones of the fore-arm become greatly modified in consequence, as described in Chapter XV. It will now be understood how, though the outer side of the humerus corresponds with the inner side of the femur, in ordinary quadruped progression, yet the outer side of the manus corresponds with the outer and not the inner side of the pes.

To these general conditions there are certain modifications met with in some animals, and certain exceptions in others.

The modifications with regard to the anterior extremity are that the humerus may be quite horizontal, or its distal ends may incline upwards, or, as is much more frequently the case, it may incline somewhat downwards, so that the dorsal surface is posterior and the ventral surface anterior : the forearm in the ordinary resting position may be quite vertical, or inclined with its upper end backwards : the whole of the manus may rest entirely on the ground, as in the so-called "plantigrade" or rather "palmigrade" animals, or the proximal part, the tarsus and metatarsus, may be raised and placed more or less vertically, the limb resting either on all or only on the terminal phalanges, according to the completeness of the "digitigrade" mode of progression.

Similar modifications apply to the hind limb. The femur is usually inclined with its distal end downwards, so that the dorsal or "extensor" surface is anterior, and the ventral or "flexor" surface posterior. In the Elephants it is very nearly vertical. In most animals which occasionally assume the upright position, as the Kangaroos and some Rodents, the femur is ordinarily inclined upwards at its distal extremity, so that the knee is above the acetabulum, and the pelvis slung as it were between the two hind limbs. In Man, on the other hand, in standing or walking the femur is nearly vertical with the distal end downwards, and the pelvis is supported on the top of the limbs.

The positions of the limbs which are quite exceptional are those of certain aquatic animals.

In the Cetacea (Fig. H) none of the segments of the anterior limb undergo any deflection from the primitive straight condition, nor is there any rotation of the bones of the forearm. The only changes which take place are a partial rotation backwards from the shoulder, and a slight turning downwards of the preaxial border. In the Sirenia and the

Seals, there is a slight bend at the elbow and the wrist, but little or no rotation of the fore-arm.

In the hind limb of the Seal (Fig. 1) there is very little flexure at the joints, and the whole limb is turned backwards instead of forwards from the hip, and at the same time rotated on its axis, so that the preaxial border becomes turned downwards. The skeleton of this limb, therefore, and that of the fore limb of the Cetacean, being retained normally in almost exactly similar positions, are well adapted for demonstrating the correspondence between the respective bones of which they are composed (see Figs. H and 1).

The necessity of the modifications in the direction of the axes of the heads of the humerus and femur spoken of previously, will easily be understood by a consideration of the relative positions that these bones are adapted to assume. Thus the axis of the head of the humerus in the majority of Mammals is inclined towards the postaxial side of the shaft of the bone, while that of the femur is inclined towards its preaxial side.

Hitherto nothing has been said about the shoulder and pelvic girdle, because the correspondence of their parts is not so easily explained, nor so generally recognized, as that of the segments of the limb proper, and yet they seem to me to be scarcely less clear.

It has been already shown (Chapters XIV. and XVII.) that the lateral half of each girdle consists primarily of a bar or rod placed vertically, and divided into an upper and a lower segment, the point of attachment of the limb being close to the junction of these two segments. The upper segment in the fore limb is the scapula, in the hind limb the ilium ; the lower segment in the fore limb is the coracoid, in the hind limb the ischium and pubis.

In every Mammal both scapula and ilium may be resolved into bars or rods of three-sided or prismatic form. The two extremities of each bar are placed, as regards the general position of the trunk, dorsally and ventrally. The dorsal or upper extremity is capped by the suprascapular epiphysis in the shoulder girdle, and by the corresponding supra-iliac epiphysis in the pelvic girdle. The ventral or inferior extremity enters into the formation of the glenoid or the acetabular articular cavity, as the case may be, and joins the coracoid or the ischial element of the girdle.

The bar, supposed to be in a nearly vertical position, has three surfaces and three borders. In what may be, at least theoretically, considered their primary position, the surfaces of each bar are—(1) Inner or vertebral, turned towards the vertebral column; (2) preaxial, corresponding to the preaxial line of the limb (Fig. 125, A *pf*, B *is*); (3) Postaxial, corresponding to the postaxial line of the limb (A *ssf*, B *gs*). The borders are—(1) External, in a line with the middle of the dorsal surface of the limb, and terminating below at the upper margin of the glenoid or acetabular cavity (A *gb*, B *ab*); (2) antero-internal, terminating below in the acromion or in the pubis (A *s*, B *pb*); (3) postero-internal, terminating below in the coracoid, or the ischium, as the case may be (A *cb*, B *ib*).

The correspondence between these parts of the scapula and ilium will be better understood by placing them in a tabular form, the middle column showing the names expressed in the generalized or ideal condition applicable to both in their primitive condition, and the column at each side giving the special terms applied to each part in its variously modified forms.

SURFACES.

SCAPULA.	IDEAL.	PELVIS.
Prescapular fossa. Supraspinous fossa.	1. Vertebral.	Sacral surface. Inner surface of ilium, behind linea arcuata interna, including the articular surface for the sacrum, and the portion of the bone above and below this.
Postscapular fossa. Infraspinous fossa.	2. Preaxial.	Iliac surface. Internal iliac fossa.
Subscapular fossa.	3. Postaxial.	Gluteal surface.

BORDERS.

SCAPULA.	IDEAL.	PELVIS.
Glenoid border. Posterior border in most animals. Axillary border in Man.	1. External.	Acetabular border. Anterior border.
Spine.	2. Antero-internal.	Pubic border. Linea arcuata interna.
Coracoid border. Anterior border in most animals. Superior border in Man.	3. Postero-internal.	Ischial border. Posterior border.

As the humerus in ordinary quadruped Mammals is rotated backwards from its primitive position, and the femur is rotated forwards, so that the preaxial side of the first becomes external, and the really corresponding side of the other becomes internal, so it is with the scapula and ilium. Each has undergone a rotation on its own axis, through nearly a quarter of a circle, and in the opposite direction (see Fig. 126, E and F), so that the inner surface of the one comes to correspond with the outer surface of the other, the anterior border of the one with the posterior border of the other. The long axis of each is also differently inclined, the upper end of the scapula leaning backwards, while that of the ilium is inclined forwards, which makes the resemblance between them at first sight more obscure.

These views are considerably strengthened by a consideration of the disposition of the muscles connected with the various bones in question.[1]

The principal differences between the shoulder and pelvic girdle of the Mammalia are two :—(1) The rudimentary condition of the inferior or ventral section of the girdle (the coracoid) in the former, as compared with the vast development of the corresponding part of the lower extremity ; (2) the free condition of the anterior as compared with the posterior girdle. It is neither attached to the vertebral column above, nor does it (except in the Monotremata) join the opposite part in the middle line below. To compensate for this, a clavicle is superadded to the anterior girdle in many Mammals, for which there is no exact homologue in the lower extremity.

It has been shown in Chapters XVI. and XIX. that the terminal segments of each limb present a remarkable general correspondence, with certain constant differences.

[1] See "On the Correspondence between the Parts composing the Shoulder and the Pelvic Girdle of the Mammalia " (*Journal of Anatomy and Physiology*, vol. iv. p. 239, 1870).

There can be no question but that the carpus and tarsus, the metacarpus and metatarsus, and the various digits beginning at the pollex in the one, and the hallux in the other, are really homologous; the circumstance of the constant absence of one of the bones of the preaxial digit in both fore and hind limbs is most significant.

In the carpus and tarsus, the serial homology of the four bones of the distal row in their respective order is geneially admitted, but with the other bones there is still some difference of opinion. Gegenbaur has, however, given good reasons,[1] derived chiefly from the results of tracing both limbs back to their less modified condition in Reptiles and Amphibia, for considering the astragalus as equivalent to the scaphoid and lunar united, or the scapho-lunar bone of the Carnivora, &c. ; the calcaneum as representing the cuneiform, and not, as often supposed, the cuneiform and the pisiform (the latter being only a sesamoid) ; and the navicular of the foot as representing the os centrale, found only occasionally in the manus of Mammals.

[1] " Untersuchungen zur Vergleichenden Anatomie," 1tes Heft, Carpus und Tarsus, 1864.

INDEX.

THE END.

R. CLAY, SONS, AND TAYLOR, PRINTERS, BREAD STREET HILL.

CPSIA information can be obtained
at www.ICGtesting.com
Printed in the USA
BVHW03*1302110518
516009BV00001B/2/P